D1562556

Tilton Territory

A *Historical Narrative*

Warren Township
Jefferson County, Ohio
1775–1838

———————•———————

(TILTON)

DIGBY.

———————•———————

by
Robert H. Richardson

DORRANCE & COMPANY • *Philadelphia and Ardmore, Pa.*

Copyright © 1977 by Robert H. Richardson
All Rights Reserved
ISBN 0-8059-2362-4
Printed in the United States of America

CONTENTS

ILLUSTRATIONS

INTRODUCTION

History is that intriguing study of confusing, contradictory, conciliatory and, sometimes, conjectured events that constitute the past and conjure the future. In this documented narrative, an attempt has been made, through authoritative and unembellished accounts, to relate the early happenings in Warren Township of Jefferson County, Ohio. Factual evidence, accurate and uncontestable, that pioneer settlements were well established, officially governed, and recognized by the federal government prior to the formal founding of Marietta, Ohio, in April of 1788, will also be presented.

Certain historians of note—particularly the late W. H. Hunter, who wrote so extensively and accurately in Volumes VI and VIII of the *Ohio Archaeological and Historical Publications* under the title of "The Pathfinders of Jefferson County, Ohio"—are and were well aware of the early settlements in the Northwest territory.

It is to the utter amazement of the author, that, in all of its discernible history, the sovereign state of Ohio and its highly respected antiquarians and archaeologists have given, unquestionably and probably without intent, only a minimum of recognition to the county of Jefferson and the township of Warren. Most certainly, these eminent researchers and scholars are acquainted with the Adena and Hopewellian cultures—the exploits of Gist and Boone and Kenton and Clark and Wayne—all of whom, at one time or another, trekked the virgin hills and valleys of the county and the township.

It is also beyond question that John Tilton and his wife, Susannah, who had a settlement on Buffalo Creek in Ohio County, Virginia, in 1772 (confirmed by a deed signed by Governor Patrick Henry), moved westward in 1775, crossed the Ohio River, and settled on land now encompassed in the town of Tiltonsville.

In his research, the author has learned much about the Tiltons—particularly John and Susannah, their sixteen children, and their pioneer friends and neighbors. It is almost as if he grew up with them, lived with them, and even laughed and cried with them. And that is what this first volume will reveal—the activities of these early settlers in Warren Township between the years 1775 and 1838. It is anticipated that a second volume, containing many early pictures of people and places, will be published. This volume will complete the nineteenth century and update the twentieth century history of Warren Township.

It should be noted that certain incidents related in this first volume are based on stochastic judgment and logical deduction after thorough study and analysis of all documents and evidence pertaining to such incidents. Quite naturally, much of the dialogue has been constructed to maintain the interest of the reader, but in no way does it detract from the facts as they are presented—nor does it distort the truth. This book is not fiction—it is history.

The author will not attempt to enumerate all of the many friends, acquaintances and associates who have been a source of inspiration and information, both of which were of much value in compiling the manuscript. In the second volume, however, recognition shall be properly accorded, since the style and format will be more conducive to acknowledgement.

Robert H. Richardson

Tiltonsville, Ohio
May, 1976

PROLOGUE

A HILL IN LEICESTERSHIRE, ENGLAND, where Roman soldiers had built a fortress during their invasion of that country, is named "Tilton" after the Anglo-Saxons who occupied the hill. Thus, the Anglo-Saxon name of Tilton is interpreted to mean "the place where the soldiers have been." In the eleventh century settlers were identified by their surnames, and the residents of the settlement were named after the place of residence.

In the Domesday Book, published in 1086 A.D., after William the Conqueror had ordered a census and tax list be prepared to include all of the inhabitants of Britain and their property holdings in A.D. 1066, the first reference is to Tiletone, a place where there were four acres of meadow and five acres of woods valued at two carucates (a fiscal term). Robert of Tiletone held three carucates of land in Tiletone. In translation, this quotation from the Domesday Book reads:

> In the derneane there are 2 plow horses and 8 villeins [a villein was one of the rural laboring class but his exact function and standing probably varied from shire to shire or even manor to manor; also, villeins were more important than "bordars" or "cotters" and, of course, "serfs" were slaves] with a priest and 1 bordar having 3 plow teams. There are 8 acres of meadow and it was valued and still is valued at 20 shillings. These lands were held by AElmar with sae and sohe.

It is interesting to note that the Domesday Survey contains the names of about fourteen hundred "Tenants in Capite" (those who received their land directly from the King) and about seventy-nine hundred "Meane Tenants" (those under "Tenants in Capite"). Not listed were the names of about two hundred and sixty-four thousand rural laborers. Except for a few titled women and female slaves (ancillae), women were not mentioned, nor were the wives or children of the rural laborers.

The third reference to the Tiltons in the Domesday Book translates as follows:

> Hugo held Tillintone from the Archbishop as 1 carucate of land. Friendai sub-leased it from him. There is one plow team with 3 villeins and 2 bordars. It was valued and still is valued at 10 shillings. This land is to furnish alms to St. Marie from Sudwelle. Getda held it under King Edward.

The three references in the Domesday Book indicate the location of manors in Tilton (Tiletone—Tillintone). The first, above indicated, was directly under the king; the second was under Robert, the king's stewart, and the third was on lands assigned to the Archbishop of York.

King Henry II ruled England from 1154 to 1189. It was during his reign that Sir John Tilton, a knighted gentlemen of wealth, gave certain sections of lands in Billesdon and Kirby, in Leicestershire, to the lepers of St. Lazarus at Jerusalem and the infirm brethren of Burton-Lazara; the gifts were confirmed by the king.

Sir John, who was living in 1216, served with honor and distinction in the Crusades, and on his tomb, adjacent to the Tilton Church in Tilton, England, are engraved his heraldic arms. The Tilton Church was founded by the Tilton family in 1190, at which time the traditional Norman tower was built. The spire was constructed in 1380, the south aisle in 1390, and the clerestory in 1490. The church was rebuilt by the Tiltons in the sixteenth century and is now high Anglican.

During the reign of Henry III in 1256, some members of the Tilton clan moved to Digby in Lincolnshire and, in so doing, the family name became Tilton de Digby and eventually Digby. Some famous personages bearing the name of Digby ultimately came to be, and many of these were of Tilton lineage. The lives of King Edward I (1272-1307) and King Edward III (1327-1377) were saved by loyal members of the Tilton family who were very close to the throne. In 1485, during the War of the Roses, seven faithful Tiltons held positions of stature under King Henry VII, and during the successful encounter against Richard III, several Tiltons died.

In the fifteenth century, Sir Everard Digby de Tilton was the high sheriff of Rutlandshire and lord of Tilton and Drystroke. He died in 1509.

The infamous Gunpowder Plot of 1604 involved Guy Fawkes, a soldier of note, who, although he had not originated the scheme to blow up the king and Parliament in revenge for the passage of laws directed against the Catholic faith, was quite active in the rebellion. Sir Everard Digby, who had been born in 1578, was hanged, in early 1606, as a conspirator.

In the late 1630's, during the mass immigration of English Puritans to America and at which time King Charles I and Oliver Cromwell were feuding, two younger members of the Tilton family, William and John, joined the migration and settled in Lynn, Massachusetts.

William, the progenitor of the New England Tiltons and an ancestor of Millard Fillmore, thirteenth President of the United States, was a well-educated, aristocratic leader, as was John. William remained an influential citizen of Lynn until his death in 1652.

It is the ancestor of John Tilton, who, after becoming disillusioned with the intolerant religious beliefs of the puritanical New Englanders, left the Lynn Colony with his wife, Mary, Lady Deborah Moody and many of their friends, with whom this book will be concerned.

John Tilton was the first Englishman to found a colony in what is now King's County, Long Island, which was then under the rule of the Dutch. He negotiated with the Carnarsie Indians, purchasing parcels of land in 1645, 1650, and 1654. John was quite active in the development of Gravesend, serving as town clerk for twenty years. Eventually, he and his wife, "Goody," as she was called, became quite sympathetic to a religious sect known as "Quakers," ultimately becoming members of this denomination. John and his wife remained as lifelong residents of Gravesend. He did explore the central part of New Jersey and was instrumental in purchasing a large section of land, comprising Monmouth and parts of Ocean and Middlesex Counties from the Indians in 1664 and 1665.

John and Mary Tilton were the parents of three sons and four daughters: John, Peter, Sarah, Esther, Abigail, Thomas and

Mary. Thomas, the youngest son, was born on March 1, 1652.

John Tilton died at Gravesend in 1688, and shortly thereafter, in 1690, at the age of thirty-eight, Thomas moved to Delaware. He was a frugal man and eventually purchased land in the Lower Part of Duck Creek Hundred, married a young woman, and raised a family.

The question has been raised many times as to why Thomas Tilton, his brother-in-law, John Painter, and his nephews, John and Henry Tilton, went to Delaware. The answer is theoretical but conclusive. Contrary to popular opinion, there was not religious freedom in America in the late seventeenth century. Thomas and his relatives, who relocated in Delaware, could not accept the religious convictions of the Quaker sect nor the strict, authoritarian rule of the dominant powers in central New Jersey; thus, the move.

Thomas and Mary Tilton had five sons: John, who was lost at sea, Thomas, James, Nehemiah and Joseph. Little is known of Thomas Tilton, the third son of Thomas and Mary Tilton, other than the fact that he was born in 1714 about two years after the birth of Joseph, his mother, Mary, being considerably younger than his father. According to the *Delaware Archives—Military, Volume I,* wherein is recorded a "List of Officers for the Regiment of Militia for Kent County, upon Delaware—1756," Thomas was an ensign in the Lower Part of Duck Creek Hundred.

On the basis of evidence recorded, it can properly be deduced that James married in the late 1730's and had at least one son, James, born in 1743. James graduated as a doctor on June 21, 1768, from the medical department of the College of Philadelphia, Pennsylvania. Dr. James Tilton served as a surgeon in Colonel John Hazlett's Delaware Regiment during the Revolutionary War. He was commissioned on January 13, 1776, and honorably discharged after one year. On June 13, 1813, he was appointed physician and surgeon-general of the United States Army and, once again, on June 15, 1815, he received an honorable discharge and was pensioned for disabilities contracted during his service. Doctor James Tilton died on May 14, 1822, at the age of seventy-nine.

Nehemiah, the youngest son of Thomas and Mary, was born about three years before his mother's death in 1720. He married and had a large family and devoted much of his life to military activities. He distinguished himself during the "War for Freedom," eventually earning the rank of colonel. Suffice it now to disclose a letter written by Nehemiah to his brother (probably Thomas):

Shamany Creek 2 Miles above Bristol, 1776 Decr. 24th 3 OClock P.M.
Dr Brother
We arrived here Sunday last, and by the time our baggage was in Quarters one of the Phila. Light have come express for Capn. Rodney, he mounted his horse & rode to Bristol, The Commanding Officer (Colo. Cadwalader) informed him a number of men was to cross the Delaware that night, and desired his company would be ready at 12 OClock. The Capn. informed him we had marched a considerable distance & had no provisions cook'd, but would be ready to cross the next evening. The Philadelphia Militia Peraded at 10 OClock that night to the number of 1200 men & would of cross'd had not (as I believe) General Washington ordered the contrary, tho' the common Reason is that the commander of the troops in Jersey had desired they should not cross till a few days hence. Our Troops in Jersey was skirmishing with some Hessians all day on Sunday last, yesterday I was in Bristol & Capt. Dean informed me they were then engaged & had been since daylight in the morning,—Two Brigades of Regulars (part of General Lee's Division) is moved from head Quarters near Trentown to this place & the Gundolas is ordered up also which give reason to think the general expects the enemy incline to move lower down the river.—Capt. Rodney is now at Bristol should he bring any news will insert it.—We quartered at two houses, Andrew Allens &—Coxe his wifes father; about 200 years distant from each other—Mrs. Allen Mr. & Mrs. Coxe are exceeding kind Mrs. Coxe gave a Turkey & goose to the Company at her house & Mrs. Allen has done the same for Christmas Dinner tomorrow.—The Capt. has a small room to himself at Mrs. Allens & as we have

but one bed between us I live with him.—
7 OClock Capt. Rodney Returned & nothing New . . . I
think I have not been so hearty these 7 years past.
I am your Affectionate Brother,

NEHEMIAH TILTON
N.D.
Remember me to Mrs. Hanson on Sussey.
N.T.

As far as can be determined, none of the sons of Thomas and
Mary Tilton moved west to settle, although military responsibilities sometimes required them to travel in various directions
beyond the boundaries of Delaware.

It is Joseph, a son of Thomas and Mary Tilton and the father of
one of the main characters in this narrative, with whom concern
must be sustained. Joseph was born in 1712. He married, moved
across the border to Kent County, Maryland, and accumulated
rather extensive land holdings in that area about fourteen miles
from Baltimore. He had at least two sons—John, born in 1738,
and Thomas, born about two years later. He lived a good life and
died in 1794.

It was this John Tilton, whose great-grandfather had come
from England and was recognized as a noble stalwart in the
founding of Gravesend, New Jersey, and was a pioneer in the
organization of Monmouth County, New Jersey, who helped settle the Northwest Territory. John married a young girl, Susannah
Jones, from Elkridge, Maryland, in 1759. In 1766, John and his
young wife gave up the comfort and security they possessed in
Maryland and, joining a pack horse train, they looked forward to
future adventures and the golden dream of Utopian wealth and
happiness in the primitive Middle Ground—the land of the Indian.

By the year 1775, they had conditioned themselves to life on
the frontier, and it was only because of their tremendous strength
of character, forbearance and faith that they made their dream
come true.

I

THE DECISION

IT WAS EARLY MORNING. The first rays of sunlight were beginning to creep over the eastern hills and filter through the dense, dew-laden foliage of the forest. The rabbit, the deer, the squirrel, and the muskrat were active. The cabins in the clearing were dark and silent. It was springtime, and the locust trees were heavily endowed with their white-beaded clusters.

Sunrise created a bevy of activity in small settlements on the western frontier, and very soon now, smoke would be curling from the cabin chimneys and fireplaces outside the cabins. Doors would open and men would come forth, rifle in one hand and axe or hoe in the other. The axe and the hoe were used to prepare and provide the necessities of life. The rifle was, to some extent, used for the same purpose—but primarily as a guardian of survival. While the animals scurried for cover, the men, in unison, explored the tiny village and its outskirts to assure that vengeful Shawnees or Mingoes were not in the area. After the murderous events of recent months, every precaution was taken. Upon being certain of their immediate safety, all able-bodied members of the community undertook their arduous duties which were necessary to subsist in a land which offered only its natural beauty, virgin soil, and strong hope for the future.

These were the settlers. The adventuresome traders and explorers, like Gist and Boone and Kenton,[1] had come before. They liked what they saw; they thrived on the challenge of the unknown; they learned the skillful and wily ways of the Shawnee warrior; and they used this knowledge in conjunction with their native abilities to survive and prosper in the land of the Indian.

John Tilton opened his cabin door and, with dark, piercing eyes, surveyed the area. The scene was silently somber. Several of the small log homes near the Tilton settlement on Buffalo Creek were empty now, the families having moved in various directions to seek their destiny in other areas of the sparsely populated lands west of the Alleghenies.

Tilton wondered about his friends. Some had moved south, along the north branch of Wheeling Creek; others, west, by way of the Buffalo Creek; and some had retreated eastward toward Redstone; none had returned. After a restless night, he knew what he must do—and soon.

John Carpenter's[2] cabin, where he had staked a good claim and established his settlement, was only a hundred yards from Tilton's. Tilton set aside his gun and, cupping his hands to his mouth, relayed the soft cheep of the cardinal.

Although the signal was well known, the pioneers were cautious. Carpenter opened the door of his cabin with extreme caution and came forth, long rifle in hand.

The frontiersmen moved toward each other. To distinguish between them was difficult, with their weather-beaten faces, calloused hands, similar clothing made from the coarse fabric then available. After nine years on the frontier they had, for the most part, adopted the typical and most appropriate costume. The outfit of the frontiersmen varied little whether he was scout, hunter, soldier or settler.

The over-the-shoulder garment fell almost to the knees and had a sewn-on cape for head protection in bad weather. This garment was usually constructed of linsey or deerskin and was sable in color. It was also loose at the breast and was controlled by a rope or belt as required for hunting or scouting. Loose-fitting linsey leg coverings were apparent. A moccasin-type deerskin shoe based the rawhide-wrapped leggings that Tilton wore. Carpenter, although attired similarly, could be distinguished by his tawny, wildcat-skin moccasins.

The men approached each other.

"Anything wrong, John?" asked Carpenter.

"No, nothing wrong, but I didn't sleep well last night," said Tilton, "and I made a decision."

They were now face to face.

"Is it important?"

"Yes."

Carpenter motioned with his gun. "Let's check the area and then we'll talk about it."

The two pioneers proceeded with their morning ritual. Tilton to the south and east—Carpenter to the north and west. Every sound had a meaning—the breaking of a twig, the gobble of a turkey, the song of a bird. Continuous surveillance and constant caution were, above all, necessary for survival in this frontier land where danger in the form of man or beast lurked almost constantly.

Silently, on moccasin-clad feet, they explored their assigned areas. There was no obvious evidence of danger from Indians or white renegades. The time would come.

The two scouts returned and signaled that there was no sign of immediate danger. Upon receiving this assurance, the cabin occupants began their daily chores. Few cabins had inside cooking facilities or chimneys, and most meals were prepared outside the cabin. Bear fat from deerskin pouches was liquified in heavy iron kettles. Rabbits, groundhogs and venison, from a previous day's catch, were prepared, and corn pone, the basic staple food of frontier families, was baked on the hearthstone or in the hot ashes of the cooking fire.

The family of John Tilton, although more substantial, materially, than most frontiersmen, followed the same routine in their daily life. Susannah Tilton, wife of John—she of the beautiful auburn tresses and flashing smile—was only twenty-five. Tall and talented, she had grown in stature and respect as a mid-wife and mother. Her experiences after sixteen years of marriage had served to bring forth the best qualities and virtues of pioneer women. She knew the healing power of each herb, each leaf, each root. Having already borne six children, three sons and three daughters, she was quite qualified to deliver and care for the babies born in the wilderness—and had done so on many occasions.

Susannah was extremely devoted to her family and held her husband, John, in the highest esteem. And now she stood in the open doorway of their cabin and watched the men who had returned to the clearning. She saw her husband and John Carpenter move toward a log bench near Carpenter's house. The firm look on her husband's face gave further indication of the restlessness he had been experiencing lately—and she knew the time had come. She closed the door.

Joseph, the eldest son, not yet nine years old, was dressed now in a garb similar to his father's. He went outside to feed the two cows and two horses which the Tiltons owned. Thomas, who was born in early 1768, and was now seven years old, was splitting kindling for the stone fireplace in the cabin. Jackson, the five-year-old, was still asleep, wrapped in a coverlet of linsey-woolsey, as were four-year-old Polly and two-year-old Sally. Susannah gently picked up the baby, Susannah—John had insisted on naming their third daughter after his wife—and began nursing her.

She held her close and remembered.

It had been a long and arduous trek from Maryland. She and John had been married there when she was only nine years old in 1759. The little village of Elkridge where she was born and lived was somewhat vague in her memory. She never knew her mother, who had died young, and her father was overjoyed when John Tilton had asked for her hand in marriage. He knew the Tilton reputation and the high regard in which every Tilton was held. Age was no barrier. It mattered not that he was twelve years her senior. He was educated—he could read and write. His father, Joseph, had extensive land holdings in Kent County, and no doubt John could provide well for his young wife.

Susannah, young though she was, was quite infatuated with handsome, young John Tilton, even though they had known each other for only a short time. She was mature in thought and structure and was quite willing to become the wife of John Tilton. The marriage took place in St. Anne's Episcopal Church[3] just across the state line in Delaware. Many of John's relatives attended the wedding: his uncles, Thomas, James and Nehemiah were there; his brothers and sisters and some cousins; and, of course, his father and mother.

The young couple lived happily together on a section of Joseph

Tilton's estate which he deeded to John. Of all his brothers and sisters, John was particularly close to his brother Thomas, who was nineteen when John was married, John and Susannah were quite content in their Maryland home which was several miles north of Baltimore—at least until the summer of 1766.

In the meantime, traders and explorers were returning from their travels in the relatively unknown west. They told tales that old men would not believe, that men of middle age were intrigued by, and that young men were inspired to investigate. Ripe, golden, bounteous lands, virgin soil where corn would grow to its full productive height in one month, game so plentiful that a cool springhouse could be adequately stocked for winter in practically no time at all—this is what they said; there were things they left unsaid!

And so it was in late July of 1766, with Susannah three months pregnant, that John Tilton decided to give up his eastern holdings and seek his fortune in the west.

There is no mystery about their quest. It is an inborn trait for man to pioneer—to accept the challenge of the unknown. For many, it was the desire to acquire land, to build a cabin, to provide a living, to be strong and independent. For twenty-eight-year-old John Tilton, young, strong, adventuresome, it was more. Security he wanted not; the challenge of seeing and invading and occupying the land of the Indian, with all its hazards and hardships, he wanted.

Good and faithful wife that she was, Susannah wanted what her husband did. And also, being of the same high-spirited English stock as he, she anticipated the westward trek.

After selling his land and house and all excess livestock and furniture, for which he received a good price, John Tilton retained three strong horses and two good milk cows.

Joining a pack horse train organized to move westward, Susannah rode on one of the horses, which also carried the table vessels and cooking utensils. The second horse was loaded with several cases of provisions and tools for cultivating the land and building cabins. Two large crates woven from tree branches were filled with clothing and bedding, and a barrel of water was tied securely to balance the load. The two milk cows which followed provided milk for the children in the train and for others whose tastes were so inclined. John walked ahead of the lead horse, upon which his wife was riding, rein in hand.

The pack horse train, consisting of about fourteen horses, seven cows and five families, moved slowly along the Potomac River, finally reaching Fort Cumberland. After a night's rest, they struck out along Nemacolin's Trail,[4] and with every mile the travel became more arduous and tiresome. During the latter part of their journey, they were greeted by a number of frontiersmen exploring the lands along the Youghiogheny River, and eventually the packhorse train disbanded at Burd's Road.[5] Some of the settlers moved north toward Fort Pitt. After some discussion, the Tiltons decided to take the Burd's Road route, and soon they arrived in the small frontier town of Redstone Old Fort.[6] Here they found a strong, substantial structure called Fort Burd in honor of Colonel James Burd, who had directed its construction in 1759. They were also aware of numerous settlements in the outlying areas along the Youghiogheny, and they decided to settle here, at least temporarily. John built a small cabin not far from the Fort. He came to know many of the early settlers, including the Gists, the Paulls and the Browns.[7] From these, he learned much.

Only about two months earlier, a regiment of His Majesty's Soldiers from Fort Pitt had come to Fort Burd and posted a notice to the effect that the settlers were encroaching on Indian lands, and, unless they returned to their particular colonies in the east immediately, their possessions could be justly claimed by the Indians and force would be used to drive them east of the Allegheny mountains.

The governors of the two states involved, Penn of Pennsylvania and Fauquier of Virginia, issued joint proclamations to the same effect. The final boundary line between Pennsylvania and Virginia had not yet been established.

The threat of expulsion and loss of property had little effect upon the influx of adventurous and determined pioneers. The white population in the regions surrounding Redstone and the Monongahela Valley was expanding—without resistance from soldier or Indian. But the Indians, particularly the Delawares and Shawnees, were quite unhappy with the invasion.

After about a month in their abode at Redstone, the Tiltons

decided to move farther west. They were more concerned about the regimental forces than about the Indians. They loaded their gear upon the pack horses and, with the two cows in tow, traveled westward across the Monongahela, along a swift-flowing stream known as Buffalo Creek. In due time a green clearing of terrestrial beauty appeared not far from the headwaters of the creek.

The sun was slowly dropping behind the western hills. Susannah was tired.

"This is it, John," she said. "I believe we have found our land of milk and honey."

And so it was. Susannah, wife and mother-to-be at the age of sixteen, had spoken, and John agreed. The earth was black and rich, the water was pure and clear, and the forests were a contrasting array of unblemished nature.

The horses were quickly unloaded and foddered. The cows were milked and a hitching post was erected to prevent the animals from straying off during the night. A tentlike temporary shelter was set up and bedding was prepared.

John and Susannah slept. They had not taken time to eat supper. Tomorrow would be a busy day. They must acquaint themselves with the area and select a site for their cabin. Susannah was well into the fifth month of her pregnancy. It was September. The moon was bright and full. The silence was unbroken—but deadly.

The night passed without incident, and only the occasional hoot of an owl interrupted the solitude. They slept soundly, perhaps from fatigue; perhaps a feeling of self-satisfaction enveloped them; perhaps a peaceful dream consoled them.

Upon arising early the next morning, they further assessed the dew-laden area of their encampment. It was as they expected. They were alone in the wilderness, but the beauty and serenity of the silent forest was unparalleled in their memories. Even the waters of the Buffalo were quiet, and only an occasional chitchat of a brown sparrow or the cheep of a red cardinal broke the silence.

John collected some twigs and dry tree branches from the edge of the forest and started a small fire. Susannah fried cornmeal mush in an iron skillet and baked pone in the hot ashes.

"Perhaps the soldiers will not come to this area," said Susannah.

"I think not," agreed John, "and I intend to build a strong house and stock it well with meat and forest fruits. We will be secure and comfortable 'til spring."

And John did as he said. He felled trees, converted them into logs of the proper dimension, built a cabin and sealed it well with moss and clay from the creek bed. As expected, the winter was harsh and cold, with icy winds and heavy snows.

It was on just such a winter's night that Susannah Tilton gave birth to her first child—a boy. The date was December 30, 1766. And John was her only source of consolation and relief. He gently massaged her thighs and stomach before and after the child was born.

"We shall call him Joseph, after your father," she suggested. And so it was.

The Tiltons lived in quiet contentment at their early settlement west of the Monongahela River. Upon completion of the Mason and Dixon Line in 1767[8] which established only the southern boundary of the colony of Pennsylvania, it became known to the settlers at Redstone and to the Tiltons, John having made several trips back to that town, that their lands were within the colony of Pennsylvania.

Upon becoming aware that the Redstone and Monongahela settlements were officially recognized as part of his province, Governor Penn summoned the members of the assembly and made them aware of their responsibility to devise a means of dispossessing the settlers in these areas, and to exert every effort to prevent war with the Indians.

The Indians often visited the settlements and were always friendly and respectful. Certain white settlers were not. Bald Eagle, an old and steadfast friend of the settlers, was murdered; Indian Stephen was also killed in the Mon Valley. These and other similar incidents had stirred the Delawares and Shawnees to retaliatory threats.

In February of 1768, the Pennsylvania Assembly took drastic measures and enacted a law to compel withdrawal of the settlers. The law stated that many disorderly people, in violation of His

Majesty's proclamation, had presumed to settle upon lands not yet purchased from the Indians. This action, the law proclaimed, had created great concern among the Indians and could endanger the peace and safety of the privince. The law further stated that if any settlers, after notice or proclamation sent to them, should not remove themselves within thirty days, or if any should settle after such notice, every such person being legally convicted of such, should suffer death without benefit of clergy. It also proclaimed that anyone encroaching on these unpurchased lands to make surveys, or to cut down or mark trees, should pay the sum of fifty pounds and be imprisoned for three months.

The law, although written in somewhat terrifying terms, exempted certain areas in the Fort Pitt and Fort Burd areas and was quite ineffective in forcing the stout-hearted pioneers east of the Alleghenies.

In the spring of 1768, Susannah gave birth to a second son, Thomas, and once again her husband imparted a sense of warmth and safety and well-being, even though other emigrants from the east had now moved into the area and erected crude log structures.

In the summer of 1768, John, leaving his family in the care of other settlers in the region, returned once again to Redstone to barter or buy certain provisions. There were about one hundred fifty families abiding in the area of the fort and the Youghiogheny and Cheat rivers. Many new cabins had been built along the river banks, and upon effectively accomplishing his trade, which included one of his horses, John decided to tour the immediate area to ascertain news from the east and the disposition of the colonial government.

He was much surprised and exuberant when he found that one of the cabins was occupied by his brother Thomas. The brothers were almost in tears as they embraced each other.

"Thomas," said John, "my joy in seeing you exceeds all bounds. Tell me—why are you here and how are our father and mother and the others?"

"I have taken a wife, John," replied Thomas, "and we have a three-month-old son. We have only been here about three weeks. I like the people and the clear water and the green forests and the smell of the wild foliage. Our father is fine; mother was sad to see us go. I have hoped for this moment—seeing you—talking to you. How is Susannah?"

"She is fine, and we now have two sons, one only about five months old. We are settled just west of here across the Monongahela River. Other families have moved into that area. You must come over. Perhaps you should desire to move there. At least, the soldiers from Fort Pitt have not pestered us and the few Indians we have seen and talked with have been friendly."

"That I will," said Thomas. "And now you must supper with us before returning."

John enjoyed the hospitality and lighthearted, but revealing, conversation which occurred while they were eating.

"I must be going," he said. "The sun is well down in the western sky, and Susannah expects me before nightfall."

John mounted his horse and the brothers bade each other farewell.

Upon returning home, John related the happenings of the day to Susannah and she, too, was surprised that John's brother had married and come west. She looked forward to seeing Thomas and his family.

In fact, hardly a month passed during the next three years that the brothers and their families failed to get together for a day of reminiscing and relaxation from their daily toil.

Thomas had decided to stay in the Redstone area. The pressure of the military to force the settlers to return to the east had subsided. He and his family were quite happy in this frontier town. He had expanded and strengthened his cabin, and the land he farmed was productive. The Thomas Tilton family had become quite friendly with most of the Redstone residents.

In the fall of 1769, John and Susannah became the parents of a third son, whom they named Jackson. It was a time of joy—all too fleeting. The rainbow-shaded forests were a monument of beauty. The cabin was well stocked with the necessary provisions to sustain life. But John was restless. More often now, he explored the surrounding countryside and became quite competent as a hunter, scout, and woodsman.

Polly, the first daughter of John and Susannah Tilton was born in the summer of 1771. Meanwhile, the settlers near the head-waters of the Buffalo became more numerous. Jacob Wolfe[9] came and, with the help of John and other adventurers in the area, built a strong fort about a mile west of Tilton's cabin. This was, indeed, a source of consolation to many of the residents in the immediate area, since the Indians appeared to be assuming an air of superiority; certain incidents of their savagery had been reported.

The winter of 1771-72 was uneventful, at least for John and Susannah Tilton. And in early spring, John was determined to move further west. They packed their belongings, loaded the pack horses, and struck out westward along the Buffalo.

"Good luck and God protect you," called Wolfe, as they passed his fort. "You are always welcome to return if the situation demands."

"Thanks, Jacob," replied Tilton, "but, as for now, I must see what lies ahead."

The Tilton contingent moved slowly along the north bank of the Buffalo. After traveling about seven miles west of Wolfe's Fort, they crossed the creek and decided to make a settlement. John tomahawked a large claim, built a cabin of sufficient size to accommodate Susannah and their four children, and cleared the area to plant a patch of corn.

Other settlers soon came and claimed adjacent lands. Among these were the Carpenters, the McCormicks, and the Wellses. John and Susannah were happy to have other settlers in the area; neighbors provided a great source of consolation.

In the summer, a young man named James Maxwell[10] came north from Wheeling and stopped at the Tilton settlement seeking temporary shelter.

"I won't be here long," he said. "Movin' on down the creek."

"And what might you find there, Mr. Maxwell?" asked John.

"I know what I'll find, Mr. Tilton. A great blue river, three times as wide as the one east of here and a land that neither plow nor axe has touched—and the distance from here to there is not great."

John Tilton listened well and remembered.

True to his word, James Maxwell did not remain long at the Tilton settlement. Susannah had provided goods, food, and adequate shelter in a lean-to adjacent to the Tilton cabin.

"I have enjoyed being here with you and your family, Mr. Tilton, and I really appreciate the comfort you have afforded me, but now I must resume my quest."

"It's only been a week, Maxwell; you are certainly welcome to stay longer."

"No. But I shall remember you well," replied Maxwell.

At that point, he struck out on foot, well-provisioned, strong, and filled with determination.

In the fall of 1772, existence and harmony in the wilderness had not been as productive as John and Susannah had expected. Although after six years in the western frontier, they had conditioned themselves to pioneer life, they were not content, and at this point in time, the Indians were becoming more aggressive and oppressive. Previous treaties apparently were meaningless to them. Consequently, the Tilton settlement, south of the Buffalo, was attacked by roving bands of Shawnees and Delawares. Constant vigilance and alertness were necessary; and quite often a savage redskin with mischievous intent had felt the wrath of John's hunting knife—the sharp edge of his hatchet or a lead ball from his long rifle—but only if he threatened the life or limb of his family or friends. He grew wise in the antics of the wily savages as did most of the other settlers along the Buffalo.

As for Susannah—she of the auburn tresses and flashing eyes—she had mastered the art of using the rifle and ball and was always a keen competitor in the shooting games in which the settlers engaged from time to time. She plowed the lands, planted the corn and potatoes, harvested the crops, prepared the meals, and cared for the children. She bore her children, helped others in bearing theirs and conducted herself as a strong and capable lady of the wilderness.

In early fall of 1773, the second daughter of John and Susannah Tilton, Sally, was born on the Tilton homestead near Buffalo Creek. John Carpenter's wife, Nancy, acted as midwife during this event, and in time the Tiltons, Carpenters, McCormicks, Harrises, Wellses[11] and others in the area came to know one another quite well.

John Carpenter was a member of Major George Washington's

retinue when he visited the French fort in western Pennsylvania in 1753. Later he was a member of the Virginia Riflemen and a captain in command of a garrison on the Virginia border. Upon pursuing a party of Indians, in conjunction with the soldiers, he came upon a burning structure which the Indians had set afire. The Indians were intent on leaving the area when Carpenter and his men encountered them. In the ensuing battle, most of the Indians were killed and Carpenter entered the burning cabin. Here he found a young woman who had been tomahawked by the Indians, lying on a bed. Her husband had been murdered by the savages. She eventually recuperated from her wounds and became the wife of John Carpenter. They were quite content, especially after a son, Edward, was born. Not long thereafter, they moved westward, settled on Jacob's Creek, and became traders. In the summer of 1773, when John was about forty-one years old, the Carpenters were near Tilton's settlement on the Buffalo. John Carpenter enjoyed solitary hunting and exploratory expeditions which often lasted throughout all the daylight hours in a single day or more. Always he returned with a good supply of fresh meat, which he would share with others in the area who might be in need.

With the advent of Dunmore's War in 1774, which was the direct result of false reports to pioneers in Wheeling and the surrounding areas that war with the Indians was imminent, and the treacherous murder of the Mingo Chief Logan's family at Joshua Baker's camp in the east side of the Ohio across the River from Yellow Creek, the Indians of the valley took up the hatchet to wreak vengeance on the white settlers. Bloodthirsty bands of Mingoes, Shawnees, and Delawares invaded western Virginia.

The Tiltons and other settlers in that vicinity retreated eastward to the apparent safety of Jacob Wolfe's Fort and remained there until late in the year. In December, when the threat of Indian depredations had diminished, John and Susannah and their children returned to their settlement and found their cabin intact. Even the provisions which they had left behind, stored in the attic, were unmolested. Here, they spent the winter of 1774-75.

After almost nine years, John Tilton was, once again, restless and somewhat disturbed. He continued to expand his talents as

an expert hunter and trapper and scout. And, as of late, the
existence of himself and his family was seriously imperiled by
marauding Indians, wild panthers and bears, and avaricious and
treacherous renegades. After the end of Dunmore's War and with
the signing of the treaty of Camp Charlotte[12] now in effect, the
cabins and land claims along the Buffalo were slowly becoming
abandoned.

———————

    Susannah finished feeding the baby and returned her to her
crib. At the stone fireplace, she prepared the morning meal of
cornpone and mush. John would be home soon. The children
were up now. She was arranging the food on the rough-hewn
wooden table when John returned. He greeted the children and
kissed his wife.

    As they ate, his face was firm but his dark eyes sparkled.

    "Susannah," he said, "I was just talking to Carpenter. He plans
to stay here for a while. Others, east of here, are talking about
moving to Wheeling or returning to Catfish.[13] Do you have any
thoughts on the matter?"

    "My thoughts are yours, John."

    John smiled; he had known what she would say.

    "Good," he proclaimed. "Today, we will begin our
preparations; we shall move west to see for ourselves this great
blue river called the Ohio."

II

THE GREAT BLUE RIVER

THE PACK HORSE TRAIN WAS ALIGNED and loaded with all the essential equipment and provisions that two strong horses and two cows could carry. The Tilton family bade "Good-bye and God's help in the future" to their friends. Then, with John and the two older boys leading the way, the seekers of land, adventure, and the great blue river, moved westward along the Buffalo.

Susannah and her baby daughter rode securely on the lead horse, while Jackson, Polly, and Sally straddled the horse that followed, in a strong hickory-thistle enclosed saddle. The path was narrow and the pace was slow, but John Tilton's whole being was filled with a feeling of exhilaration. He was constantly aware of his surroundings and the dangers from Indians and wild beasts that might be lurking in the forest. At the age of nine, Joseph was strong and wise in the ways of the woods, having grown up in the wilderness. He, too, could sense a silent foe. He had developed the hunter's instinct, and his tread was as soft as his father's. The boys enjoyed hearing their father tell stories about the Indians which he had heard from other settlers or events in which he himself had been involved.

"Tell us a story while we are walking, father," said Joseph.

Thomas persisted, "Yes, the one about the great chief who came here last year when we were all hidden in Mr. Wolfe's Fort."

Their father smiled. He loved his family and he enjoyed telling stories to the children—Susannah listened, too.

"I will tell the story as I know it," said Tilton, "and I have learned it from others. Let your imagination wander. Last year was a dark and bloody year for people such as we, who seek good land in fertile valleys. I will tell you of the great chief from the time of his birth—I know not where he is now. I saw him only once when he passed Jacob Wolfe's Fort last summer. I am not anxious to see him again. This you will understand soon. Listen— and be constantly on your guard."

John talked as they walked, relating in simple terms what he knew of the great chief. There was much he did not know, but the boys listened intently.

Camouflaged by the high grass and heavy foliage—the white-tipped brown eagle feathers only occasionally visible—the tall, bronze Indian moved swiftly, almost ubiquitously, from oak to oak. His eight companions followed closely. Ever alert to the slightest sound—the call of a bird or the gobble of a turkey—his onyx eyes pierced the twilight.

Dressed only in soft deerskin leggins and high, tightly laced moccasins, his face was firm and strong, not reflecting his forty-nine years of life. Silver bands encircled his wrists and the upper part of each arm, and around his neck hung a decorative silver necklace.

This was Tah-Gah-jute,[1] Chief of the Mingoes—a nomadic branch of the Cayuga tribe. His more common name to his brothers, the red men, and to his former friends, the white men, was—Logan!

Logan was born at Shamokin on the Susquehanna River in 1725, the second son of Shikellemus, the principal chief of the Cayugas. He was named Logan in honor of James Logan, Secretary of the Province of Pennsylvania and a devoted friend of the Indians.

Logan had moved from the Cayuga country to settle near the Juniata River in central Pennsylvania. Here, he married a Shawnee maiden after the death of his father in about 1749.

Logan, his family, and a small band of his Mingo followers, came west of the Alleghenies in 1770 and established a hunting camp at the mouth of Yellow Creek[2] in the Ohio Country. Statuesque and wise, and possessing great oratorical ability, his word was highly respected by both Indians and whites. He had explored the Middle Ground where, up to this time, few white men had ever dared venture. He was welcomed in the village of Cornstalk, the great chief of the Shawnee; he knew and advised

Elinipsico, son of Cornstalk, and Blue Jacket, the white boy who became the ferocious war chief of the Shawnee.[3] White Eyes and Captain Pipe, Delaware chieftains, were his friends as was the infamous white renegade, Simon Girty.

White frontiersmen were always welcome in his camp, and Simon Kenton and David Duncan were often there.

Logan did not know fear. He was courageous and brave while possessing a unique tender quality. Judge William Brown[4] said of Logan, "He was the best specimen of humanity I ever saw or met with, either white or red."

To illustrate the nature of Logan, it is known that one day when Judge Brown, one of the early pioneers in Redstone Valley, was away from home, Logan stopped at his cabin. Mrs. Brown, although somewhat apprehensive, greeted him warmly. She had a little daughter who was just beginning to walk and told Logan that she wished she had a pair of shoes for her. Upon leaving, Logan asked if the little girl might spend the day with him. Although concerned, Mrs. Brown was afraid to refuse, and off they went, the tall, stately Mingo and the tiny, innocent girl. The day was a long and anxious one for Mrs. Brown. Near eventide, Logan returned with the little girl on his shoulder. She toddled to her mother, on her feet she wore a pair of new moccasins.

In early 1774, the Earl of Dunmore, Governor of Virginia, instructed his agent at Fort Pitt, Dr. John Connolly, the treacherous Tory, to bring about a treaty with the Indians and enlist them to serve in future encounters on the side of the crown. Connolly's plot is well documented. He sent circulars to the settlers along the Ohio and to Captain Thomas Cresap at Wheeling, saying that the Shawnees were not trustworthy and had declared open warfare upon the white men.

Connolly's false insinuation caused considerable consternation among the settlers and, being the faithful soldier that he was, Cresap was determined to defend the western Virginia settlements.

In late April, two canoes carrying Indians were seen passing an island near Wheeling. Cresap and several of his men gave chase, and when the Indians encamped at the mouth of Captina Creek, the whites attacked, killing one Indian and wounding several others.

This was one of the events that led to what has become known as "Dunmore's War"; the other was the atrocious murder of Logan's relatives and friends who were stationed at his hunting camp on Yellow Creek.

The latter deed, an insidious crime in the eyes of red men and white men alike, was planned and perpetrated by one Greathouse, the Mahon brothers, and about twenty-seven other white men of low moral character and an even lower sense of decency. It occurred at Baker's Bottom on the Virginia side of the river almost directly across from Logan's camp.

Thus, the peaceful Mingoes, always in accord with their leader, Logan, were lured across the river for a friendly feast of fun and games. After plying the Indians with rum, all were massacred in a most ruthless manner, the only exception being a ten-year-old boy, supposedly the son of Colonel John Gibson and Logan's sister.

Upon returning from the hunt, Logan beheld the scene in disbelief. He blamed Captain Cresap for the deed, not knowing that Cresap was fifteen miles away at the time, in Redstone. After burying the dead, he lifted his tomahawk and swore revenge:

> I, Logan, will not rest until I have taken ten white scalps for every one of my relatives slain!

No longer was Logan the friend of the white man, the advocate of peace: he was Logan the avenger.

It was July, 1774. Logan moved silently and swiftly toward the Creek of the Buffalo. The Mingoes moved westward past Wilson's Fort and Rice's Fort[5] on the south branch of Buffalo Creek. Seeing no activity and no whites, they moved on, finally approaching Jacob Wolfe's Fort.

The occupants of Wolfe's Fort had been forewarned of his approach. Chinks in the stockade wall revealed the regal bearing of the Great Mingo. He was only about fifty paces from the main bastion of the fort. No evidence of life was apparent—the silence was deafening.

Logan and his party left the scene without a sound and turned northeast toward the west branch of the Monongahela. Upon approaching that area, they saw three men—Major William Robinson, Thomas Hellen and Coleman Brown, who were pulling flax in a field near the mouth of Simpson's Creek. The unsuspecting flax pullers were quite unprepared for the burst of gunfire which killed Brown instantly. Robinson and Hellen ran for safety, but Hellen was soon captured and bound. Robinson continued running, with Logan in pursuit.

"Stop, I won't hurt you," cried Logan.

"Yes, you will," Robinson replied.

"No, I won't; but if you don't stop, I'll shoot you."

Robinson continued running, but while looking back over his shoulder he fell over a log. Quickly, Logan was upon him and immediately made himself known to his captive.

"You must come quietly now with your white brother. No harm shall come to you."

Upon reaching the Mingo town on the Muskingum River, Robinson was forced to run the gauntlet, which consisted of two long lines of men, women, and children, facing each other and standing about four feet apart. All were armed with clubs, sticks, and switches. The victim was forced to run as far as he could between the two rows of Indians, who thrashed him unmercifully as he passed. Very few white men had run the gauntlet and lived to tell about it.

Upon instructions from Logan, Robinson was permitted to pass through without serious injury. He was then tied to a stake to be burned, but after much discussion, pro and con, the masterful eloquence of Logan prevailed and his bonds were loosened.

It is said that Hellen was adopted into the tribe.

Shortly, thereafter, Logan took Robinson to the village of Newcomer, the principal chief of the Delawares, on the Tuscarawas.[6] Here Logan requested the major to write him a strong note, expressing his feelings concerning Captain Cresap. Using ink made from gunpowder, the note was written as follows:

Captain Cresap:

What did you kill my people on Yellow Creek for? The white people killed my kin at Conestoga, a great while ago, and I thought nothing of that. But you killed my kin again on Yellow Creek, and took my cousin prisoner. Then I thought I must kill too; and I have been three

times to war since; but the Indians are not angry, only
myself.

July 21, 1774   (Signed) Captain John Logan[7]

The note was found, tied to a war club, in the cabin of a settler
on the Holston River. Four months later, Robinson returned to
his Virginia home.

The children were tiring. The little pack horse train had been
moving steadily, traveling only about four or five miles. It was
late afternoon and the sun was two-thirds down in the western
sky. Unknown to John Tilton, the great blue river—the
Ohio—was only a short distance farther west.

"We will rest here and eat supper," he said.

The small clearing he had chosen was, indeed, a picture of
tranquility. Yellow daffodils, wreathed in a mantle of soft green,
nodded gently and the sparkling, clear water of the creek flowed
smoothly, with only an occasional ripple, created by its
inhabitants, breaking the silence. A jungle of locusts, oaks, and
pines adorned the hills on each side of the creek.

After gathering dry twigs and branches, the boys had prepared
a fire for cooking, and Susannah baked leaf-covered potatoes in
the hot ashes and stirred a clover-laden rabbit stew in an iron pot
suspended over the fire.

In a short time, Susannah had filled the pewter bowls that she
had brought from Maryland and carefully preserved during their
tenure on the frontier. They ate quietly with only occasional
laughter and chatter from the children breaking the silence of the
shaded clearing in the wilderness. The horses and cows grazed
nearby. John and Susannah sat near each other on a grassy
mound.

After sixteen years of marriage, she never ceased to amaze him
with her vitality and her invigorating spirit which seemed to have
been inculcated in the children. As wife and mother, she never
questioned his decisions, yet she was strong-willed and when she
spoke or acted, it was with forcefulness and wisdom.

When Susannah had finished washing the iron pot and was

packing the utensils on the horses, the soft padding of a single horse could be heard coming toward them from the east.

Without hesitation, John grabbed his gun and directed his family to take cover in a nearby cluster of trees. This they did quickly.

In moments, a lone white, buckskin-clad rider appeared.

"Hold your fire," called the horseman. "I'm Sam McColloch[8] from Fort Van Metre just south of here. Wondered if I might be of some assistance."

Tilton relaxed. The name was familiar.

The rider climbed down from his horse, tethered it on a low-hanging branch and walked with noiseless ease toward the little camp. John handed his rifle to Susannah and moved toward the stranger.

"Tilton's the name," he said. "John Tilton."

"You can tell your family to come out, Mr. Tilton. I mean no mischief. I've been watching you about half an hour."

John followed his suggestion, and soon they were all gathered around McColloch.

Susannah asked, "Would you like some pone and milk, sir?"

"That would be fine, Mrs. Tilton, haven't eaten since morning. My brother, John, and I do most of the scouting for the fort. Things been rather quiet on this side of the Ohio in recent months.

"So I understand," said John. "Did you say Van Metre's Fort?"

"Yes. It's about four miles south and sets about five miles east of the river. Quite a few families are quartered in that area."

John was suddenly alert.

"And the river you speak of—is it wide and deep and blue?"

"That it is," said McColloch, "but I suggest you not cross. The fertile valley to the west is filled with savages and bears. Furthermore, a treaty with the Indians forbids our entering that virgin country."

"And how far from the river are we, Mr. McColloch?"

"Not far. You could reach it in about half an hour at the pace you travel. I suggest you stake a claim in the commonwealth—and, oh yes—I should tell you. Word has arrived that we are now at war with England. We now have two enemies, Mr. Tilton—the Tories and the Indians."

"I suspected as much," said Tilton. "The rumors were such when I was in Redstone not long ago. The soldiers of Fort Pitt had ceased their attempts to drive us out. As for staking a claim, we did so about three years ago and our settlement is established about five miles east of here."

"You should also be aware, Mr. Tilton, that I have just received my commission in the Army of Independence as a major. I trust I can depend on you to fight for freedom?"

"Without question, major."

"Then I'll be on my way. Meanwhile, you best return to your settlement and a strong cabin—the need for such will not be long in coming. I am grateful for the food, Mrs. Tilton, and God be with all of you."

With this admonition, coupled with courtesy, McColloch walked back to his horse, mounted easily, and moved off in the direction from which he had come.

The Tiltons watched until he disappeared. Ignoring the advice of McColloch, John said, "We will move on and bed down before nightfall."

Moving at a more rapid pace now, they were soon aware of the widening of the creek, and suddenly, almost in disbelief, they gazed in wonderment on the great blue river—*La Belle Rivière*, the French had called it—"The Beautiful River."

The golden rays of a setting sun were like flaming arrows reflecting on an azure surface of tranquility. John, Susannah, and the children of vision drank in the beauty of the western landscape. The lofty trees, decorated in multi-hued green—tan-sunned beaches—the coves and inlets, formed an indelible impression on their minds.

In an adjacent clearing, they camped for the night. Long after Susannah and the children were asleep, John Tilton pondered the events of the morrow, and moonlit shadows danced gracefully as the dark folds of night encompassed them.

III

INDIAN COUNTRY

AT DAYBREAK, JOHN WAS THE FIRST to awake. It was late in May and the early morning air was cool and fresh. The pleasant scent of pine was invigorating, and after assuring himself that Susannah and the children were safe and comfortable in their blankets of deerskin, he gathered some dry brush wood from the hill and built a small, almost smokeless fire.

After sharpening a point on the end of a slender pole, he quickly speared and prepared enough catfish for their breakfast.

By this time, Susannah was awake and watching her husband. The children were stirring. Securing an iron skillet from one of the pack saddles, she greased it with bear's fat and awaited John's approach.

"Hail and good morning. I bring you choice morsels from yon river."

Susannah smiled. She relished the eloquence he exhibited on particular occasions. "And the same to you, sir," she responded. "I am sure they will be delicious."

The boys were awake now and laughing softly. They were amused by this display of gallantry. And always it served to set them at ease, because even at such lean ages, they were apprehensive and aware of their environment.

As they were eating, John said, "We will not cross the river today. I think it would be well if we expanded our claim on this eastern side and return to our cabin, as Major McColloch suggested."

Susannah agreed.

"We'll mark that large maple near the river and travel south."

"The beach is narrow and the hill is high," replied Susannah. "Would it not be wiser for you and Joseph to go by foot and stake the claim? Thomas will stay, and we are well concealed in this sheltered grove."

As usual, the wisdom of Susannah prevailed. Before leaving, John filled the pouch in his hunting coat with dried strips of venison and bear meat and a nugget of pone. He tomahawked a large "T" on the maple near the river, and bidding his wife farewell, John, followed by Joseph, moved south along the river bank.

While wending their way along the sandy beach of the river and occasionally moving up along the hillside into the back country, carving the Tilton "T" on the sturdy trees as they trekked, they arrived at the mouth of a creek.[1]

"This must be the creek of which Major McColloch spoke," said John. "We will move east along the creek bank and stake out a good claim."

They walked silently about two miles before sitting down in a shaded glen to rest and eat. The sun was high in the sky, and John wanted to return to the place whence they had started before nightfall. He would have liked to explore farther up the creek to locate the fort that McColloch had described. At this point, they had seen only a small log cabin[2] on the south side of the creek. He decided there would be time enough later for that expedition.

Soon, father and son were moving to the northeast. The terrain was hilly and heavily overgrown with trees and vines. To maintain a relatively true course, they often had to cut their way through the dense foliage. They had seen neither Indian nor white man. In due time they came upon a familiar setting. They had arrived at the Creek of the Buffalo, and the irregular outline of their tomahawked claim included the land encompassed in their earlier settlement. Without hesitating, they forded the stream and headed toward the Ohio.

Susannah was happy when her husband and son returned. Although she had no doubt they would accomplish their mission, there was always the possibility of some unforeseen danger.

"We have staked a good claim," said John. "Much of the land is hilly, but there are many clearings and the soil is good."

Susannah prepared their supper. Her husband sat in silence, gazing at the great blue river and the land to the west. He seemed deep in thought.

She of the beautiful auburn tresses and flashing smile could discern that something was troubling him.

"John, all is not well with you," she said. "Tell me."

He walked toward her and sat down. "I have thought much today, Susannah. We came here nine years ago to make a new life—to find new land and adventure. While at Redstone, the soldiers from Pittsburgh often pestered us to go back east, until we moved further west. Our goal has not been accomplished, and time is fleeting. Who is to say what will come next? I have a strange and strong feeling. If you do not object, tomorrow I will build a raft and cross the river."

Susannah smiled. "My place is with you, John, and the children. All that you said is true. I do not object. However, you do recall Major McColloch telling about a treaty with the Indians, I'm sure."

"That I do. But I know well most such agreements mean nothing. Many have been made previously and been broken by both parties. Who is to say the meaning of this treaty? And besides, we can always return to this side of the river, should the need arise."

Susannah nodded. John embraced her tenderly and kissed her.

After finishing their evening meal, while twilight settled over the green valley, all retired in their secluded camping area.

The night passed quickly, and at the first sign of daybreak, John was awake. Ever cautious, he slowly crawled from beneath his deerskin cover and silently observed the countryside. It was a tranquil, clear morning. Only a gentle breeze from the south caused a slight ripple on the river. Susannah was awake now and, after assurance from John, that all was well, together they prepared a breakfast of mush and pone.

"I think it would be well if I crossed the river alone," said John. "If I deem what appears to be a rich and fertile bottom land as the place for our abode, I shall stake a claim and return before the sun sets."

"We are well concealed in the small hamlet," confirmed Susannah, "and it would be hazardous for all to cross with the horses and cows."

John ate quickly and, procuring his felling ax, he proceeded, in a most skillful manner, to cut and drop four tall oaks that were not too distant from his camp. By this time, Joseph and Thomas had joined him and, with their tomahawks, they cleared the branches from the fallen trees. John cut the trees into logs about twelve feet long and notched the end of each log, which was about fourteen inches in diameter. Working as a team, they rolled the logs near the edge of the river. In the meantime, Susannah had been preparing long strands of fresh deerhide. With these thongs, John and the boys bound the logs together firmly, using the notches which had been cut for that purpose.

By the time they had completed the raft, which was about twelve feet square, the sun was one-third of the way across the sky. John selected and prepared a long, stout pole and fortified himself with jerky and pone. The raft was pushed slowly into the broad expanse of the blue water and John, propelling pole in hand, waved farewell, saying, "I'll be back in due time—take care 'til I return."

He could not see, nor could the children, the little tears in the flashing eyes of Susannah as her auburn tresses waved gently in the breeze.

John Tilton was strong, and in a short time he was almost to the middle of the river. Although he had headed directly across, he found the current also strong, and he drifted southward. As he approached the western shore, he realized he had floated some distance from his original objective. When only about thirty feet from the shoreline, he saw a creek[3] flowing out of the western hills. He shoved hard on the pole and immediately was engulfed by a swift eddy of water that caused him to momentarily lose his balance and almost fall from the raft. As he passed the creek, the whirlpools and rapidly flowing water subsided and, spotting a quiet inlet, he forced the raft ashore and climbed off onto a sandy, pebbly beach.

John's crossing of the river had taught him much—and he would remember. Unknowingly, he had traversed about six miles south of his place of origin. He was undaunted, and the peaceful glen that led to the cove where he had landed intrigued him. He quickly pulled the raft upon the beach and moved cautiously up the gentle rolling hillside that led away from the river.[4]

When he reached the top of the bank, he was amazed at the vast area of lush green bottom land that reached to the base of a high hill. The land was dotted with an extensive variety of trees and bushes and vines and small clearings. He saw rabbits and turkeys and deer and squirrels and he knew that this was, indeed, a land of plenty—and a land of adventure. He dented the earth with his heel and his tomahawk; it was rich and black. He knew that this was the land in which he must settle and farm and live.

Noiselessly, he walked the paths untrodden by the white man and marked with his hatchet a large claim along the river, finally arriving back at the glen where his raft was beached. Bouyant in spirit, he descended to the beach and, seizing his long pole, slid the raft into the river. He knew the currents now, and his destination was true. He poled a straight course. Upon nearing the eastern side, he shoved in close to shore, where the current was not strong, and moved north toward his small camp on Buffalo Creek. Almost immediately, he came upon a creek which he recognized as the one in which Van Metre's Fort was located and he saw the large "T" which he had carved on a white beech near the river.

After much exertion, tiring even for a man of his endurance and strength, he arrived at his destination and was greeted with a discreet, but joyful, display of happiness.

"Tomorrow, we move," he told Susannah, as they snuggled on their bed of leaves. "I have found what you want and I want." Susannah was happy. The owls hooted; the wolves howled; the night was dark—but Susannah was happy.

In the morning, John explained his plan.

"The raft is large and sturdy enough to carry us safely across the river," he told Susannah. "We will travel downstream to Van Metre's Creek. The boys will lead the horses and cows along the river bank to the same spot. Here we will fence the horses and cows, on land which I have claimed, until we have need of them. At this point, we will cross the river and I will show you the beautiful countryside which I have selected to build a cabin."

Soon the horses were packed and the four animals aligned and tied for single file movement. The boys were in a joyful and playful mood. The spirit—the happiness, the joy, and the love—exhibited by their parents, created a surge of youthful energy within them and they reacted accordingly.

John poled the raft at a pace consistent with the progress of the boys and their pack horse train, always keeping them in sight and constantly aware of any obstacle they might encounter.

The voyage downstream was smooth and uneventful. Four-year-old Polly, even at such a tender age, possessed many of her mother's frivolous characteristics. She sat on the rear of the craft and dangled her bare feet in the water.

Upon arriving at Van Metre's Creek, John shored the raft. Using strong saplings, he fenced in a sufficient portion of his Virginia claim to pasture the horses and cows. Susannah and the older boys assisted in this construction, and upon its completion, they all boarded the raft with a minimum of provisions, and crossed the great blue river.

Joseph had provided himself with a long, stout pole similar to his father's, and the second crossing was much easier, even with the added weight. John avoided the eddies and swift currents as much as possible, and he had no difficulty in beaching the raft in the same cove he had discovered the day before.

They climbed the bank in high anticipation—and their hopes were well rewarded. This was truly a wonderland of terrestrial beauty. Together, they explored the spacious claim that John had marked.

"The ground is high, and the soil is rich," explained John. "We will build a home here, clear the land, and plant our corn."

And so they did—beginning the same day. The high grass in the selected area was cut short by hoe and knife. Vines and dense overgrowth were removed and unwanted trees were felled or girdled for death. By eventide, a well-defined clearing had been established and many fallen trees had been stripped of their branches, preparatory to building a cabin.

At this point in time, they had not seen any person, red or white, since Major McColloch had visited them. Both shores were peaceful and serene. But life on the frontier had conditioned the Tiltons to be watchful and vigilant. And so they were.

Just prior to sunset, they returned to the eastern side of the river, watered and fed the livestock, prepared their beds of leaves in a secluded ravine—and slept.

The next day, after crossing the river, they cut the fallen oak and ash trees into lengths of about fifteen and twenty-four feet. The boys had gathered round stones and rocks from the river bank and beach and secured them in a depressed area outlined by their father. These would serve as a foundation for their house in the wilderness.

The trees selected for the cabin were tall and straight, averaging from six to eight inches in diameter. John notched the ends of the logs on opposite sides, using his ax to form semicircles. The base logs were placed in position and anchored with oak stakes. The straight, notched logs were piled with accuracy, strength, and expediency under the expert direction of John. He had built cabins of this type before and had helped others construct similar abodes. At a height of about five feet, he intentionally chinked the logs on all four sides of the rectangular structure to permit the insertion of a rifle and a view of the surrounding area. Prior to erecting the top section of their pioneer home, John split the logs, using an ax and wooden wedges and formed a solid ceiling before erecting the rafters and triangular end sections. This storage area, accessible by a log ladder and an open entrance, would serve as ample space for food supplies and necessary provisions during the winter. At one end of the cabin, a hearthstone of rock was assembled and a hole cut in the ceiling and roof to let the smoke out, as this masonry base would be used for cooking and heating. If all went well, an outside chimney of stone would eventually be built. Puncheon flooring was laid flat, blocked and levelled, and fitted neatly around the hearthstone.

The boys had carried a mud-based moss from the shallow river coves and sealed the narrow slits between the logs. When the mud and moss were dry, the cabin would be well protected from the elements and wild beasts—the only openings being the intentional chinks and the doorway which John had trimmed with oak planks. The door, which could be secured by a heavy timber on the inside, would swing easily on the wooden hinges—pegged and greased with bear's fat.

The interior of the cabin was furnished with only the minimal necessities. Beds of strong, young saplings were secured along one side and Susannah, weaving the magic of a frontier wife and mother, prepared soft mattresses of linsey-covered leaves. Joseph and Thomas, using their tomahawks to good advantage, built a rough-hewn table outside the cabin and rolled some logs into position around the table. An A-framed cooking trammel was constructed over a bed of flat stones.

In all, the preliminary preparations for living in Indian country had taken about five days.

Meanwhile, John had defaced the opening clearing near the cabin by opening three rows of virgin soil. He planted two rows of corn and a row of beans.

Although a man of confidence and optimism, he was also realistic. He knew the dangers that threatened their survival west of the great blue river. Consequently, every accomplishment and all preliminary preparations required for the family's existence were performed on the basis that the present adventure would be temporary—but eventually permanent.

By the end of July, there had been no major incidents of primary concern. True, he had killed three bears and two panthers that had visited his cabin and threatened his family, but these actions only served to fatten the larder in the top of the cabin. The corn and beans were thriving, and a constant vigil, on the part of the older boys and their parents, protected their productive potential. They kept the rabbits, the groundhogs, the crows, and other creatures of the wild from destroying their crops.

John had explored the area to the north and south quite extensively. To the north, he had crossed the creek that had tempted him and threatened his survival on his first crossing of the river. He moved farther north and came upon a small cabin which appeared to him to have been vacated some time ago.

He did not know that this cabin had been built by his friend, James Maxwell, about three years ago. He did not know that Maxwell had lived there, alone, for about two years, and then, through fear of the hostile Indians during Dunmore's War, had returned to his home in Virginia.

Maxwell's cabin had deteriorated considerably. It was quite evident to John that heavy snows and lack of maintenance had rendered the cabin unworthy of occupancy. He knew not whether it had been built by Indians or whites, but the corner notching, with which he was familiar, indicated the latter.

John Tilton was a man of vision and his Anglo-Saxon blood demanded foresight, coupled with adventure. Susannah—she of the flashing smile and auburn tresses—was of the same temperament. And so it was that they decided to provide protection and provisions for their horses and cows in Virginia during the coming winter. An adequate log barn was constructed, and long hillgrass and corn were stored in a similar adjoining structure. In the spring of '76, they would decide on future actions.

The winter of 1775 was truly a wonderland of beauty and peacefulness as they lived an undisturbed but lonely life on the western flatland of *La Belle Rivière*. The cabin attic was well stocked with venison, rabbit, bear meat, corn, and beans. The snows were heavy, and sometimes the snow lay three feet deep on level areas and six feet deep in drifts. The river was frozen solid to a depth of four feet for over two months, and periodic excursions across the ice were made to care for the horses and milk the cows. Games in the snow and on the ice-covered river were enjoyed by all, including Polly and Sally, while the baby, Susannah, was warm and content in the cabin.

Fresh snow always invited a tracking hunt by John and often Joseph or Thomas, and invariably the Tilton storehouse in the top of the cabin was enlarged by six or eight fat rabbits, a deer or several pheasants.

Sometimes, in the evening, John was thoughtful and meditative.

"I am sometimes concerned about the war Major McColloch spoke of," he confided to Susannah. "I wonder about the colonist cause to which I am sympathetic. In the spring, I shall go to Van Metre's and even to Wheeling, if need be, to determine the situation."

Even the remarkable attributes of John Tilton could not discern the future—in which he was to play an important part.

IV

THE HARVEST
AND THE HAZARDS

BY LATE MARCH OF 1776, the frozen river had thawed and, although the nights were still cold, the temperature during the daylight hours seemed to be steadily rising. The Tiltons had survived their first winter west of the Ohio in good health. An occasional cold to one of the children was quickly subdued by the ministrations of Susannah, using bear's fat to grease the chest and throat, along with a dose of sassafras tea. Nevertheless, springtime would be welcome.

When it arrived and the trees were budding and the grass began to lose its muddish hue and turn to green, activity around the small cabin increased. The children became frolicsome, and John and Susannah prepared the seeds for the spring planting.

At the proper time, long furrows of black soil were dug, and a large patch of corn and beans and pumpkin was planted. It would make a bountiful harvest in the fall.

During an evening of solitude, as the sun was declining behind the western hill and the red embers of the cooking fire were still red, John and Susannah were alone, the children having bedded down for the night.

"Tomorrow, I will cross the river and find Van Metre's place," said John. "I feel that it is important to know the state of our safety and our security in this country. Throughout these long, cold months, we were unmolested by any human being. Who knows what the morrow may bring? You know the perils that could engulf us at any time."

Susannah concurred, "Things have been quiet. It is a lonely life. In a month or so, we will have another child. It would be well if we had friends nearby."

At sunrise, John crossed the river on his raft, foddered the horses and cows, which had weathered the winter in good condition, and traveled eastward along the northern creek bank. He soon arrived at a large oak on which he had marked his claim.

He continued his journey. Suddenly, he saw a small cabin to the north, from which smoke was puffing through a hole in one end. He cautiously approached and hailed the inhabitants, rifle in readiness.

Almost instantly, the cabin door opened, and a tall, buckskin-clad pioneer, gun in hand and wildcat-skin moccasins on his feet, emerged.

John, concealed by a large beech, surveyed the occupant of the doorway from head to toe. Suddenly, with a cry of joy, he ran forward, leaping and crying, "Carpenter! Carpenter!" The pioneer in the cabin cautiously crept outside.

"Carpenter, I knew you almost instantly," said John. "No one else wears wildcat-skin moccasins."

At this rejoinder, both ran toward each other and embraced in friendship.

"Tilton," said Carpenter, "Where have you been? I thought you and your family had long ago been dispatched by some savage. Come in—come in—eat—rest—and tell me."

They entered the cabin arm in arm, and John was greeted by Mrs. Carpenter and questioned, "And what of your family, Mr. Tilton—my good friend, Susannah, and the children?"

"All are well at this point, Mrs. Carpenter. We wintered west of the great blue river—the Ohio. We have made our spring plantings of corn and beans and pumpkins. The land in this area cannot produce a plentiful harvest; it is brown and not productive, for the most part."

"What of the safety—is the place secure?"

"At the moment—yes," replied John. "But I know not for how long. I was headed for Van Metre's to determine the prospects of remaining on the western lands or returning to my claim on this side of the river."

"Van Metre's is only two miles east-creek," interjected Carpenter. "I saw John McColloch only two days ago, and he said the war for independence from the crown was not going well."

"John McColloch," asked Tilton, "the brother of Major Samuel?"

"The same," said Carpenter. "He traveled to Wheeling about a week ago, and the settlers at that town are concerned. A fort called Fincastle was built there two years ago; it is a strong bastion and I hear they now call it Fort Henry in honor of our esteemed governor."

"And what has created this concern?" asked Tilton. "I've seen no evidence of Tories in this area—or even Indians."

"That is true," said Carpenter, "but rumors are rampant that the English and Indians are gathering in the northern areas of the territory to drive south and assault Fort Henry and any other colonist village in this area."

Tilton pondered these statements of his friend.

"Perhaps 'twould be well, John, if I built a cabin on my claim about a mile west of here. Susannah is heavy with child, and quite evidently the McCollochs and residents of Van Metre's Fort are well informed."

"A sound decision," said Carpenter. "Even if only temporary, the times require it. Also, Susannah, good doctor though she is, should be much comforted by the presence of Nancy."

"I'm sure she would be," said John. "Your wife would be of much consolation. I shall take my leave now and return tomorrow to build a new home."

Upon arriving at his western house, John related his experiences of the day and announced his decision to build another cabin. Susannah was quite joyful to hear that the Carpenters were alive and well, and she did indeed relish the fact that they would soon be neighbors. John did not mention his concern for their safety, but this was also a factor in his decision to return to Virginia. They would not be far from Van Metre's Fort.

After a tasty meal of corn bread and fried catfish, flavored by green beans, they retired and slept comfortably until sun-up.

In the morning, all available food provisions and utensils were loaded on the raft and ferried across the river to be loaded on the two pack horses. In their many crossings of the river, the Tiltons had learned that certain sections of the broad expanse were too deep for poling, and short paddles had been whittled to shape by Joseph. After retrieving the remainder of his family, since all could not be conveyed in one trip, the Tiltons were once again traveling pack-horse style, eastward along the creek. They moved carefully, although by now John knew the best route, primarily because of Susannah's advanced pregnancy. Well before the sun was directly overhead, they arrived at the southeast corner of Tilton's claim.

Here, the horses and cows were pastured in a pole-fenced area north of the creek and John, Joseph, and husky eight-year-old Thomas, began the business of clearing an area on high ground near the creek, on which to build a log house. The boys gathered flat stones and rocks from the creek bed, as they had done previously for their cabin to the west, and laid them flat and firm on a rectangular outline. The construction proceeded smoothly while Susannah, using pestle and mortar, pounded corn for pone in a shaded area.

The structure was closer in design to their one-time home at the headwaters of the Buffalo. John decided to add an outside chimney, which he did in the following manner. Since flat stones and rocks were plentiful in the immediate area, he formed a broad base of clay and stone and rough-hewn square logs, mortared together with creek clay. He created a sturdy edifice, narrowing it gradually from the base until it was about two feet higher than the peak of the gable roof. The chimney was further strengthened by bracing a long oak pole, about three inches in diameter, three feet below the top of the chimney and anchoring it securely, as a diagonal support, in the ground.

Inside the log house, John cut a large opening about five feet square and constructed a spittle, or pot holder, over the stone base. Puncheon flooring was installed; beds were built on the east end of the house; and a rough table of oak was constructed, as were a number of three-legged stools. On the side of the structure adjacent to the creek, he cut and framed a two-foot-square window and shielded it with a thin deerskin blind that could be rolled up to let fresh air inside or sealed tightly at night.

During the construction period, Major McColloch had stopped by on several occasions, and John Carpenter was also there as time allowed. Both were of some assistance in completing the Tiltons' log house. Frontier sons and the remarkable attributes of John Tilton were, indeed, an asset to the frontiersmen along Van Metre's Creek.

In late May, Susannah gave birth, with Nancy Carpenter in attendance, to a baby boy, whom they called John. Nancy was quite helpful in her ministrations, but it was John who supplied Susannah's greatest relief. He, as always, massaged her thighs and stomach with his rough hands, and soon the pain was gone—his kiss was gentle and consoling, just as it had been seventeen years before.

At first the baby boy appeared strong and healthy, but no mother's milk—no herbs nor oil—could deter his destiny. Within two weeks he died and was buried not far from the Tilton house.

Susannah, she of the flashing eyes and auburn tresses, bore her sorrow in silence. Dry-eyed, she trusted in the omnipotent Providence of Almighty God. This strength of character she had possessed at a very young age, and it remained with her until the end.

As the summer progressed, John made periodic visits to his garden in Indian country. Sometimes, one of the boys would accompany him. They hoed the corn and loosened the soil around the bean plants, and the crops flourished. An abundance of basic vegetarian foods was developing for harvesting in the fall.

As time permitted, the Carpenters visited with the Tiltons on Van Metre's Creek. It was on such an occasion that Carpenter reported that he had recently been to Wheeling and talked to Colonel Ebenezer Zane, the proprietor.

"Colonel Zane said that the Indians in the territory to the northwest were somewhat undecided as to whether they should join our fight for freedom or side with the English Tories. As you may know, the Commander in Chief of our Continental army is General Washington, who knows this area well and traveled down the Ohio River for some distance before returning to Fort Pitt.[1] I understand that he has been authorized by the congress of our new country to offer just rewards to the Indians for the capture of English prisoners."

"And what of success in this venture?"

"Ah, 'tis sad," said Carpenter. "The Shawnees and Delawares and Mingoes resent our so-called intrusion on their land, even though we have paid for it many times over. The British agents are giving them money for white scalps. I fear that the savages will soon be upon us, and we had best prepare to defend ourselves."

Although cognizant of the facts reported by Carpenter, John, with an intensity of purpose that burned deeply in his breast, was not about to abandon his field of bounty across the river.

And so it was that in late September, John and Susannah and their sons, leaving the girls in the care of the Carpenters, and leading their two horses, returned to the thriving crops they had planted in the spring. Woven baskets of flexible hickory branches had been formed into large containers for returning the cultivated produce.

They crossed the river and husked the large, tender ears of golden corn, plucked the bean sprouts, and broke loose the ripe, orange pumpkins from their vines. The baskets were filled, floated across the river on their trusty raft and paraded to their Virginia log house for storage in the attic area provided for such purpose. The transfer of the fruitful harvest took almost four days, but finally the fields were stripped and the stalks cut down to preserve the richness of the earth for future plantings.

A portion of the mellowed corn was laid out on a split log base for drying, and several large tree stumps were hollowed out by auger and axe. After three or four days, the dried corn was husked from the cob and deposited in the hollow stumps. Pine poles, about five feet long and four inches in diameter, were used as pestles, and the cratered stump served as a mortar. The dried corn was pounded into a fine golden meal appropriate for making corn bread or pone.

Supplies of venison and bear meat and wild turkey were added to the larder but in smaller quantities, since hunting was productive during the winter months.

The Tiltons, secure in their winter-proof log house, were quite unaware of certain events that would eventually have a dramatic effect upon their existence on the western frontier.

They did not know that under the date of September 4, 1776, Colonel Dorsey Pentecost, of the Continental army in the District of West Augusta, Virginia, had written to Colonel David Shepherd, the eldest son of Thomas, who was born in Berkeley County, Virginia, near Shepherdstown, where his father was one

of the earliest settlers of the Shenandoah Valley, along with the
Hites and Van Metres. In 1770, David Shepherd journeyed to
the west and settled at the forks of Wheeling Creek. He was of
high rank in the newly established county of Ohio which included
Wheeling and all of the contested area in northwestern Virginia.
Colonel Pentecost wrote to Shepherd, who at one time had acted
as his commissary, as follows:

> Sir—It is has been thought Expedient for the Protection
> and Safety of the frontiers to Station a Number of Men at
> Different places on the Ohio between Fort Pitt, and the
> mouth of Grave Creek,² and at a Council of war held this
> day you have been Appointed Commissary for the Victual
> Etc. Such of the Militia as are now or may be Imployed
> on the present Emergency, and I having also laid your
> Appointment before the Committee of the County which
> they have been pleased to approve, I am therefore to
> Desire that you immediately proceed to provide Such
> provisons Etc as shall be wanting on this occasion, taking
> care to supply them in due Time, & purchase on the best
> Terms you can on the faith of Government. I need not
> suggest to you the Great Nescesity there is of Exerting
> Your self, but am full assured that you will Exert your
> best Endeavors in facilitating the Business at this Time of
> alarm and Great Calamity
>
> I am Sir your Most Hme Servt
> Dorsey Pentecost C. Liut

The Tiltons did not know, although Joseph had reported seeing
two large canoes of Indians paddling upriver, that all of the tribes
of the Six Nations and the Delawares and Shawnees and Mingoes
and others had assembled their principal chiefs and speakers at
Pittsburgh the past fall and attempted to work out a treaty of
peace. Representing the United States in this endeavor were
Colonel Lewis Morris and James Wilson for the congress, and
Thomas Walker, James Wood, Andrew Lewis, and Adam
Stephen for Virginia, who were appointed as the Commissioners
of Indian Affairs. Spokesmen for the Indians were: White Mingo,
a Seneca; Captain White Eyes, a Delaware; Shaganaba, of the
Tawaas; Flying Crow, of the Six Nations; The Half King, a

Wyandot; Cornstalk, a Shawnee; and other representatives of the Six Nations and Shawnees.[3]

At this point in time, John Tilton's face-to-face contact with the Indians of the green valley had been minimal. His primary relationship had been a rifle ball through the eye of a red savage or a knife blade across the throat or through the heart.

He would have been much impressed by the speech of the Delaware chief, Captain White Eyes, who spoke to the commissioners at Pittsburgh on October 9th, 1775, as follows:

Uncles the Six Nations and Wiandots our Grand Children the Ottawas and Shawanese The time we purposed to speak to our Brothers the White people is Elapsed it is Owing to a Misunderstanding which happened this Morning among ourselves our Uncles the Six Nations propose Speaking in the Morning I shall now speak on Behalf of the Wiandots the Shawanese the Tawaas and my own Nation he then addressed the Commissioners in the following words *Brothers* we are much obliged to you that as soon as we Appeared you wiped the Sweat from us so that we were Quite refreshed you wiped the Tears from our Eyes and removed all bad Impressions from our hearts so that we are Quite at Ease you have also told us that you have gathered all the Bones of our Deceased relations and Buried them deep in the Ground and planted a tree upon them that our Children of foolish young People may never see them to their Disquiet In the name of our Uncles the Wiandots our Grand Children the Shawanese and Tawaas and our own Nation I Acquaint you we are Much rejoiced and return you our Sincere thanks *A String*[4]

Brothers listen to me I now Inform you that we are Extreemely rejoiced at what we heard the day before Yesterday from you and that all the White People Account themselves as one Body and that Virginia is not alone for the future when we look on you we shall Esteem you all one People our reason Brothers why we were very much rejoiced to hear you are United is when our Brothers the White People first came upon this Island I thought they and us shou'd be the only people who shou'd live on it we made room for you to set down by Us Accordingly

Brothers I have now Acquainted you what we thought

when you first Arrived on this Land I now think our Treatment to you then is the Cause of the King over the Big Water, Striking you at this time I therefore desire you not to think much of it but think good until we hear from him I now also Acquaint you that my Uncles the Wiandots have found themselves the Shawanese Tawaas and Delawares together and have made us as one People and have also given me that Tract of Country Beginning at the Mouth of Big Beaver Creek and running up the same to where it interlocks with the branches of Guyahoga Creek and down the said Creek to the mouth thereof where it empties into the Lake along the Side of the Lake to the Mouth of Sandusky Creek and up the same to the head until it interlocks with Muskingum down the same to the mouth where it Empties into the Ohio and up the said River to the Place of Beginning (White Eyes has here described the limits of Delaware Territory.)

I also now Acquaint my Uncles the Six Nations that my Uncles the Wiandots have given me that Tract of Country as we have now Acquainted you what Lands belongs to us I desire you will not Permit any of your foolish People to sit down upon it that I cannot suffer it least other Nations should be Uneasy *A Belt of Wampum*

Brother I am Extremely rejoiced to hear what you said to me the day before Yesterday and also to hear you call upon God to witness and Assist us in future meetings to talk of the Friendship which is between us and the reason of my being rejoiced is that we are poor and Ignorant and know but little of Gods Wisdom but you have him in your heart and are more capable of Judging than we can be and as you have made Mention of that Heavenly friendship which proceeds from God I am very much pleased and take hold of it and the reason of my being so ready and willing to take hold of it is that our wise forefathers began the Blessed Work I also inform you that I am Extremely rejoiced and think it was God Almighty that has put it into your hearts to offer us this and that you did not despise us the poor and ignorant *A Belt*

I now *Brother* Assure you that I am much rejoiced you offer me your hand to take hold of I Gladly Accept it and shall not let it fall to the ground and I hope God Almighty will Endow me with Wisdom to treasure it up in my heart as my Brothers the English do we now desire you Brothers to

be strong and finish the Business we are come about that we
may be able to Inform the other Nations what we have been
about and when we have finished this good Work there will
never be any Occasion of Difference between our Children
and your Children but that they will have reason to remember it and call it the Blessed Council of Peace *A Belt*

Brothers, I am very much rejoiced that you Acquainted
me it was a long time since we had met and as some of our
great Men might have died desired we would inform you
that there are three tribes of us—Kalalamint (Turtle Clan—
the tribal leaders), Walapachakin (Wolf Clan) and Ohokon
(Bear Clan) or Capn Pipe are the chiefs Appointed for the
Delaware Nation *A Belt*

Brothers listen to your young Sisters the Delaware
Women we are very Much rejoiced to hear you and our
Children renewing the friendship between you and them
this is what your Sisters have said to you and our paying Attention to them is the reason why we did not go to War with
any Nation whatsoever as God Almighty did not Create us
to War with one Another we now also desire you will
Acquaint your Mothers our Elder Sisters the White Women
what we have said and when any of our Children shall be
born in the future we will point to heaven and tell them
these our sentiments *A Belt from the Women*

The speech of Captain White Eyes is looked upon as one exam-
ple of Indian eloquence, and it was well received by Colonel
Morris and the other commissioners.

John Tilton, too, would have been deeply moved by the brief
talk, at the same conference, by Chief Shaganaba of the Tawaas
and a son of Pontiac, the renowned Ottawa chief:

Fathers I thank you that you have Wiped the Tears from
my Eyes the Sweat from my body and thoroughly cleansed
me I was at first Unwilling I acknowledge to come to this
Treaty from evil reports I had heard and which I have now
found to be falsehoods my father and many other Cheifs
have lately Tasted of Death Accept my hearty thanks for
your kind Condolence on that Occasion I Present you my
right hand in token that I rejoice to see you United nore
shall my Children be Untold of it Accept this String of
Wampum as a Pledge of my Sincerity and Friendship my

Fathers knew you but Unhappily are no more I have now found the road to your Hospitable Mansions nor shall it be Untrodden by my People in the future. *A String*

The treaty with the Indians was concluded on October 19, 1775, and the commissioners filed their report on October 21st. It was reported at Williamsburg, Virginia, on November 18, that Thomas Walker, one of the gentlemen appointed by the Virginia Convention to treat with the Indians, had returned and stated that the Nations were peacefully disposed toward the colonists' cause.

It was because of these meetings during the fall of 1775, that the winter of that year was relatively peaceful, although several depredations did occur the next year. According to Colonel George Morgan,[5] Indian agent for the Pittsburgh area, another treaty was agreed to by the Six Nations, the Delawares, Shawnees, Munsees and Mahicans—the number of representatives being 644 in the fall of 1776. Morgan appears to have been too optimistic. It should be noted that the western tribes—the Wyandot, Chippewa, Miami and Ottawa—were not present, and that murders were still being committed.

On June 29, 1776, Patrick Henry was elected the first governor of the colony of Virginia. Shortly thereafter, the District of West Augusta was defined by the Virginia Assembly, at the same time dividing it into three counties—Ohio, Yohogania and Monongalia.

As a result of much correspondence with the Virginia Militia officers in 1776, Governor Henry became much concerned for the safety of the inhabitants of western Virginia, and on December 13, he ordered Colonel Dorsey Pentecost to prepare the militia and provide them with arms and ammunition.

Unbeknown to John Tilton, there lived, about three miles southwest of his log house, a young native of Ireland named David Rogers; he had built a cabin there, along the bank of the Ohio, in 1775. In 1776, he represented the West Augusta District in the Virginia legislature and was appointed captain in the continental service. He, too, was designed to play an important role in settling the Indian issues in the Upper Ohio Valley.

The cold, winter days, with their freezing temperatures ac-

companied by biting winds, eventually dissipated into the
warmth and gentleness of spring zephyrs. The Tiltons, the Carpenters, and the occupants of Van Metre's Fort had wintered
well.

Little did they know or envision the events of 1777, which has
been depicted as a dark and bloody year in the history of the
nation.

V

THE PATRIOT

ON MARCH 4, 1777, DAVID ROGERS was appointed county lieutenant of Ohio County, Virginia; David Shepherd was commissioned colonel and Samuel McColloch was commissioned major of the same county. McColloch had held the rank of major in the militia of the District of West Augusta, Virginia, for almost two years.

The situation at Wheeling appeared somewhat desperate to Colonel David Shepherd in early 1777. Rumors were rampant. The various Indian tribes of the great Northwest Territory had joined the cause of the English and were intent on the destruction of the settlements on both sides of the Ohio. Informants moving north toward Pittsburgh had proclaimed that the savage Shawnee were once again on the warpath. Under Chief Blackfish they had harassed the settlers in Kentucky, killing William Ray and capturing Thomas Shores. The fort at Boonesboro was also under seige, and before refuge was found within the fort, two persons were killed.

Consequently, Colonel Shepherd wrote to Governor Patrick Henry, as follows:

Weelin or Ohio County March 24th 1777

Sir—By a Letter Directed to Majr David Rogers and Likewise the Order in Council of the 12 of February it was ordered that this County Should Send fifty men to the Little Kanawa and fifty men to the Mouth of Whelin, application being made to me I Called a council for that purpose of the field officers and captins of the County and after Considering the State of the County and Our Militia not Consisting of more than 350 Affective men and having a frontier of Eighty Miles and that Laying the Nearest and most Exposed to the Indians and the Late

alarming accounts from the Indian towns I Receivd In-
teliganc by way of the Kanaway that they have Burnt one
white prisoner at the Shawnee towns Lately which alarms
the people very much suposed to be a Soldier Named
Elijah Matthews taken at Grave Creek, under those and
many other Surcomstances of the Like Nature, and no
garison being Built at the Little Kanaway and there Never
been any men at that Station I hope Sir under those Sir-
comstances you will not Consider our Disobaying of or-
ders a breach of trust or Disafected to the Commonwelth
ass our pressing Necessity forced it to we therefore
thought it proper to order fifty of our militia to Whelin
and fifty more to grave Creek and twenty five to the
Beach Bottom[1] which places appeared to us to be the most
fiting to Defend us against the Indians and protect the
Inhabitants of this and part of the other Countys. according to your former order we have sent spies towards
the Indian Country one part[y] of which Come across a
party of Indians in Camp and fired on them wounded one
which got of[f] by the assistance of the Rest a deep creek
being betwen them they got clear they Lef their Kittle a
Number of Bows and arrows and had all the apperance of
woryers [warriors].

At the same time, Shepherd sent a member of the militia to
secure additional ammunition, as noted in the following message:

Weelin March 24th 1777

Sir—Please to Send by the Barer Daniel McClane
the Barril of Powder which I chose and Likewise 163 lb of
Lead and 300 flints I should take it ass a great favour if
you could supply me with a Bar off Steel to Repair
gunlocks and other things for the use of the militia that is
Stationed on the River I hope you will give Some direction for the Victualing the Militia that will be Stationed
at Grave Creek Whelin an the Beach Bottom ass in our
Council it was not thought proper to Send men to the Little Conway and Leave our frontiers Defenceless and ass
there was No garison built there Neither had we Directions for that purpose if we had the men to Spare it was
thought proper

By the time of purple violets and nodding daffodils, John Tilton and his family were quite unaware of the Indian atrocities in Kentucky and southwestern Virginia.

It was in early April of 1777, when he and John Carpenter and Major McColloch were discussing the general state of the frontier, that Colonel David Shepherd appeared on the scene. They were about two miles east of Van Metre's Fort at which point, Shepherd, accompanied by six outriders, made his appearance.

McColloch, who knew him well, greeted him.

"Colonel Shepherd, I greet you as a friend and compatriot. These are my neighbors—John Tilton and John Carpenter."

Shepherd saluted the three frontiersmen, each of whom reciprocated.

"This situation is not good, Major," said Shepherd. "Recently, I wrote Governor Henry to this effect. Blackfish and his Shawnee warriors are causing havoc to the south. Even here, there has been mischief by the Indians. The treaties have been broken. I have requested that men of the militia be stationed at Grave Creek, Wheeling, and Beech Bottom. I caution you to be ever on your guard."

"My brother and I are constantly patrolling this area," responded McColloch. "I've seen no evidence of the red savages. I trust you know the Hedges at Beech Bottom are encroaching on Tilton's land."

"I think not," interjected John. "We circumvented that area as I know it and, furthermore, it matters not; our primary purpose must be to establish a strong line of defense."

"Well spoken, Tilton," Shepherd responded. "I have also sent David McClane to secure a barrel of powder and a good supply of lead and flints. The governor has told us to protect our allies, the Delawares, and to share with them our provisions. It is the savage Mingoes and Shawnees and the tribes from the northwest that will give us trouble."

"What of the war in the east, Colonel?" asked Carpenter. "Is there any word of its outcome?"

" 'Tis too soon to tell. Seems as though most of the Indians have sided with the English. Again, I say, be cautious. Now we will return to Wheeling. I must confer with Colonel Rogers."

John Tilton returned to his log house near the Creek at eventide. Susannah and the children welcomed him warmly. As they ate their evening meal of corn bread, potatoes, fried fish which the boys had caught during the day, and pumpkin tea, John related what he had learned from Shepherd.

"Colonel Shepherd is much concerned about our safety even on this Virginia soil, and he would be even more concerned if we were lodged in our cabin west of the river. The attic is still stocked sufficiently, and it will be replenished, as needed, from our hunting in this area. Our cabin to the west and our land is in good state. I think it would be well if we wintered here, at least until we are able to see more clearly the picture of the frontier as described by Colonel Shepherd."

Susannah did not smile. The children were silent. They had looked forward to another adventuresome winter in their home across the great blue water.

"I am sure the colonel is well advised in this matter," replied John's wife. "But, as yet, we have not witnessed this danger. I and the children will miss the planting and harvesting—and, as for myself, I would just as soon shoot through the eye of a red savage as the black eye of a black bear."

The comment from Susannah was strong, and the boys were much in agreement; but, in the end, John convinced them to remain at their present homesite.

"We must not be selfish; we must be considerate of our friends. There is a rich patch of land on a hill to the north. We will plant corn seed and a row of beans. If the fruit is born, our larder will be increased. But I am more concerned with your safety and the safety of our friends in this area. I must make myself available for duty as a soldier and fight for liberty, should the need arise."

Thus, the issue was settled. The land was cultivated and the seed planted, and the Tiltons were again unaware of certain events that took place in the summer of 1777.

In April, David Rogers was reelected to the Virginia Senate, after having been Ohio County Lieutenant since March 4th of the same year. He moved back to Pennsylvania, and Colonel David Shepherd was appointed lieutenant of Ohio County, Virginia, in June.

In April of 1777, the Shawnees, Wyandots and Mingoes, having decided to join the British cause, invaded the lands of

northwestern Virginia. They killed and scalped a man named
Ogden, who was a late immigrant from New Jersey, at the
Shadrach Muchmore settlement about forty-five miles south of
Fort Pitt near the Ohio River. In the same month, Roger McBride
was killed about ten miles up Wheeling Creek. Colonel George
Morgan, Indian Agent for the Middle Department made comment of these murders in a communique dated April 10. About
the same time, another white pioneer was killed on the western
side of the river opposite Wheeling. The widow Muchmore and
her three children were killed and scalped near where their log
house stood opposite Yellow Creek on the Ohio.

Two days later, the British-inspired savages penetrated inland,
killed three men near Dunkard Creek at the mouth of the Cheat
River, and disposed of three others in the same area; the bodies of
the latter three were never found.

On the occasion of these atrocities, Samuel Mason[2] commanded
a company at Fort Henry, and leading a small regiment of the
county militia, he pursued the murderers about twenty-five
miles, at which point they encountered the savages and gained at
least a partial revenge.

During the summer of 1777, the immediate area around Van
Metre's Fort and Tilton's log house was, somehow, undisturbed.
The necessary precautions were taken in all their activities. Tilton
and Carpenter frequently visited Van Metre's Fort and came to
know well the other occupants of the fort, including Major
Samuel McColloch's younger brother, John,[3] and his sister
Elizabeth.[4]

In late summer, the rumors persisted that a confederation of
Indians from the territorial tribes were assembling in the northwest part of the land west of the Ohio preparatory to striking a
devastating attack upon the settlements at Wheeling and north of
there on both sides of the Ohio River. The talk of invasion by the
Indian army became widespread, and the settlers strengthened
their blockhouses and forts, determined to protect their families
and retain possession of their settlements.

When General Edward Hand,[5] the commandant at Fort Pitt,
became aware of the situation, his scouts having confirmed its
validity, he immediately advised the frontiersmen to prepare for
the event. With a feeling of trepidation, efforts were further ex-

tended by the river-front and back-country pioneers to entrench themselves for some measure of security. They knew not when the Indians would strike, until late August, when warning trails of smoke appeared high on a hill slightly north and west of Fort Henry.

On the evening of August 31, Captain Joseph Ogle, accompanied by a number of scouts, returned to Wheeling and reported that he had seen no sign of the Indians. He and his men had been scouting the surrounding area for several days. The crafty Indian mind had anticipated these maneuvers, and the army of savages had avoided the usual trails of travel. They moved south along the hilltops under cover of darkness and assembled on the river bank about two miles below Wheeling Creek. Here, they crossed the river, planned their method of attack in the morning, and proceeded to take their positions on the broad bottom land. In all, the Indians numbered about two hundred, mostly members of the Shawnee, Mingo and Wyandot tribes.

September 1, 1777, was indeed a dark and bloody day at Wheeling. Doctor James McMechen, upon deciding to return to the east, asked several of his companions to get the horses. While about this task, they came upon six Indians who had been posted not far distant from the village. The men retreated, but before gaining the safety of their cabin, John Boyd was killed and the others, Andrew Zane, Samuel Tomlinson, and a black man returned safely and notified the soldiers that there were six Indians outside.

Captain Samuel Mason and his fourteen-man contingent were ordered by the commandant of Fort Henry, Colonel David Shepherd, to go forth and investigate the situation. After proceeding a short distance, they encountered the six Indians and opened fire. Immediately, the whole army of Indians revealed themselves, and, with loud, piercing shrieks, attempted to engulf the small band of gallant patriots. Mason ordered a retreat and he, personally, battled his way through the savage throng and succeeded in gaining the safety of the fort. Out of his fourteen men, only two—Hugh McConnell and Thomas Glenn—escaped; the rest were slaughtered.

A blinding fog hung heavy in the air during that fateful first day of the siege. The occupants of the fort could not see the

tragedy occurring to the south. Before Captain Mason had returned, Captain Joseph Ogle and his company of seasoned
frontier veterans moved out to assist Mason. After advancing only
a short distance, they heard the mournful cries of the wounded
and dying, but without hesitation they moved toward the point of
conflict, only to meet a deadly fate. With hideous, demoniacal
screams, the red savages repeated their ravage against Ogle's
troops; only a few escaped the ambush. After a ferocious
struggle during which a number of Indians also died, Captain
Ogle, Sargeant Jacob Ogle, and Martin Wetzel, were still alive.

As the sun continued to rise in the east, the Indian army
regrouped and advanced toward the fort, where most of the
villagers had taken refuge, demanding surrender or death.

The fort at Wheeling was, indeed "Indian-proof," as described
by Colonel David Shepherd. It was a parallelogram of square
pickets, pointed at the top, with bastions at the angles. Enclosed
within its walls were barracks and an officer's cabin for the
military, and a storehouse, well, and cabins for the families. Outside the fort, there were a number of log houses and several head
of livestock.

The Indians appeared in no hurry to storm the fort. They con-
tented themselves with scalping their white victims, killing the
livestock in the immediate area, and burning the houses outside
the fort.

Finally, they assembled their troops and marched toward the
fort. At first, they attempted to negotiate a surrender, but the occupants, in unison, declined their proposal, determined to fight
and hold their position. Several times during the first two days of
the siege, the savages attempted to gain entrance by sheer force of
numbers; using a log as a battering ram, they rushed the fort to
test its pickets and doors. Each time they were unsuccessful, and
gunfire from the portholes dealt death to many of the screaming
redskins. Attempts to set fire to the fort also proved fruitless.

On the morning of the third day, Colonel Andrew Swearingen
and a party of fourteen men came to the relief of the small
garrison in the fort. They had come by night in a large bargelike
canoe from Holliday's Fort, twenty-four miles to the north.

Meanwhile, Major Samuel McColloch, at Van Metre's Fort,
had also become aware of the situation at Fort Henry. Without

hesitation, he entreated the militia members in the Short Creek area to follow him in defense of their kinsmen and friends. "Tilton! Carpenter!" he called. "Mount your horses and bring rifle and ball—the fort at Wheeling is under siege!"

Susannah was calm as her husband said, "The toil of our hands is in jeopardy. The boys are strong. I must ride with the major."

The Lady of Legend, she of the auburn tresses and flashing smile, concurred, "Go, John, and God be with you."

After riding hard, they arrived at the beleaguered bastion shortly after Colonel Swearingen, and the gates of the fort were opened with rejoicing as the forty mounted patriots moved inside. At the time of their appearance, the bloodthirsty enemy reappeared and McColloch, riding at the side of the company, was prevented from entering the fort. He attempted to skirt the savages and reach the top of a high hill to return to Fort Van Metre. However, he was soon surrounded on three sides and, under the circumstances, urged his gallant white steed down an almost perpendicular thirty-foot precipice. No Indian would attempt such a feat, and they watched in complete dismay as he rode off in safety toward the north.

With the arrival of reinforcements, the leaders of the Indian army knew their chance of besieging Fort Henry was greatly diminished, but it was only after Tilton and Carpenter and the other defenders had laid low between forty and fifty of the frustrated marauders that the Indians headed back whence they had come.

Only one person in the fort was slightly injured, and upon being certain of their immediate safety, Tilton and his compatriots left the fort and returned to their homes.

At his log home, John, returning on the morning of September 4, was greeted with exclamations of joy and happiness. Susannah, after embracing him, prepared a hearty meal, and as he ate he related his adventure at Fort Henry.

"'Tis good that the gallant major escaped," said Susannah. "He has indeed been a source of consolation in this territory of lurking death. I trust the inmates of the fort are secure."

"At the moment, they are, but who knows for how long. But what a tragedy that so many brave heroes should fall in ambuscade outside the fort. Some said that the leader of the Indians

Girty's Grove: Simon Girty, March 7, 1776

Girty's Grove: Jim Girty, May 7, 1777

Girty's Grove: Totem Symbols on a Beech

Girty's Grove: A Beech Tree Home

Photos Courtesy
Lewis Petras

was Simon Girty[6]—you know, the white man and a member of the Continental forces."

"You have spoken before of this Girty. What do you know of him?" questioned Susannah.

"I only know what I have heard from others," replied John. "I have not seen him, but they say he is truly a vicious-looking character. If he was there, he is most certainly a deserter and a defender of the king—and against freedom for the colonies. One of the soldiers at the fort said Girty grew up among the Indians and will always be a savage in his heart."

John did not know that there were four Girty brothers: Thomas, Simon, James, and George. In 1775, while living in the valley of Sherman's Creek in Pennsylvania, all were captured when the Indians destroyed Fort Granville on the Juniata. They were transported to Kittanning, where their stepfather, John Turner, was burned at the stake, and their mother and stepbrother, John Turner, Jr., were taken by the Delawares. Thomas was released from Indian captivity when Lieutenant Colonel John Armstrong attacked Kittanning in September, 1756. The other three boys were taken west by the defeated Indians, and all eventually had returned when English domination over the French had been assured. Simon, who had been with the Senecas, was fifteen years old when he returned. George was claimed by the Delawares and James by the Shawnees.

Three Girty brothers, all except Thomas, established themselves as renegades when all deserted to the British. Simon, presumably, joined the British in March of 1778. Although this is recognized as his official date of desertion, there is evidence that he was active against the white settlers for at least a year before then. The grove of white beech trees,[7] well concealed on a western hill in Warren Township, distinctively denotes the presence of Simon in March of 1776, and Jim in May of 1777. This hilltop was a frequent source of rendezvous for Indian war parties, and many of the trees were hollowed out by fire and tomahawk to provide protection from the elements.

James returned to the Shawnees and joined his brother on the side of the hated British Tories. Simon Girty died on February 18, 1818, and British soldiers fired a salute over his grave.

" 'Tis a shame," said Susannah. "He could have been of much help on the side of the colonists."

"I agree," enjoined her husband. "But, at the moment, I am concerned for our immediate safety. There is no telling when the Indians will invade this area. There are no restrictions on their warpath. The larder must be replenished from the field, and we must make ourselves secure against any future onslaught."

As darkness settled in the valley, the occupants of the Tilton homestead retired and slept—except for John. The dim light from a quarter moon revealed no sign of life as he scanned the country-side from the window. He secured the window and reset the heavy oak timber that barred the door. With a feeling of ap-prehension, he sat down on his bed, placed his rifle near at hand, and stretched out his weary body beside his wife. He held her hand and slept fitfully.

VI

ENCOUNTER

DURING SEPTEMBER OF 1777, there was no evidence of Indian depredations in or around the expansive claim of John Tilton, lying along Buffalo Creek and south to Short Creek (formerly referred to as Van Metre's Creek). The small crops of corn and beans had been harvested and stored without molestation or significant incident.

The Tiltons were intent upon returning to their western cabin beyond the great blue river. Joseph was now eleven and Thomas nine. Young in age, but old in the ways of the hunter and the woodsman, they anticipated, with great longing, another autumn and winter like the one they had experienced two years earlier.

To this purpose, they entreated their father.

"Back across the river, father, to our small cabin and rich land," suggested Joseph. "I amd strong now and so is Thomas—even Jack. Our mother, likewise , is in favor. The game is more plentiful—the deer and rabbit and turkey may be caught with a rope. Is it wise at this time?"

Susannah smiled and nodded silently—even she could not have made a more eloquent plea.

John was impressed. But he knew what they did not.

"Good wife and children," he responded. "I, too, rejoice and look forward to returning to our western home. And this we shall do in the spring, if all is well. At the moment, a group of vengeful Shawnees are encamped on the hill just west of our claim. Not that I would not welcome the opportunity to engage them in mortal combat, if the odds were right, but they outnumber us five to one. Our larder is well stocked, our friends are close—and, as you know, I have always preferred peace to war. As I say, hopefully in the spring the Indians will be gone, and we will once again resume our livelihood under the yoke of Almighty God, in the land we have claimed on the west side of the broad Ohio."

The word of John was final in this instance, and the daily duties of this early pioneer family proceeded in harmony and love.

The Indians of the upper Ohio Valley practiced a code of morality quite different from that of the whites. There has never been a race of historic origin, however, that did not believe in some form of Supreme Being; this God, they associated with visible creatures and nature: the hills, the birds, the sky, the sun. They were highly superstitious and believed that the great eagle or an owl could convey their actions and deeds to the Great Spirit —called *Moneto* in the Shawnee tongue.

They believed in immortality and a state of existence after death that would be similar to their life on earth. Consequently, when a brave warrior or chief died, his weapons of war were buried with him to permit him to exist in an ethereal land of perpetual pleasure.

The grief of the Indians for an infant or young child was almost inconsolable, as depicted in the following paraphrase:

A young Indian couple lost a son when he was about four years old. The parents were so disconsolate at his death that they engaged in the testimonies of grief with extreme vigor, which resulted in the death of the father. Upon the expiration of her husband, the mother of the boy dried her tears and became quite consoled and cheerful.

Upon inquiry as to her change of mood, the mother explained that the child was so young when he died, and unable to support himself in the land of the spirits, both she and her husband were apprehensive that this situation would be far from pleasant. But upon the death of the father, who had a great love for his son and was a good hunter, she discontinued her mourning. She added that her lamentations had ceased because the child was now under the protection of his father and her only wish was to be with them.

The Indian respect for the aged members of the tribe was also carried to the extreme. "The aged," they said, "have lived through the whole period of our lives and long before we were born. They have not only the knowledge which we possess, but a great deal more. We, therefore, must submit our limited views to their experience." David Zeisberger[1], the missionary of the Moravians said, "I am free to declare that, among all the Indian nations that I have become acquainted with, if anyone should kill an old man or woman, for no other cause than that of having become burdensome to society, it would be considered an unpardonable crime."

The Indians had their tribal laws and rules. For committing adultery, a woman, for the first offense, had her hair cut very short, and for a repetition of this act, her left ear was cut off. For anyone being declared an outlaw, it was not only proper, but also a responsibility of every member of the tribe, to kill the offender on sight.

Such were the beliefs and ways of the red savages who roamed the hills and valleys of the upper Ohio in the eighteenth century.

———

In the fall of 1777, Ohio County, Virginia, included an extensive land area in northwestern Virginia; and the boundary line between Pennsylvania and Virginia had not been established firmly. Concurrently, the Commissioners of Ohio County enlisted Daniel McClain, Alfred Caldwell, Silas Hedges, Zachariah Sprigg, William Scott, and Thomas Waller to compile a list of soldiers and administer an oath of allegiance to the Commonwealth of Virginia to those so inclined. An extensive tour of the county was conducted to enroll and swear in the advocates of freedom.

And so it was that on the afternoon of October 6, 1777, Zachariah Sprigg approached the log house of John Tilton and hailed the inhabitants.

John came out, followed by Susannah. The boys, who had been playing near the creek, scurried to the doorway of the house.

"May I be of service to you, sir?" asked Tilton. "Behind me are my wife and children, and we are founded on a staked claim."

Sprigg responded, "I know of you, Tilton. I know you were at Fort Henry last month when the Indians tried to take it. You have claimed much land here between the Buffalo and the Short. I trust you have not been harassed in any way, and that all is well with you and your family."

"Yes, sir. My friend, Carpenter, lives only a mile east of here, and the Van Metres are not too far distant."

"Colonel Shepherd and the commissioners have entrusted me to bring under oath all able-bodied men who are sympathetic to the cause of independence. Are you so disposed, Tilton?"

"Yes, sir."

"Then repeat after me: 'I, John Tilton, will serve as a soldier in this war for independence, and, by Almighty God, I swear allegiance to the Commonwealth of Virginia.' "

John repeated the words as Sprigg had spoken them and then suggested, "Would you care to rest, sir? I know not your name, but I can provide you with some cool water and food."

"Thanks, I appreciate the offer. I will rest for a short time. I must be off soon to consult Hedges and Harris and others for the same purpose. Carpenter and those at Van Metre's, I have already enlisted. Oh, yes, my name is Sprigg—Zachariah Sprigg."

Susannah obtained cool water from a hillside spring and set out chunks of dried venison and corn pone.

In due time, Sprigg acknowledged the hospitality of the Tiltons and resumed his tour.

"Farewell, my friend Tilton, perhaps we'll meet again."

"Good-bye, Mr. Sprigg, and God be with you."

And there it was that John Tilton, faithful husband, respected father, and patriot for liberty, was officially enrolled as a soldier in the Ohio County Militia.

The winter of 1777-78, was spent in comparative comfort by John Tilton and his family, and many happy days were spent in hunting, visiting, contesting with one another in turkey shoots, tomahawk-throwing contests, and wrestling matches. Usually on Saturday, the inhabitants of the small Tilton settlement and the surrounding countryside would come together for a general frolic, although this event might occur on any special occasion, such as a wedding, a housewarming, or even a burial.

Hunting was of particular appeal to John Tilton and his two oldest sons. They took great pleasure in arising early on a crisp, cold winter morning, dressing warmly in their rough but appropriate linsey-woolsey clothing and fur-lined moccasins and venturing forth at daybreak in search of game. The ground might be snow-covered and unblemished, and under these conditions, the deer or rabbit, or any other creature of the wild, could be tracked quite easily.

The boys had already learned to imitate the cry of a bleating fawn, the gobble of a turkey, and other significant sounds which would ultimately bring their prey within the deadly range of rifle or bow and arrow. John had taught them early. They knew well that each sound echoed by the forest could provide either food or death from a cunningly concealed red savage.

It was indeed a rare occasion when they did not return at eventide with venison and rabbit and turkey to further stock their storehouse of food and provide additional skins for clothing and bedding.

During the frolic, which sometimes lasted several days, shooting contests were extremely popular, provided that powder and shot were in good supply. The frontiersmen took great pleasure in shooting the head from a wild turkey, contained in a narrow enclosure of logs approximately ten feet long and covered with thatched tree boughs so that only the head was visible. It was in this event that even some of the women participated, and the unswerving aim of the beauteous Susannah parted many a red-jowled head from its feathered body.

The wedding frolic offered a particular occasion for all members of a frontier settlement and the residents of the adjacent forts, blockhouses, and cabins. This was a highly anticipated event, and the pioneer men, women, and children bedecked themselves in their best buckskin and linsey-woolsey clothing; laid aside their fears of attack from Indian, renegade, or beast; and engaged in merrymaking and self-indulgence over an extended period of time—sometimes as long as three days.

The bride and groom were usually young in years but mature

in the ways of existence in the forest. And true love became a reality with the birth of the first child.

On the day of the wedding, the groom and an assemblage of his frontier friends gathered at his father's cabin. The wedding took place at high noon, and it was important that they arrive at the bride's house before that hour. The march to the bride's house normally involved passage along narrow trails, and although the custom was double file, this practice was often impeded by narrow lanes or intentional obstructions set up by some of the groom's "friends."

The marriage ceremony was performed by a minister, justice of the peace, or sometimes by the father of the bride, if neither of the other two were available. If the ceremony was conducted by the bride's father, it was confirmed by the first circuit rider or itinerant minister to reach the area.

Following the marriage ceremony, a sumptuous feast of turkey, venison, and bear meat, boiled and roasted, and complimented by corn pone, cabbage, potatoes, and "roasting ears" was prepared and served under the spreading elms. Everyone in attendance enjoyed the dinner, which was usually laid out on a large slab of timber, hewn flat with a broadaxe and set on four strong legs fitted into holes made by an auger. Ancient pewter dishes and plates, wooden bowls and trenchers, and well-worn pewter spoons were much in evidence. Other necessary utensils were often made of animal horns; the scalping knife, which every pioneer carried, was put to good use.

Dancing until dawn always followed the wedding, and the fiddlers played three or four hand reels or jigs. The initial dance was always a square four and was followed purposely by a lively dance called "jigging it off." This rapid, circling, side-by-side and front-to-front jumping contest was performed by couples who intermittently chained into circles. It was concluded only when the fiddler became tired of fiddling or the dancers dropped or retreated from exhaustion.

The frontier wedding was truly a hilarious and enjoyable occasion, and John and Susannah were welcome attendants at several of these frolicsome events during the winter of 1777 and early 1778. And John took part in the raising of the house which, upon completion, became the humble abode of the young couple.

The population of western Virginia increased as children were borne with intention and purpose on the frontier. Susannah contributed further to this cause in late 1777, when she brought forth her third son, whom they called Lorenzo. By this time, the youngest child of John and his wife was their daughter Susannah, who was almost three years old. Lorenzo grew strong and healthy, and his mother nurtured him well, so that by the spring of 1778 he was active and robust.

The locusts had dropped their white blossoms and the walnuts were beginning to bud when the Tiltons decided to return to their tomahawked claim in the territory northwest of the Ohio River.

As they sat around an outside fire, enjoying the fruits of their larder and a happy hour of banter and stories before nightfall, John suddenly became serious.

"As I promised," he said solemnly, "it is now proper that we return to our land beyond the great blue river. The menacing Indians have dispersed, and as throughout the winter, the area of our settlement appears safe for occupation."

Joseph and Thomas and Jackson responded with a warhoop of approval. Susannah smiled. And the exhilaration of the boys brought forth a giggle of happiness from Polly and Sally.

And so it was that in early June of 1778 they returned to their squatter's homestead west of the broad Ohio. There was no problem in locating the claim they had staked almost three years earlier—the Tilton "T" was still prominent, and the cleared area was still much in evidence. But the cabin had been reduced to ashes and rubble!

Although they were somewhat dismayed, particularly the children, they were not discouraged. John had suspected as much; he knew the ways of the savage redskin. He knew their customs and their likes and dislikes; he knew their treachery and the meaningless value of their treaties. With reckless abandon, he proceeded to clear the charred area and reconstruct the pebble base foundation for a new home. Susannah and the boys joined him in his labor, and in due time a strong, rough-hewn log house was erected. As before, provisions brought from their Virginia home were stored in the attic, and a patch of rich black earth was cultivated. Although it was mid-June, John was hopeful that crops would prosper rapidly and could be harvested before winter.

Such was not to be the case.

It was early in October of 1778 that John Tilton had his first encounter in the Ohio country with a small band of scalp-hunting Shawnees.

Certain events had taken place during the previous year, including the dastardly murder of the principal chief of the Shawnees, the strong leader and eloquent speaker Cornstalk. His son Elinipsico, and Chief Red Jacket were killed with the same barrage of bullets from the guns of Captain John Hall and his company of Rockbridge volunteers. This tragedy occurred in the spring of 1777 at Point Pleasant, while the three Shawnees were on a mission of peace, and this event only served to further segregate the Shawnee Nation from the Americans. It is said that Cornstalk had some premonition of his ultimate destiny and that on the day prior to his death, while speaking to a council of officers awaiting the arrival of General Hand from Fort Pitt, he pronounced:

> When I was young and went to war, I often thought each might be my last adventure, and I should return no more. I still lived. Now I am in the midst of you, and if you choose, may kill me. I can die but once. It is alike to me, whether now or hereafter.

Meanwhile, all of the western and northern tribes of the confederacy, including the Six Nations, the Mingoes, Wyandots, and Shawnees were joining the cause of the Tories, primarily because of the handsome duty the British were paying for white scalps. Upon recommendation of the congressional commissioners at Pittsburgh, the Continental Congress ordered several regiments of Continental troops into the upper Ohio and western Virginia areas, preparatory to striking a devastating blow against the marauding redskins.

Before the invasion, Fort McIntosh[2] was erected about twenty-eight miles south of Pittsburgh at the mouth of the Beaver River; a treaty was signed at Pittsburgh on September 19, 1778, between the somewhat neutral Delawares and United States commissioners, Andrew Lewis and Thomas Lewis. In October,

General Lachlan McIntosh,[3] commandant of the Western Department, brought together one thousand soldiers and militiamen
at the fort on the Beaver, including Colonel Daniel Brodhead[4] of
the Eighth Pennsylvania Regiment and Colonel John Gibson of
the Thirteenth Virginia Regiment. According to the Articles of
the Fourth Treaty of Pittsburgh, the Delawares presumed to
grant authority for soldiers of the Continental army to march
through their territory.

It is apparent that this treaty of Pittsburgh was quite
misleading to the Delaware chiefs. It provided an alliance between this friendly tribe and the Americans and permitted the
construction of a fort in Delaware country to provide protection
for the women and children while the men of the tribe were
fighting the allied British and Indian forces. During McIntosh's
forage toward Detroit, the highly respected Chief White Eyes
was reported to have died of smallpox, but George Morgan, Indian Agent for the Middle Department, infers that he was murdered by some of the militia and secretly buried.

McIntosh and his troops, although poorly equipped for such an
expedition because of the minimal provisions available from a
poor harvest, regardless of the consequences, proceeded to cross
the Ohio and march westward. They traveled about seventy
miles, and, reaching a high plain on the west bank of the
Tuscarawas River, they erected Fort Laurens, which was completed in December, 1778. It soon became apparent that McIntosh could not continue his march to Detroit; his horses were
worn out and he lacked sufficient life-sustaining necessities for his
army. With a small garrison of approximately one hundred and
fifty militiamen left under the command of Colonel John Gibson,
to hold the fort, the balance of his soldiers quickly returned to
Fort Pitt and, subsequently, to their homes. The sufferings and
hardships and humiliation and death at Fort Laurens were yet to
come.

John Tilton and his sons, Joseph, now almost twelve, and
Thomas, ten, were cultivating their small garden, which was

almost ready for harvesting, when John, always cautious, spotted the six Shawnee warriors descending the western hill and moving toward his cabin.

Instantly, he recognized the perilous situation. By throwing clods of dirt, he gained the attention of his sons and motioned them to seek refuge in the cabin, which was only a short distance south. They obeyed and he followed, in a crouched position, concealing himself in the cornstalks, which were over four feet high. When all were inside, he sped, with the speed of a young doe, the final fifty paces, eluded two rifle balls, and, upon entering the cabin, secured the door with a heavy timber.

Forewarned by her sons, Susannah was well prepared to do battle with the savages. With ball and powder they were well stocked, and it was a lead ball from the long rifle of Susannah that sent the first redskin to come within range to his eternal reward.

The remaining warriors spread out and intermittently sprayed the Tilton cabin with bullets and flaming arrows. None were effective. John dispatched another Shawnee warrior from a chink in the north side of the cabin.

The remaining savages proceeded to set afire the corn patch and trample the pumpkins and squash, always being careful not to come within range of gunfire from the cabin. After completing the ravage of the crops, the four Shawnee warriors abandoned their purpose and headed north toward Mingo Town.

Upon assurance that the savages were gone, John ventured forth. The fire was still crumbling their abundant vegetation, but all was lost. The corn and beans and pumpkins and squash were blackened and burned beyond use.

And so it was that John Tilton and his family endured the hardships and privations forced upon them by the Indians during the winter of 1778 and 1779. They subsisted basically on the wild game that John was able to provide and the scanty vegetable provisions which they had transported from Virginia.

The worst was yet to come!

VII

CARPENTER'S FORT

JOHN TILTON AND HIS FAMILY remained on their toma-hawked land claim in the Territory Northwest of the Ohio River throughout the winter. They were persistent in their ideals that this land of rich, productive soil, untainted beauty, and peaceful solitude would eventually become their permanent homestead.

In the spring of 1779, Susannah was again pregnant, and her knowledge and experience indicated that the baby would be born in about two months.

As they sat around the evening cooking fire outside the cabin, while Joseph and Thomas were fishing, she proposed:

"Would it not be well if we returned to our eastern settlement so that the child might have his rightful citizenship in a recognized colony of the American States?"

"Probably," said John. "But are there not other reasons?"

"I must confess to you, my husband," replied Susannah, "that I am of more comfort at this time in life when others are near."

"It will be as you wish, beloved wife. Tomorrow, we shall prepare to return to our Virginia settlement. I, too, am anxious to see our friends and learn the state of this land—however, I would entreat you for another son."

Susannah's eyes flashed and her long, auburn tresses waved gently in the evening breeze. The boys returned with a good catch of blue catfish, which provided the main course for their supper. As the flaming sunset dimmed, all retired. Susannah smiled and rested comfortably in the arms of her husband.

The next morning, after breakfast, John informed the boys of their decision, and together they prepared to vacate their cabin. The larder in the attic was cleared, and all necessary provisions, utensils, and tools were loaded on the raft and conveyed to the opposite shore. After camping the night, they trekked northwest toward their Virginia log house, arriving there when the sun was in mid-sky.

They found the house unoccupied and in a good state of repair. After a good cleaning and some resurfacing of the walls and roof with creek clay, they resumed occupancy. The beds along the wall were reinforced, and the interior fireplace on the west wall was inspected and made ready for use. The rough-hewn square table was refurbished, and additional three-legged chairs were constructed.

The Carpenters, Wellses, Van Metres, McCormicks, and Mc-Collochs were still within a two-mile radius, and old acquaintances were quickly renewed with revelry and merriment.

In late spring, Susannah gave birth to another baby girl whom she named "Drusilla." At this point in time, another son was not to be.

John shielded his disappointment and exhibited every indication of happiness and satisfaction at having another daughter. Although other women, including Nancy Carpenter, were in attendance part-time, John, as always, was Susannah's greatest source of joy and contentment.

The family of John and Susannah Tilton was, indeed, growing. Joseph was approaching the age of thirteen; Thomas was eleven; Jackson nine; Polly eight; Sally six; Susannah four; and Lorenzo not yet two. And, as a family, they prospered. John and the boys provided adequate meat for the table. The two cows were still strong and productive. The garden of corn and beans and pumpkins and squash flourished. They were not annoyed by Indians, and they enjoyed the companionship of their friends as the days and months passed swiftly.

During the years of 1779 and 1780, the eastern section of land between the Buffalo and the Short was comparatively free of Indian attack, and the settlers developed a growing feeling of security.

Such was not the case in the Mon Valley and points south. Many Indian atrocities were committed in this area during the warmer months of 1779. A Mrs. Freeman was killed and scalped as she went forth from West's Fort, near Hacker's Creek,[1] to pick some greens. At about the same time, a large band of Indians

arrived at Coburn's Creek and attacked a group of whites returning from the field near Coburn's Fort. John Woodfin and Jacob
Miller were both killed and scalped. This same group of vengeful
redskins later appeared at Stradler's Fort² and lay in ambush,
awaiting the return of the pioneers who were occupied at work in
adjacent fields. When the settlers returned in the evening,
bearing a number of hogs which they had killed for the occupants
of the fort, the hidden Indians fired upon them and killed several
people. The remainder of the settlers returned the fire, and a skir-
mish of death took place. Before the Indians revealed themselves,
many of the whites had been killed, and the battle became completely one-sided in favor of the red savages. Thus, the outnumbered and unprepared men of the fort fled to its confines
with great dispatch. Eighteen of the pioneers had been killed and
scalped and, after some time had passed and upon assurance that
the enemy had departed, the men in the fort went forth and
buried the mangled remains of their friends.

In his frequent discussions with Carpenter, the McCollochs,
and Colonel Shepherd, John Tilton learned of other instances of
attempted barbarism along the branches of the Monongahela and
its many small tributaries. One of these concerned the individual
combat and heroism of David Morgan, a relative of Colonel
George Morgan of Revolutionary War fame. At the time of the
incident, which took place near Prickett's Fort³ on the upper
Monongahela, Morgan was more than sixty years of age.

He was one of the earliest settlers on the frontier and was considered a man of strong qualities and good character. It was in
early April of 1779, that he requested his sixteen-year-old son,
Stephen, and his daughter, Sarah, about fourteen, to feed the
stock on his farm, which was about one mile away on the opposite
side of the Monongahela. He was not feeling too well that morning, and he felt completely safe in requesting this favor since Indians had not been sighted in this area for some time.

After the children left the fort, Morgan fell asleep and dreamed
that Stephen and Sarah had been scalped. He awoke, and upon
becoming aware that they had not returned, he started in search
of them. Upon arriving at the farm, he saw the children actively
engaged in preparing a choice plot of ground to plant melons.

Seated on a log he watched them awhile. Suddenly, he saw two Indians come out of the farmhouse and start toward his son and daughter.

Gaining the attention of the children, he motioned them to return to the fort at once. This they did without hesitation, and the Indians, soon becoming aware of their retreat, yelled a loud war whoop and gave chase. At this point, Morgan, of whom the Indians were unaware, shouted to divert their attention, and they immediately sought protection in the trees.

Morgan sought to escape by running from tree to tree, but age and his impaired health were against him. After several hundred yards, the savages closed in on him rapidly. He finally determined to shoot one and fight the other as best he could. Thus began the movement from one protective tree to another by Morgan and his pursuers.

One of the Indians, attempting to get closer for a clear shot at the old pioneer, ran behind a small tree and, seeing himself vulnerable, tried to flatten himself behind a fallen log. He was still not completely concealed however, and Morgan, with unerring aim, shot him through that part of his body which was visible. The savage, thinking he was injured beyond recovery, instantly unsheathed his knife and stabbed himself twice in the chest. True to Indian warrior philosophy, it was better that he die by his own hand than by that of his white adversary.

Again, Morgan began running toward the fort. The remaining savage followed him swiftly, and just as he raised his rifle and fired, Morgan glanced over his shoulder. The bullet missed, and the engagement now became one of mortal hand-to-hand combat. The Indian attacked his older opponent with great ferociousness and hideous cries. Morgan tried to defend himself with his rifle. The tomahawk of the savage struck with great strength, knocked Morgan's gun free from his grasp, and cut two fingers from one of his hands. The struggle continued, but the Indian was much younger and of greater strength. Incensed at the death of his companion and his own failure to dispatch the "old" man sooner, he fought with a rare display of ferocity. Morgan, however, had no intention of yielding his life easily. He strained every muscle and with strength that can be garnered only in such a desperate situation. When younger, he was quite competent as

a wrestler and still was able to throw the Indian easily. But the
savage rebounded, and in a moment he was atop the courageous
Morgan and attempting to get his knife.

The Indian had a cloth apron tied around his waist, which
prevented him from getting hold of the knife handle. While in
this position, Morgan grabbed one of the redskin's thumbs with
his teeth and bit firmly into the flesh. While in such a state, the
Indian finally freed his knife, but most of the handle was exposed.
Morgan quickly grasped the handle and jerked the blade through
his antagonist's hand, almost severing it at the palm. The pain-
crazed redskin attempted to escape, but Morgan's teeth were
grinding his thumb to the bone. He plunged the knife into the side
of the Indian, inflicting a mortal wound, released the thumb, and
the savage fell writhing to the ground.

Morgan caught up with his children before they reached the
river, and together they made their way to the fort. After relating
the incident, a number of men went forth from the fort, found
the wounded Indian, and quickly proceeded to kill and scalp
him.

Many other Indian raids and atrocities were committed in the
upper and central regions of the Monongahela Valley and the
creeks that flowed into it. But for some unexplainable reason, the
area of John Tilton's settlement between Buffalo and Short Creek
remained unmolested. It appeared as though Divine Providence
had cast an impenetrable cloud over the western area of Virginia
between Wheeling and the Buffalo.

The men of this area soon learned of other Indian depredations, and as members of the Ohio County Militia, they lost
their earlier feeling of security and were constantly alert to the
invasion of marauding savages.

It became known that in June a party of Shawnees had killed
three men—Peter Croase, James Stuart, and James Smalley—and
taken seven others prisoner near Martin's Fort, a rather humble
abode which had been erected on Crooked Run, a tributary of the
Monongahela. Shortly thereafter, two daughters of Captain
David Scott were accosted on Pike Run, which flowed into the
same river below Redstone. The youngest was killed and the
other made captive.

To the south, the family of John Schoolcraft, which was settled near Buchanon's Fort, was killed in late 1779; in all, the women and eight children were murdered and two small boys were taken prisoner.

Such was the state of the countryside east of the Ohio in the valley of the Mon in 1779.

In March of 1779, Colonel Daniel Brodhead succeeded General McIntosh as Commander of the Western Department. In short order, Colonel Brodhead wrote to the commander in chief, General George Washington, requesting troops and provisions to strike an effective blow at the British and Indians in Detroit. Under date of April 21, 1779, Washington directed him to make the necessary preparations. This task was extremely difficult. The Indians of most tribes, even the Delawares, were not receptive to such a scheme. The men of the militia were more concerned with guarding the homefront. And few soldiers of the Continental army were available.

On January 4, 1780, Washington countermanded his instructions to Colonel Brodhead on the basis that all services of Continental regulars and volunteers in the cause of liberty were required in the east. He explained that he was unable to reinforce Fort Pitt even in case of disaster.

A month later, on February 4, 1780, Washington reaffirmed the impossibility of complying with Colonel Brodhead's urgent request, on the basis that all his Continental troops would be required to assist our French allies. In the area of Fort Pitt and the surrounding countryside, provisions were scarce. Washington, in referring to this problem stated:

> You must therefore, of necessity, confine yourself to partizan strokes, which I wish to see encouraged. The State of Virginia is very desirous of an expedition against Detroit, and would make great exertions to carry it into execution. But while the enemy are so formidable to the southward, and we making such strides in that quarter, I fear it will require a greater force of men and supplies to check them than we, since the defeat near Cambden, shall be able shortly to draw together.

Thus, Brodhead was frustrated in his attempts to muster men and provisions for a northwestern march against the British and Indians at Detroit. This attack would come later from another direction, and Brodhead was slated for other aggressive and patriotic activities.

It was the summer of 1781. John Tilton was restless and John Carpenter was in a similar state. As they stood in the forest primeval and overlooked their land and possessions, Carpenter revealed certain of his past experiences.

"I know well the nature of the territory west of the great river. I have been there often on hunting quests. This area is no longer inhabited by the Indians, and Colonel Shepherd has not returned from his expedition to the west. What say you, John? I and my wife are somewhat disconsolate. I would like to build a cabin across the river on a creek I found, and soon thereafter bring my family to it."

"The ground is rich and black," said Tilton. "The great river and streams are pure and clean. Only several days ago, I was at the river's edge. I could see my cabin, which appeared strong. I have a great feeling to return. Our daughter, Prusilla, as you know, born about two months ago, is doing well and appears quite healthy. Often, my wife and children reproach me for not returning to our claim west of the river."

Carpenter was quiet and thoughtful. "I am in favor of adventure," he suddenly proclaimed. "From others and from exposure to the western lands, I have become aware of the dangers as I know you have, John; but would the end result not justify the means?"

"Only if we are strong enough to repel a savage foe," rejoined Tilton. "Even the Delawares have turned against us, and the unyielding Shawnees and Mingoes are not far away. I have staked over nine hundred acres in the territory west of the Ohio. Nevertheless, I will consult Susannah and, if she be receptive, we shall return with you to the Ohio country."

John returned to his home where Susannah was engaged in

preparing their evening meal. The aromatic odor of roasting venison, potatoes, beans, and corn bread was quite evident, and soon all were assembled at the table, which had been moved outside.

The day had been hot. But now a gentle breeze from the south caused the leaves of the elm and maple to waft gently, and the hint of rain was strong.

The younger children were fed accordingly; the baby, Prusilla, having nursed at her mother's breast earlier, was content in her linsey-lined crib inside the log house. The evening meal was truly the kind of feast which all frontier families enjoyed. It was, traditionally, a time for everyone in the household to come together, and after the blessing there was much idle chatter and merriment. Thomas could not resist dropping a cold bean down the back of Polly's linsey shirtwaist, and after shaking it free, she proceeded to clout him, rather smartly, on his head. They both laughed. Fun and adulation, amid composure, prevailed. Near the end of the repast, the children became silent and listened to a serious conversation between their parents.

"John Carpenter is in favor of seeking adventure and establishing a home west of the river," said John. "I explained the good things in the western valley, and he is quite receptive to challenging the dangers that exist. I did not know before today that he had hunted in that area for several years now. Would it be unwise if we accompanied him and once again occupied the cabin which I know still stands?"

"He is strong and courageous," responded Susannah, as her heart beat more rapidly and she concealed her excitement. "However, I, too, feel that our western claim provides the brightest future. And I would tell you now, John, that, once abroad, I will remain, unless compelled by force to return to this area."

"I agree with you, dear wife. As always, I cannot turn away from the wisdom of your words. Reports from Wheeling indicate that conditions in the east are favorable, but the Indians of this territory remain bloodthirsty and dangerous—as well as the British Tories. The Shawnee and Delaware and Mingo are within a one or two day striking distance from our cabin. But Carpenter is determined; he aspires to build a strong fort."

Susannah's eyes flashed and she twirled her auburn tresses. "Very well," she consented. "But this time, all must be abandoned in this Virginia land."

"I will retain my claim and register it at Wheeling. It may be beneficial in the future. But, as you have consented, we shall prepare to return to our home west of the Ohio."

On the following day, John informed the Carpenters of their decision, which was received with much joy and happiness. Preparations for the relocation were immediately begun. John's two horses and cows were made ready, and Carpenter, who had decided to take only a meager assortment of necessities, loaded a strong wooden skid, which, upon being tied securely to the trailing horse, was easily conveyed across the winding southwest path to a point near the river just north of Short Creek.

Before the sun had descended beyond the western hills, the men and boys had felled and prepared, by trimming and notching, enough trees to construct a large raft for conveyance of all persons, livestock, and provisions across the river.

The night's rest in a sheltered grove of locusts was of little consolation to Susannah. She slept, but lightly. As a mature thirty-one-year-old woman of the wilderness, her hopes and dreams of the future were without fear or doubt; as a mother, she was secretly concerned about the safety of her children. The baby, Prusilla, snuggled close and her head rested on one arm of her mother. Their bed of leaves and linsey was not uncomfortable. But every so often a tear would stain the unblemished cheek of the fair Susannah and her beautiful auburn tresses became rumped and disarrayed as she turned from side to side.

With the coming of the sun came activity. Tilton and Carpenter, with the help of Joseph, Thomas, and Jackson, had soon lashed together, with rawhide thongs and strong vines, a sturdy craft for conveyance across the river. Propelling poles and paddles were fashioned with tomahawk and knife. By midmorning the first crossing was in order. Susannah and the children, stationed aboard the craft, were expertly floated across. Joseph, knowing the route well, led the way to their humble abode of yesteryear. The men ferried the horses and cows and provisions across, and in a short time all were assembled near the cabin.

After a little over two years absence, the Tiltons found their cabin in relatively good condition. It had not been molested by Indians, and a few spatches of moss and mud to the exterior conditioned it for occupancy. By nightfall, beds inside the cabin had been prepared; the high grass and creeping vines that had grown to considerable proportion around the cabin had been cleared by sickle, knife and tomahawk; and a circular clearing around the cabin enhanced the beauty of the flat land above the river.

Tilton and Carpenter took turns in sleeping and watching during the night to protect against the invasion of some uninvited visitor—be it wild animal or red savage. None came.

With the advent of dawn, Tilton informed his wife as to their intention.

"Carpenter and I will explore the area more thoroughly. He is anxious to stake a claim and build a cabin. Perhaps we shall be fortunate enough to secure fresh meat. Joseph is quite capable of providing any protection you may require during our brief sojourn, since we shall return about midday."

"I urge you, be careful, John. The children and I will widen a path to the river and, also, the land must be cleared. The weeds in the area we plant have thrived during our absence."

"I have cautioned the boys to be alert to dangers, and they fully realize the possible meaning of every breaking twig or turkey gobble."

Tilton and Carpenter rode north through the lush, green bottom land and soon arrived at a creek[4] about a mile north of the Tilton cabin. They examined the region, and finally Carpenter decided.

"I will build a strong cabin, here,"[5] he announced. "The soil is rich and this creek, which I have explored about two miles up, is close by."

"It is a good choice, John," said Tilton. "You are, at this point, close to the river and not too far distant north of our cabin."

The two frontiersmen dismounted, pastured the horses in an adjacent field, and began clearing the area that Carpenter had selected. Trees and green foliage were felled and dispersed in short order, and before the sun was halfway across the sky, the land was void of cabin-building obstructions.

Upon returning to Tilton's house, each with a plump turkey taken en route, they were greeted heartily.

"The land for our cabin has been cleared," announced Carpenter. "Tomorrow we shall start building a house. For some time, I have wanted to come to this country of the Indians where the game is plentiful and the land is rich. I know Nancy will like it, too."

The afternoon was spent in cultivating the land on Tilton's claim so as to properly condition it for early planting the following spring.

After a peaceful night, Tilton and Carpenter once again mounted the horses and are headed for Carpenter's clearing on the creek. The boys wanted to come along, but their father cautioned, "There is much to be done here, and besides, your abilities with a rifle may be required—although I pray not."

With the two expert woodsmen working daily, Carpenter's log cabin was completed and ready for occupancy in about five days. Upon completing the structure, Carpenter decided to bring his wife and his son, Edward, and daughter, Elizabeth, to their new home. And in due time he returned to his cabin on Buffalo Creek, secured all of their remaining supplies on a strong pack horse, and returned to his new cabin just north of Tilton territory.

Nancy Carpenter was of stout heart, great courage, and strong character and together they, too, prepared some land for seeding with corn. Quite often one of the Tiltons assisted in this chore as time and circumstances permitted.

After only about six weeks of living in their western home, the Carpenters, while on one of their frequent visits to the Tilton cabin, appeared concerned.

"I have seen several Indians along the creek, John," said Carpenter. "This appearance is cause of some consternation to my wife and me."

"I, too, have been aware of smoke signals to the west," replied Tilton.

"I intend expanding our log home into a fort to offer greater protection. Do you think this wise?"

"A stockade and jutting second floor, with well-placed chinks, would most certainly insure our chances of survival, should the Indians decide to attack," said Tilton. "Perhaps, it would be well if my family and I joined you, temporarily, to assist in the venture."

Carpenter jumped to his feet, pummeled his friend on the back, and shook his hand. In this manner, he expressed joy at Tilton's suggestion.

In due time, the original cabin of John Carpenter was converted into a structure which would be highly effective in repelling attacks from the red savages. The split-log roof was dismantled and, using an auger and strong oak pins, the basic ceiling joists were extended on all four sides of the cabin. With the use of eight- or nine-inch-thick logs, about twenty-four feet long, flattened and creviced on each end, the upper section of the blockhouse was rebuilt and extended; the extension was about seven feet above ground level. Logs, four to six inches in diameter, were split with axe and wedge and neatly fitted, braced, and pegged to cover the roof. Yellow clay and mud and moss from the creek bank sealed the upper portion of the building, except where intentional slots were retained to permit a view of the surrounding countryside and the insertion of a long rifle. The roof was weather proofed in a similar manner.

Outside the main building, a square of tall pickets about ninety feet on each side was constructed, in addition to a small cabin adjacent to the main house, to be used for storage.

When the fortification of Carpenter's cabin was completed in August, John Tilton and his family returned to their own house and made preparations for the coming winter. Salted and dried venison, bear meat, turkey, rabbit, and groundhog were stored in their attic larder.

Carpenter's Fort was established, and a shortage of salt almost led to the death of its owner!

VIII

THE LAST BATTLE AND THE FIRST BABY

SHORTLY AFTER THE COMPLETION of Carpenter's Fort, on a day when John Tilton and his family were engaged in neighborly conversation and relaxation inside the stockade, they were suddenly jerked to attention by a loud shout outside the main entrance. Instantly, they grabbed their rifles, herded the women and children inside the blockhouse, and climbed the log ladder to the second floor, to determine the nature of the outsider.

Upon observation, they saw a white man, clad in typical frontier style and accompanied by a young woman holding a child.

"What be your mission and purpose of your call?" asked Carpenter in a loud voice.

"I have a cabin only an hour's walk north of here," said the stranger. "This is my wife. My name is Maxwell—James Maxwell."

Tilton and Carpenter stared at each other unbelievingly.

"Are you the same Maxwell who was at Wolfe's Fort and Tilton's settlement across the river some years ago?" questioned John.

The response came. "I am the same one, and there is no one here but my wife and I and our daughter."

Convinced that Maxwell was being truthful and seeing no evidence of other movement in the area, the Maxwells were admitted to the confines of the fort. Upon closer scrutiny Tilton recognized him.

"Maxwell," said Tilton, "I never thought to see you again. Why are you here? And may I, in all candor, compliment you on your choice of this young woman as your wife and the mother of the little girl."

"Many thanks, Tilton. I came to this country nine—ten years ago—built a cabin—but the Shawnees persuaded me to return to

Virginia. Although somewhat fearful of this, because I was suspected of committing a crime, I did return. I found myself exonerated, and after taking this young girl to wife, I determined to return to this land. We have been here almost a year now, and the Indians have been friendly. Our daughter, Sally, is almost three years old."

The remainder of the day, until almost nightfall, was spent in talking and eating and playing. The three settlers reminisced and discussed the future. Susannah and Nancy and Mrs. Maxwell engaged in conversation, while the children played.

Susannah was the same flashing-eyed lady of the auburn tresses that she had been from girlhood.

"Tell me, Mrs. Maxwell, are you happy in this wilderness?" she inquired.

"Oh, yes, Mrs. Tilton, my husband and I feel quite secure. The Indians visit us frequently; they call me 'Wild Rose.' Even though they may do mischief elsewhere, they will not harm us. We have a young man staying at our cabin who has been quite helpful with the chores."

Susannah was surprised.

"We have seen no evidence of friendship from the redskins, even though we have lived here off and on for the past six years. Only a few years ago they attacked us and destroyed our crops."

"They were renegades," responded Wild Rose. "My contact with them has always been peaceful. In a few days we intend visiting Fort Henry; our daughter will stay with the young man we have befriended."

"What do you know of him?" inquired Nancy. "Your daughter is most welcome to stay here."

"We know nothing of him, but his character is good and not once during his stay with us has he been disloyal or dishonest. She is safe with him."

Little did she know!

Before the dark of night, the Maxwells and Tiltons returned to their cabins and retired. The moon was full, and only an occasional cry of a wildcat, the hoot of an owl, or the guttural mumble of a black bear broke the silence.

At breakfast time, Susannah related to John what she had learned the previous evening and voiced her concern for Sally Maxwell.

"Could you not convince Mrs. Maxwell that the girl would be more secure and well-cared-for at the fort or even here in our cabin?"

"No, John," said Susannah. "She was quite certain that Sally would be safe at their cabin."

"We shall visit them upon their return from Fort Henry; they will have news of the war."

Thus it came about that while Maxwell and his wife were away from their cabin, a savage band of Indians burned their home in Ohio country, killed the young man who was their guest, and took their daughter prisoner.

Upon returning home somewhat earlier than expected, due to reports of Indian depredations in the immediate area, the Maxwells learned of the situation. There was no trace of Sally, and her mother could only deduce that she had been slain and burned to ashes. Upon reaching this conclusion, the young and beautiful Wild Rose became quite insane, and, grabbing her husband's knife, she cut her throat severely and sent her soul to its eternal destiny.

Maxwell was dismayed, despondent, and quite desolate by the loss of his wife and daughter. Leaving the scene of disaster, he informed Carpenter and Tilton of his sad state of affairs and recruited other settlers in Ohio County, across the river, to accompany him on his mission of revenge. Unfortunately, a heavy torrent of rain wiped out the trail of the savages and eventually all the settlers returned to their homes without achieving their purpose.

Maxwell then became a lone avenger, and over a period of time he killed over a hundred Indians; the name of James Maxwell became as much feared among the redskins as the names of Simon Kenton and Lewis Wetzel.[1]

Salt, one of the staples of the frontiersmen, was quite important for maintaining healthy livestock, curing animal skins, and cooking. It was almost nonexistent in the Ohio country and the land east of the river.

Carpenter and Tilton discussed the situation.

"I have two good horses back along the Buffalo near our earlier settlement, John," said Carpenter. "Even though it is now December and the weather could become a hindrance, I propose to go to Fort Pitt and return with the salt which we require."

"I agree the salt would be of great advantage to the maintenance of survival in this rich land. The snows have been light. But you know, John, the savages are on the prowl. I know that I must stay here. Joseph would be pleased to accompany you."

"No, I will go alone," responded Carpenter. "My son would also go with me, should I ask. But I feel that both my son and Joseph are needed here. I know the way, and I can travel swiftly."

"Very well. Be it as you wish. Take this as payment for half of whatever salt you purchase," said Tilton, handing him several sterling coins.

It was decided.

The next day, Carpenter crossed the river, trekked eastward along the creek, and found his two horses in good health in the fenced pasture and shelter where he had left them in the care of other settlers about six months ago. After greeting his former neighbors, he prepared the horses and started on his journey toward Fort Pitt. By evening he had made good progress toward his destination and, selecting a tree-encircled clearing, decided to rest until dawn.

While sleeping peacefully, his campfire dimmed by dying embers, he was surrounded and made prisoner by a party of dissident Delawares.

He protested. "I mean you no harm; I am on my way to Fort Pitt to get salt."

His plea was ignored. The war party entered the settlements of western Pennsylvania and commited much mischief. Carpenter's clothes became quite torn and unwearable after about two months' travel with the savages and they eventually outfitted him in a plain buckskin vest and breechcloth. In February of 1782, the red marauders attacked the house of Robert Wallace,[2] who was away at the time. They made prisoners of Mrs. Wallace, a ten-year-old son, two-year-old Robert, and a baby girl. After this dastardly deed, the Indians herded their prisoners toward the Ohio river.

At this point, Mrs. Wallace was in a state of consternation, and the infant cried constantly. The savages tomahawked and scalped them and carefully concealed their bodies about twenty miles north of the Mingo town. The two boys and Carpenter were taken to a Moravian town on the Tuscarawas and from there to the Wyandot town of Sandusky. Here the older Wallace boy died; Robert, after being held captive for almost three years, was finally rescued and returned to his friends.

Carpenter escaped much sooner, in the spring of 1782. As a pioneer and woodsman wise in the ways of nature and the stars, his basic instincts led him back to Fort Pitt, whence he returned to his family—with a good supply of salt.

There was much rejoicing at the return of John Carpenter, by both his family and the Tiltons, and the families spent many early summer evenings listening to his exploits and relating events in the area of his fort and Tilton's cabin during his absence.

In one such session, when the moon hung low and the children were safely bedded down, Carpenter proclaimed, "I am convinced that no Indian can be trusted. They give in return for fair payment and take back by force. My captors were self-proclaimed Christians, but they did not hesitate to kill or plunder. Not one of the red savages shall I ever befriend, regardless of his claims or intentions."

"I am inclined to agree with you, my friend," said Tilton. "Twice during the winter, even in heavy snow, they attacked our cabin but were soon sent scurrying to their haven beyond the western hill by sheer determination and strong musket fire from our cabin."

"The harvest should be good. I know you have assisted my family in many ways," responded Carpenter, "and I shall be always grateful. Already I see the green leaf of the corn plant rising from the ground. It will be a productive year!"

Little did he know the events that would occur in that momentous year—1782.

Only about a month after his return, Carpenter was working in his corn patch when a lone Indian fired at him. The ball, although not fatal, wounded him and knocked him to the ground. While in this state, the red savage ran toward him with the intention of scalping him. Nancy had heard the shot, and upon leaving the fort she immediately diagnosed the situation.

It appears that in this type of circumstance, the courageous pioneer woman received superhuman strength and determination. Quickly reaching the side of her fallen husband, she beat the red invader unmercifully, thus allowing John to reach the safety of the fort. The perplexed Indian limped away, in due haste, to reach the dark confines of the forest.

In time Carpenter recovered from his wounds, but by September he was still somewhat incapacitated. Meanwhile, the crops prospered, but John Tilton became increasingly aware of the smoke signals to the west. He suspected that warriors of the various Indian tribes were camping on the hilltops. His concern was soon to be confirmed. Messangers from across the river advised him that the Indians and British were preparing a massive assault upon Fort Henry.

With these thoughts in mind, he abandoned his cabin and insisted that his family move inside the confines of Carpenter's Fort.

"John, I know you are not yet physically able to grapple with our enemies; but since you insist, Joseph and I will travel to Van Metre's Fort. Susannah and Thomas and the rest of my family will stay here; they are quite accurate with the rifle and will assist you if need be. I have a strange feeling that this encounter at Fort Henry will be significant in our fight for freedom."

The last battle of the Revolutionary War took place at Fort Henry in Wheeling, and it must be recognized as a most significant event in opening the Territory Northwest of the River Ohio for settlement.

On September 11, 1782, approximately three hundred Indians, mostly Shawnees, Mingoes and Delawares, under the direction of James Girty,[3] who was at least equal to his brother Simon in ruthlessness and ferocity toward the whites, crossed the river and stationed themselves within view of the fort. In addition, they were reinforced by fifty British soldiers, known as the Queen's Rangers,[4] under the command of Captain Andrew Bradt.

With fife and drum playing martial music and the British flag flying high, the attackers presented themselves, in full view, to the inmates of the fort[5] and Girty, who seemed to have complete command of the besiegers, demanded surrender in the name of the British crown. He promised protection to all inside the fort according to the mandate of King George.

After consultation, the heroic defenders of the fort defied, with vocal torrents, the demands of Girty. At the time, there were only eighteen men within the fort fit for service, another nine being injured or ill; there were also about forty women and children in the fort.

Copeland Sullivan, an experienced Indian-fighter, who had stopped at the fort on his way with a supply of cannon balls for General Clark at Louisville, was selected to take charge of the fort, since Captain Boggs, the commandant, upon becoming aware of the approaching army, had gone for assistance.

Toward nightfall, Girty again demanded surrender and threatened to storm the fort. His pleas fell on deaf ears, and the brave defenders prepared to do battle. Each of the eighteen inmates was outfitted with rifle, tomahawk, and scalping knife. The women prepared bullets, consoled the injured, and took care of the children.

Girty proceeded to attempt the assault he had promised.

Inside the fort, situated on a platform high enough to clear the picket walls, was a small French cannon. As the massive army approached, the cannon was fired, and its projectile cut a wide swath through the ranks of the enemy, killing and wounding many. The amazed savages retreated but soon regrouped, spread out around the fort, and maintained a continuous harangue upon the patriots inside, several times attempting to set fire to the wooden palisades. None of these maneuvers were successful. The small cannon was fired from the fort quite often during the first night of the siege and dealt extensive death and destruction.

Colonel Ebenezer Zane, the proprietor of Wheeling, was determined to remain in his house with several members of his family and friends,[6] and defend it to the last. His log house was not far from the fort.

The next day the British and Indians withdrew their attack for several hours. The supply of powder at the fort was diminishing fast, as the defenders had maintained an almost continuous barrage of gunfire against the enemy.

Sullivan and Silas Zane became somewhat concerned as the powder supply dwindled.

"My brother is well stocked with ammunition at his cabin," said Silas. "But to acquire it will require a man of speed afoot and daring."

Sullivan called for volunteers to accomplish the hazardous mission.

One of the men immediately stepped forward, but it was Elizabeth Zane, the colonel's sister, who moved in front of him and said, "No! I will go; should I be killed, I can be better spared than any one of these men."

And so it was that young Betty Zane, after shedding most of her outer garments, stepped from the fort, and with the speed of a gazelle quickly gained entrance to her brother's house. Immediately, she was provided with a good quantity of vital gunpowder. Upon leaving Colonel Zane's cabin, she ran at the same pace toward the entrance of the fort.

The Indians, watching her, suddenly became suspicious and began firing, but every shot went awry and she reached the fort safely.

This act of heroism by a young girl of the violent frontier undoubtedly saved the inmates of the fort and the house of Colonel Zane from certain death and destruction. Yet the exploit was typical of the brave and strong-willed pioneer women.

As darkness approached, the Indians and Tories once again resumed their attack on Fort Henry. The barrage of gunfire at the fort and from it continued unceasingly through the night. Unsuccessful in their efforts to break the stronghold, the savages began killing the livestock, setting fire to empty cabins, and performing whatever other mischief their perverted minds could devise.

Meanwhile, Captain Williamson and seventy mounted patriots, including John and Joseph Tilton, were approaching the beleaguered fort after entreatment by Captain John Boggs. An Indian spy had seen them, and his warning had sent the remaining members of the British-Indian army scurrying toward the Ohio and the security of the untamed northwest. The inmates of Fort Henry and Colonel Zane's house greeted the arrival of Williamson and his militiamen with much rejoicing and relief. The Tiltons, humble in the background, were content that their mission had been accomplished.

John and Joseph Tilton returned to their Ohio home about September 20, after their recognition by Captain Williamson as solid defenders of the new United States of America. Although the British army had surrendered at Yorktown almost a year before, in October of 1781, the British Tories of the west were quite active until the Battle of Fort Henry in September, 1782. After this, their activities were primarily concentrated in the areas near Detroit and north of the Canadian border.

John was sad.

"Although successful in our mission at Fort Henry, we have lost a good friend and strong defender," he explained to Carpenter, as Susannah and the older children were gathered around the campfire near his cabin. "Major Sam McColloch is dead. He was killed from ambush by the red devils in late July while on a scouting expedition with his brother John."

This news served to provide a cloud of silence among the adults in the Tilton camp. But sixteen-year-old Joseph could not help relating his adventure to his brothers, Thomas and Jack.

"It was a hard ride," he told them. "The sky was red from the flames of burning cabins, and I saw the last of the Indians crossing the river. I was tempted to shoot, but refrained as the others entered the fort. You cannot imagine the joy and happiness they expressed at our arrival: children clinging to my legs and women crying, except for one,[7] who seemed to be a tower of strength and as strong as most men. When we left, after reinforcing the south bastion and the log fence, they provided us with good food and expressed strong hope for the future."

"What did the Indians look like?" asked Jack.

"They were red and black and yellow, and most were half naked," said Joseph. "But I was not afraid."

"I would have been," replied Jackson.

"Well, maybe I was, too, but I did not sense fear—I am a man and, as such, I cannot feel, or at least reveal, fear."

Jack's eyes widened and then closed as Joseph relaxed; all slept until sunup.

The winter of 1782-1783 was spent in comparative comfort by the Tiltons. The snows were deep and pure, and only occasionally would a small party of Shawnees or Delawares attempt to molest them. All such invasions were repulsed with strong and accurate rifle fire from the cabin, and in short order the attackers were sent with quiet dispatch to the heavily forested western hills—and a dead savage was buried the next day in a shallow grave along the western hillside.

The children of John and Susannah had little fear of Indians or bears or wildcats during the snow-laden winter days. Joseph, now seventeen, and Thomas, age fifteen, were strong and mature young pioneers. Everyone enjoyed a swift ride down the sloping river bank on a smooth carved wooden "sled" or a large basket of woven hickory branches. The frozen river provided a smooth, slick surface, and the primary purpose of the sport was to see who could slide the greatest distance on the ice.

Even Susannah, their mother—she of the flashing eyes and auburn tresses—took an active part in the fun and games. She and John, when he was not hunting with Joseph or Thomas, enjoyed the company and escapades of their children. Jackson, Polly, Sally, Susannah, Lorenzo, Drusilla and Prusilla, the younger children of John and Susannah, grew strong and hearty.

In early spring, the snows had melted and ice cakes were floating down the river. The rich bottom land of Tilton Territory was loosened, and long rows of corn and beans and melons and pumpkins were seeded and cultivated.

The Tiltons, having endured many hardships and labored faithfully in their fruitful virgin vineyard, had often vowed that no human would eject them. But someone would try!

An ordinance had been approved by the Continental Congress in October, 1783, by which it was understood that all land between the Ohio River and Lake Erie, east of the Big Miami and Maumee Rivers, could be claimed and occupied by white settlers. The ordinance eventually turned out to be somewhat meaningless.

Although many Indian atrocities were committed in western Pennsylvania and Virginia during the spring and summer of 1783, the Tilton and Carpenter claims west of the Ohio were free from strife. The larders of both families were well stocked, and the fall harvest was bountiful.

As the multihued leaves fell from the oak and elm and maple, the Tiltons replowed their productive lands and prepared them for planting in the spring. With the first snowfall in November, their cabin was snug and secure, at least against the onslaught of cold, blustery winds and heavy snows. The mournful howling of a wolf, the cry of a wildcat, or the weird screech of an owl did not disturb the peace and tranquility within the Tilton home.

And in the early winter of 1783, Susannah gave birth to her eleventh child—a son. They named him Caleb, and time alone would reveal his claim to fame![8]

IX

A SETTLEMENT
AND A STATE

IN THE SPRING OF 1784, after the snow had dissipated and the white-clustered blossoms of the locust had fallen, John Tilton and his family once again planted the seeds which they had carefully selected from the previous year's bounty and protected throughout the winter.

Although somewhat uneventful in Indian warfare, the year 1784 was quite significant in the colonization and settlement of the Territory Northwest of the River Ohio. William Hogland and his associates made their presence in the territory well known and Hogland's intentions and ambitions soon became evident.

Hogland was a strong, aggressive pioneer of the "forbidden" territory. He had come, with his family, to western Pennsylvania about fourteen years earlier and in 1772 was a resident of Bedford County in that state. In 1775, he was a trader on Decker's Creek, a tributary of the Monongahela named for Thomas Decker. He had witnessed the migration of land-hungry pioneers in 1779, and shortly thereafter, transported his family west of the broad Ohio and claimed a section of land south of Tilton territory and Norris Town, which was a small settlement made by Charles Norris, an adventuresome pioneer from the east, immediately south of Tilton's. He became quite prominent in the eastern section of the territory, through his political expeditions to the south and west and north. In all his discussions with the western squatters, he belittled the treaties between red men and whites as meaningless and unlawful. He defied the right of the congress to endorse his claim and others as Indian property.

During the summer, Tilton and Carpenter were in frequent contact with Hogland, the influential and determined Scotch-Irishman.

"Tilton," said Hogland on one occasion, "I know that you and Carpenter have claimed much of the land in this area, and your claims are just. However, I think, as a measure of defense, not only from the Indians but from the Continental army, that our settlements should be secured and a democratic system of government be placed in effect. I have traveled as far down the river as the Muskingum and into the back country. I have talked to many settlers, and all are in accord."

Tilton and Carpenter concurred.

There is no queston that the federal government was well aware of the establishment of the "official" settlements west of the Ohio at least five years prior to the formal organization of Hogland's "state." On October 26, 1779, Colonel Daniel Brodhead, commander of the Continental troops at Fort Pitt, advised General Washington:

> I rec'd a letter from Col. Shepherd, Lieut. of Ohio County informing one that a certain Decker, Cox & Comp'y with others had crossed the Ohio river and committed trespasses on the Indians' land wherefore I ordered sixty Rank and File to be equipped, and Cap't Clarke of the 8t Pen' Reg't proceeded with this party to Wheeling, with orders to cross the River at that part, & to apprehend some of the principal Tresspassers and destroy the Hutts.—He returned without finding any of the Trespassers, but destroyed some Hutts. He writes me the inhabitants have made small improvements all the way from the Muskingum River to Fort McIntosh & thirty miles up some of the Branches.

The migration of settlers west of the Ohio was further evident when General William Irvine[1] notified William Moore, the president of Pennsylvania, to this effect on December 3, 1781:

> There have been sundry meetings of people at different places, for the purpose of concerting plans to emigrate into the Indian Country, there to establish a government for themselves.

On April 20th of the following year, General Irvine notified Washington, by letter, that:

Emigrations and new states are much talked of. Advertisements are set up, announcing a day to assemnble at Wheeling, for all who wish to become members of a new state. . . .

Irvine further noted that a constitution had been prepared and the squatters were acquiring artillery and other supplies from the east.

For some time, congressional action regarding this "intrusion" on Indian land was lacking. Federal authorities quite evidently condoned the settlement of lands in the Northwest Territory. Finally, on September 22, 1783, the Congress issued a proclamation prohibiting all persons from settling on land inhabited or claimed by Indians, providing such lands were beyond the control of any recognized state.

The congressional action was meaningless, and in 1784 the movement of people across the great blue river increased steadily.

The political aspirations of William Hogland were about to be realized. Settlements continued to be founded farther south on the western banks of the broad Ohio and inland. John Emerson, a friend of Hogland, prepared and posted notices on March 12, 1785, to the effect that the inhabitants on the west side of the Ohio River would be given an opportunity to elect members of a convention and frame an official constitution.

The Treaty of Fort McIntosh, located on Big Beaver Creek, in January of 1785, had provided further impetus to the western invasion. Representatives of the Delaware, Wyandot, Chippewa AND Ottawa tribes attended the sessions, and the Congress of the newly founded United States of America appointed George Rogers Clark,[2] Arthur Lee, and Richard Butler to act on their behalf. The Americans were strong and convincing in their statements, which in rather strong terms stated that the Indians had no further claim to eastern lands in the Northwest Territory. The terms of the treaty were stated clearly and with full force and effect. The representatives of the United States of America were unrelenting in their demands, claiming the land by "right of conquest."

The representatives of the Indian tribes could do nothing but accept the treaty terms, which were defined on January 21, 1785.

They acknowledged that, except for a reservation between the Cuyahoga-Tuscarawas intersection at the Maumee River, all the lands in the northwest were the property of the United States of America. The Treaty of Fort McIntosh did not please or appease the Indians, particularly the powerful Shawnees—as the white settlers would soon learn.

The residents of Ohio County, Virginia, were not long in becoming aware that an organized system of government had been established on the west side of the Ohio; many built rafts and crossed the river to claim land in the rich bottom. Others moved up along the western hill and cleared the land and built cabins. And by the spring of 1785, more than fifty families had settled to the north and south and east of John Tilton's original claim.

Upon learning of the rapid influx of white settlers in western lands, the commissioners became somewhat alarmed and instructed Colonel Josiah Harmar,[3] commandant of the Continental troops in the west, to disperse the settlers and force them east of the river. Harmar, in turn, ordered Ensign John Armstrong to assemble a company of twenty regulars and drive out the trespassers along the eastern section of the Northwest Territory.

Ensign Armstrong toured the designated area and found untold numbers of white settlers and their families. On April 4, he quartered at Mingo, where Charles Norris and a party of armed patriots accosted him and demanded the purpose of his mission. Upon obtaining this information, Norris and his contingent withdrew their guns and warned the ensign that not far to the south a strong democratic system of government was now being organized and that he would encounter considerable resistance.

The next day, Armstrong moved south. He was amazed at the number of cabins that dotted Tilton Territory and the surrounding areas. Upon encountering the "governor," as Hogland was called, he inquired:

"Are you aware that you and your families and these armed men who stand behind you are trespassing on congressional lands which, as of now, are not available to you for occupancy? Certain of the Indian tribes are quite concerned, and I am authorized to order you and your friends to lay down your arms and return east of the river."

"I am unaware of any law or ordinance which prohibits our being here," replied Hogland. "We have endured the trials of Indian and wild animal savagery. We have organized in accordance with our rights as free men. By whose authority are you here?"

Hogland was adamant. The settlers prepared their rifles.

The Continental troops did likewise.

It was a tense moment.

"I am here as authorized and instructed by the Congress of these United States of America, as an officer in the Continental army, to command all settlers in this territory to return east of the river. And I intend to perform that duty."

It was a strong statement.

"On that basis," continued Armstrong, "I will give you two weeks to prepare your belongings and return to the east."

Hogland meditated—and finally, with great reluctance, he yielded and agreed to the terms. The settlers laid aside their rifles and Ensign Armstrong, convinced of their sincerity, continued on his travels to the south and west.

On this tour of duty, he became aware of additional hundreds of families throughout the territory which had braved the western frontier. Upon his return to Fort McIntosh, Ensign Armstrong notified Colonel Harmar to this effect:

> It is the opinion of many sensible men (with whom I conversed on my return from Wheeling) that if the honorable Congress do not fall on some speedy method to prevent people from settling on the lands of the United States west of the Ohio, that country will soon be inhabited by a banditti whose actions are a disgrace to human nature. . . . I have . . . taken some pains to distribute copies of your instructions, with those from the honorable the Commissioners for Indian Affairs with almost every settlement west of the Ohio, and had them posted up at most public places on the east side of the river, in the neighborhood through which these people pass.
>
> Notwithstanding they have seen and read those instructions, they are moving to the unsettled countries by forties and fifties. . . .

Armstrong also noted that across from Wheeling, along the bottom land, the settlers occupied most of the land.

The election of William Hogland, as governor of a new state in the Northwest Territory, took place in accordance with the notices posted by John Emerson. The voting, primarily by acclamation or a show of hands took place on April 10, 1785, as scheduled. At the same time, John Carpenter and Charles Norris were elected as justices.

The expanse of the territory governed by William Hogland was extensive, since four points in "Indian country" had been established to assemble for voting—the mouth of the Great Miami, the mouth of the Scioto River, a place on the Muskingum, and the house of Jonas Menzons in Hogland's Town.

A constitution was prepared; thus a uniform system for governing the settlers' claims and actions became effective. This area, over which Governor Hogland presided, included the claims of John Tilton and John Carpenter, and was, in effect, the first organized white settlement in the Territory Northwest of the River Ohio. The boundaries, although somewhat vague in the outlying areas, were definitive enough that the rules of the constitution could be enforced.

The governor's log house, featuring a large hall, was constructed in the southern section of Hogland's Town, and from that structure, he, in conjunction with the justices, conducted the activities of the "state" under a very liberal constitutional code of laws.

Other expeditions by soldiers of the Continental army to force the stalwart settlers east of the Ohio River were quite unsuccessful. Ensign Ebenezer Denny[4] visited the western settlements in August of 1785 in further effort to entice the settlers east of the river. His mission went for nought. In October of the same year, Commissioner Richard Butler passed through the area of Tilton Territory and Governor Hogland's Town on his way to negotiate another treaty at Fort Finney. He noted that on October 2 he had called at the settlement of "one Capt. Hoglan," a few miles above Wheeling, and warned him off. The governor was polite and courteous to Butler, who left the area in a jovial and friendly mood.

In November, Major John Doughty, also under the direction of Colonel Harmar, invaded the southern section of the "state" occupied by Hogland's constituents in the Muskingum area and the back country. His report to Harmar stated:

> I destroyed by fire every house I could meet with on the Federal territory, amounting to forty in all. Notwithstanding which I am firmly of opinion many will be rebuilt, for the poor devils have nowhere to go. Many of the houses that were destroyed last spring, I found re-built and inhabited.

Captain John F. Hamtramck, who was quartered at Mingo Bottom in the summer of 1786, with 160 troops, was ordered to search for and destroy the houses of the "squatters." His efforts to perform this function appear to have been without perseverance or persistence. After one invasion of the western settlements, one of Hamtramck's officers gave notification, on August 5, that he had destroyed one corn house, twelve hundred rails, over twenty-five acres of corn, and nine houses. What a braggart!

Nothing changed on the western frontier as a result of these fruitless expeditions. And the brave ones continued to infiltrate Hogland's state.

John Tilton and his family did not leave their western home, and they continued to cultivate the rich land and plant their crops.

The adoption of the Ordinance of 1785 by the Continental Congress provided that all federal lands would be divided into townships, each to be six miles square. A township would then be subdivided into thirty-six sections, each a mile square and containing 640 acres. According to the ordinance, the Geographer's Line would run due west from the point where the Pennsylvania boundary crossed the Ohio River, and from that point, north-south range lines should be surveyed by working eastward toward the Ohio River after establishing the westernmost line.

In late summer, Thomas Hutchins, the chief surveyor, came to Fort Pitt for the purpose of establishing the base line from which to project the range lines. Thirteen surveyors, one from each of the colonies, were appointed. Only eight were on hand, however, when Geographer Hutchins, after receiving confirmation from Colonel Harmar that the surveying party could proceed safely, was prepared to undertake the hazardous task. Among the eight was Absalom Martin, who represented certain prominent citizens of New Jersey and had been recommended by the governor of that state.

Hutchins was apprehensive regarding his expedition into the country of the Indian. On September 30, however, he assembled his crew of surveyors and about thirty assistants at the mouth of the Little Beaver. On that date he erected a post at the point of beginning and charted his way westward until October 8, establishing a line of less than four miles, at which time he became aware of warlike Indian activities along his line of venture. Hutchins sent messages to the chiefs of the Wyandots and the Delawares requesting their protection. When Captain Pipe[5] of the Delawares declined to comply, Hutchins ordered his surveying crew to disband and return to their homes; Thomas Hutchins did likewise.

Meanwhile, John and Susannah, cognizant of the fact that their family was growing and that this fertile and productive Ohio Valley land would be their permanent home, discussed their plans for the future.

"As you know, John," said Susannah, "Thomas has selected a site and is determined to build his own cabin at the base of the western hill. I am sure you know why."

"That I do, dear wife, and he shall build it with our help. Even at seventeen, he is strong and quite capable of providing for a wife and child."

Susannah, now thirty-five, with flashing eyes and long, auburn tresses, embraced her husband, and interpretive conversation was absent for some time.[6]

Thomas, assisted by his father and brother, Joseph, built a sturdy cabin and settled securely on a site he had selected within the boundaries of his father's original claim. It was mid-August of 1785 and the permanent settlement of Tilton Territory was assured. Charles Kimball and John McCormick had crossed the

Ohio River and built their cabins. The area north and east of Tilton's land also was becoming quite populated.

Only recently, George Carpenter, a famous Indian scout, crossed the Ohio River and staked a claim near the mouth of a rippling, shallow creek[7] about two miles north of Indian Short Creek. He built, with the help of some other settlers, a strong blockhouse and came to be well known and respected throughout the area.

―――――――――――

The evening was calm and peaceful. Roasted venison, fresh corn, mint-flavored squash and maple-syrup drenched pone graced the outside table of the Tiltons. The rough plank benches were well occupied, and John sat at one end of the table on a three-legged stool. It had been a good day. The corn and beans and pumpkin-squash had yielded abundantly, and the attic and small cellar in the Tilton home were well stocked.

John spoke to his wife after some members of the family had excused themselves and left the table.

"Tomorrow, I must go to Wheeling. We have large land holdings across the river and, while talking with our friends, Hogland and Lamb, yesterday, I became convinced that they should be duly recorded."

"John, are we not well off now in this rich land? What need have we for this Virginia land or recompense? Your purse is as heavy as it was when we traveled to this land of adventure."

"Yes, that is true," said John. "But the relative insecurity in this unsurveyed land deems the mission necessary."

"There is no power, be it Continental troops or Shawnee warriors, that will force us from this fertile valley. But, be it as you will. In matters of this kind, your decisions have been wise."

Joseph, who was still at the table, had listened intently.

"May I accompany you, father?" he questioned. "Perhaps I could be of some service."

"According to your mother's wish," responded John.

Susannah's eyes sparkled and danced.

"Yes, my son, you will go with your father and return him safely to me. I have need of much protection in this land."

The following day, John and Joseph journeyed south on horseback, crossed the river at its shallowest point, and entered the city of the Zanes. After several inquiries, they became acquainted with William Lamb, an influential citizen of the town and brother to Frederick Lamb who lived on the west side of the river in Hogland's Town.

"Mr. Lamb," said John, "I have been in this frontier land over twenty years. My settlement on Buffalo Creek was the refuge point for many travelers to the west. By right of settlement, I ask that the area be surveyed and consigned to me."

"I know you only too well," responded Lamb. "Your patriotic service to the commonwealth lends credence to your claim. I shall write to Governor Henry concerning your settlement, and the remainder of your claim in Ohio County shall be yours as a small recompense for your service as a member of the Ohio County Militia."

John and Joseph were exuberant. They knew William Lamb to be a man of his word. The original boundaries of their Ohio County claim were surveyed and submitted to the governor. Other lands marked by the Tilton "T" were measured and recorded. Although the Tilton settlement on Buffalo Creek was relatively small, the acreage of his claim was extensive. Before returning home, Lamb had John sign a right of settlement certificate, which was necessary in order to receive his land grant from the governor. Under date of September 15, 1785, William Lamb submitted the land grant request to Governor Henry and prepared the necessary title deed for the balance of the Tilton claim in Ohio County, Virginia.

John and Joseph returned to their log house in Ohio county in late September. Their purpose had been accomplished. Except for the settlement grant, they now possessed all deeds relating to their original claim.

Susannah and the children greeted them with love and affection and a certain sense of high expectation. During their absence, the Tilton home and farm lands had been unmolested. The Delawares and Shawnees seemed to have withdrawn and moved westward. It was only a matter of time before they would return. The Treaty of Fort McIntosh was unjust; they had no part of it. But they were well aware that this treaty and the Ordinance of

1785 had provided a sound basis for settlements west of the Ohio River.

Even though many of the early settlers had returned to Virginia in the spring, upon instructions from governmental troops commanded by Ensign Armstong, they had returned in the fall. Thus, when General Butler and Colonel James Monroe[8] toured the area in the fall, they found that many cabins had been rebuilt and new ones constructed.

And so it was that in late 1785 there were many white settlers in the area of Indian Short Creek and Tilton Territory, including the Tiltons, Carpenters, Kimballs, Buchanans, and McCormicks.

There is no question that large families were a necessary attribute to survival on frontier lands. Beleaguering by Continental troops or unscrupulous Indians required defense of their claims, and solidarity was prerequisite. As other settlers from Ohio County, Virginia, moved westward, Elijah Tilton, the seventh son of John and Susannah, was born in Tilton Territory. He was now their sixth surviving son.

Although many Indian atrocities were committed east of the Ohio on the west branches of the Monongahela and in the vicinity of Wheeling in 1785 and 1786, the families to the west were not seriously threatened—except once!

The tragedy that invaded Tilton Territory occurred in early 1786. All members of the Tilton household had certain chores and responsibilities. Joseph worked mostly with his father in hunting and providing the necessary maintenance of provisions for subsistence; Jackson was responsible for maintaining surveillance over the cows and horses and assuring that they were well fed and healthy; the older girls assisted their mother in gathering greens, carrying water from the river, and preparing sufficient clothing and bedding of linsey-woolsey and animal skins.

It had been a good day. The air was crisp and cold and dry, and the cows had been permitted to roam freely in search of edible fodder and foliage, of which there was very little at this time of the year. Near eventide, the animals had not returned, and Jackson set out to retrieve them and return them to the small log shelter near the cabin. He walked north and west and, although armed with a rifle, was quite unsuspecting of any danger. He found the cows near Indian Short Creek[9] and was in

the process of driving them homeward when a musket blast from
a grove of trees pierced his breast and left him lifeless. The savage
redskins hurriedly and deftly lifted his scalp, as they knew other
inhabitants of the area would respond to the sound of a musket or
rifle. Then, in due haste, they moved westward to the confines of
a silent forest.

At the point of darkness, Susannah urged her husband to go in
search of Jackson. The cows had not returned and the boy had
been gone too long. Upon entreating the help of other settlers,
they surveyed the area thoroughly and finally discovered the
body of Jackson Tilton.

Sixteen-year-old Jackson was buried the next day near a large
Indian mound[10] on Tilton's land. The other settlers were bent on
revenge, but John quieted them.

"The murderers have long gone," he said. "We could not identify them. We know not whether they were Shawnees,
Delawares, or Mingoes, and no doubt they are far away. As settlers of this land, we knew the hazards that existed. We became
complacent; we felt secure. I tell you now that a tracking party
would serve no purpose. He was my son—and even now my wife
is bitter and unconsoled. But this land is ours, and by the will of
the Almighty, we shall retain it."

It was a stirring speech; Susannah of the tear-dimmed flashing
eyes and auburn tresses, relented. The settlers acquiesced and
returned to their homes.

John returned to his cabin, restrained his tears, and held his
wife close.

———————

In May of 1786, the Congress passed a resolution authorizing
the geographer, Thomas Hutchins, to reconvene his survey of
ranges in the Northwest Territory. Hutchins returned to Fort Pitt
in June and was informed that the Indian tribes, including the
Delawares and Wyandots, were receptive to the survey of the
lands ceded by the Treaty of Fort McIntosh. The surveyors,
representing all the states except Delaware, prepared their gear,
bought the necessary provisions, hired chainmen, and made

ready to accomplish their mission. After some delay, since Hutchins had received no communique from the Indians regarding title to the ceded lands, and despite an uncooperative Colonel Harmar, who would not provide troops to protect the engineering crew, the surveyors for the United States resumed their work toward the establishment of the Geographer's Line on August 9, 1786.

It had been a bountiful and productive summer for the Tiltons, the other occupants of Tilton Territory, and the pioneer residents of the surrounding areas. Adequate rainfall and warm summer nights had caused the crops to flourish and produce abundantly.

Susannah, too—she of unlimited energy and endurance— roamed the western lands, administered to the sick, worked the farm, cared for her children, delivered babies, and had babies. William, another son, now graced the household of John Tilton, having been born on April 3, 1787, when John received word from his friend, William Lamb, that the Governor of Virginia had acknowledged his Certificate in Right of Settlement, as follows:

> Patrick Henry Esquire Governor of the Commonwealth of Virginia To all to whom these Presents shall come Greetings Know ye that by Virtue (and in Consideration) of a Certificate in Right of Settlement given by the Comissioners for adjusting the Titles to unpatented lands in the district of Monongalia Yohogania & Ohio and in Consideration of the Ancient Composition of Two Pounds sterling paid by John Tilton into the Treasury of this Commonwealth, There is Granted by the said Commonwealth unto the said John Tilton Assignee of William Lamb a Certain Tract or Parcel of Land containing Four Hundred Acres by Survey Bearing Date the Fifteenth day of September one Thousand seven Hundred Eighty five, lying & being in the County of Ohio on the Waters of Buffaloe Creek Including his Settlement made in the Year of our Lord one Thousand Seven Hundred & seventy two, & Bounded as followeth To with Beginning at a Maple corner to said

Tilton & with his line South seventy seven degrees East two
Hundred & Eighty one Poles to white oak thence North
twenty eight degrees East one Hundred & twenty six Poles
to an ash, thence North seventy seven degrees West seventy
six Poles to a Sugar tree, thence North nineteen degrees East
fifty eight Poles to a black oak and ash corner to Alexander
Wells & with his line North thirty seven degrees West one
hundred and sixteen Poles to a Hickory; thence West one
hundred & thirty Poles to a white oak thence South thirty
eight degrees West one hundred sixty six Poles to a Sugar
tree corner to John Harris and with his line South fourteen
Degrees East eighty eight Poles to the Beginning With its
Appurtenances To Have & To Hold the said Tract or Parcel
of Land, With its Appurtenances to the said John Tilton &
his Heirs for ever In Witness where of the said Patrick Henry
Esquire Governor of the Commonwealth of Virginia hath
hereunto set his Hand & caused the Cofur Seal of the said
Commonwealth to be affixed at Richmond on the fifteenth
day of July in the Year of our Lord one Thousand Seven
Hundred & eight six & of the Commonwealth the Eleventh

P. Henry

After receiving the grant from Governor Henry, John and
Susannah were officially recognized as documented owners of
about seven hundred and fifty acres of land, spaced between Buffalo Creek and Short Creek, in Ohio County, Virginia. However,
for other than monetary value, these lands to the east held little
interest for the Tiltons. They were intent on retaining their land
holdings in the fertile valley west of the Ohio, and they were also
aware that the western land was being surveyed by congressional
approval. With the influx of pioneers moving westward and
down the Ohio, news from the east was conveyed with more expediency than might be expected.

Meanwhile, Thomas Hutchins, with some apprehension, had
resumed his efforts to establish the Geographer's Line to the west.
Colonel Harmar rejected his request for a military escort—the
Shawnees and Delawares and Wyandots had not responded to his
invitation for protection—but still Hutchins, along with surveyors from twelve colonies, advanced six miles from the Penn-

sylvania boundary. Absalom Martin, representing New Jersey, started a line southward at that point and established the western boundary for the First Range. At six-mile break points, other surveyors followed Martin's procedure and paralleled his course to the south.

The first indication of antagonism from the Indians appeared about the middle of September when Hutchins, after dispatching William Morris of New York south along the western line of the Seventh Range, moved into the Tuscarawas territory of what was to be the Eighth Range.

Reports had reached Hutchins that the Indians were combining forces southwest of the Tuscarawas, their full intention being to attack the surveying teams. The geographer was greatly concerned and sent word to the surveyors to discontinue their efforts and return to Virginia, and he and his small retinue of soldiers did likewise. Eventually, all of the surveying companies and Hutchins came together at the home of William McMahon,[12] east of the Ohio.

In early October of 1786, Hutchins now had at his disposal about seventy well-provisioned troops, and by the middle of November four ranges had been completed and the east-west township lines established. However, the harsh winter weather and the fact that the clothing and provisions of the troops were now depleted, caused another discontinuance of the survey, and once again the surveyors convened at McMahon's house and finalized their maps and sketches, which outlined range and township boundaries.

Finally, in late January of 1787, Hutchins returned to New York, made his report to a Congress of the United States which had become somewhat disillusioned with the rectangular land survey procedure, and requested leave of further assignment in the Northwest Territory.

His request was granted, and it remained for two men, Absalom Martin and Israel Ludlow, who had spent the winter in the west, to continue the Survey of the Seven Ranges. Shortly thereafter, they were joined by James Simpson of Pennsylvania, and by the middle of May, although some progress had been made, they requested military assistance.

A new army post had been established at Fort Steuben, about

fifteen miles north of Tilton Territory, in the First Range, and it was from this detachment that the surveyors expected protection. Colonel Harmar felt otherwise. He did, however, send up sixty soldiers from Fort Harmar, and after meeting in Ohio country opposite Wheeling, the troops and surveyors set out to complete their work.

Shortly thereafter, Ludlow encountered the western line of the Seventh Range at a point seven miles above the mouth of the Muskingum River. The completion of the Fifth and Sixth Ranges was soon accomplished by Martin and Simpson. The troops returned to Fort Harmar; Ludlow, Martin, and Simpson relieved their parties and returned to the Virginia home of William McMahon. They remained until the end of August, mapping and describing, as best they could, the rectangular sections of land established by the survey. The three surveyors traveled to New York and consulted with Hutchins, who incorporated earlier data on the Fifth and Sixth Ranges. After taking almost a year, Hutchins completed a general plan of the Seven Ranges and presented it to Congress in July of 1788. The first and last rectangular land survey, as authorized by Congress, was complete.

Upon completion of the Survey of the Seven Ranges, there was no public auction of these lands. The only sale of land under the Ordinance of 1785 occurred in New York City between September 21 and October 9 of the year 1787. Two townships along the Ohio were sold, but investors in the interior were not interested as long as the one dollar per acre minimum price prevailed.

The only exception to this feeling occurred in 1787 when Absalom Martin, an authorized congressional surveyor, purchased a tract or parcel containing over three hundred acres of land five miles south of the Tiltons' settlement along the Ohio River.

And so it came to be that, on July 13, 1787, Congress passed an ordinance for the government of the Territory of the United States Northwest of the River Ohio. It is one of the most important ordinances: the most comprehensive, the most democratic and the most influential ordinance ever adopted. It is composed of fourteen sections and six articles. It provided that the Territory be one district (subject to congressional division into two); it provided for a governor, who was to be commander in chief of the militia, and a secretary; it provided for the establishment of laws and the appointment of judges and civil officers by the governor; it provided a method of determining representatives from the Territory and defined the general assembly or legislature to consist of the governor, a legislative council, and a house of representatives; it extended the fundamental principles of civil and religious liberty in conformance with federal statutes; it made possible freedom of religion, trial by jury, and the development of schools; it clearly stated that the Territory was a part of the United States and subject to the Articles of Confederation; it provided that from the Territory should be formed not less than three nor more than five states and outlined the boundaries; and, finally, it provided that neither slavery nor involuntary servitude should be permitted in the Territory.

The Ordinance of 1787 is truly a monumental tribute to the intelligence and foresight of the founding fathers of this nation.

Meanwhile, William Hogland continued his role as governor in the eastern section of the great Northwest Territory. The residents of this unnamed state were quite content with his administration. He and his wife had at least two sons—Henry and Aaron. On May 27, 1787, Henry married Elizabeth Carpenter, the eldest daughter of John and Nancy Carpenter; and some time later, on September 29, 1787, the following announcement appeared in the *Pittsburgh Gazette:*

> (Marriages) Mr. Henry Hogland, son of governor William Hogland, west of the Ohio, was married to the highly amiable Elizabeth Carpenter, eldest daughter of John Carpenter, esq. landlord of Norristown, west of the Ohio. The marriage was celebrated at the Governor's hall, on Friday, the twenty-seventh day of May, at twelve o'clock, and the evening was most agreeably spent in dancing, firing of guns, and drinking of toasts to the success of the new state, and prosperity to the new and first married couple in it. . . . Capt. Swearingen[13] and the governor were seated at the head of the table.

John and Susannah Tilton were special guests on this momentous occasion, and it was a day and night they would long
remember.

Thus, the Tilton settlement became secure. Explorers and men
seeking adventure in the west passed through and made their
claims south, north or west of the Tilton Territory, respecting
John's right of settlement. Many requested permission to squat on
Tilton's land temporarily, and usually the request was granted.

The village grew and prospered, and sometimes at the evening
meal Susannah, a shining star in the rather gloomy wilderness,
would look at John and her children, glance at the neighboring
cabins, and remember when they had first came here twelve
years ago to a rich, green, untrodden valley. Her happiness and
sorrow on the western frontier were mixed, but the pleasure and
contentment provided by John and the children far outweighed
the anxiety and sadness she had experienced.

At the age of thirty-seven, she was still young, as evidenced by
her flashing eyes and the flaming tint of her auburn tresses. She
looked at John as he ate his venison and beans and pone. She
could not ask for more than he had given. His skill as a woodsman, farmer, militia scout, advisor, father, and husband were
undisputed. She had nurtured and watched their children grow.
Joseph, now almost twenty-one, was strong and resourceful and a
great source of consolation to her when John was absent for one
reason or another.

The sun was receding behind the western hill, and the twilight
sky was sprayed with streaks of red. Susannah glanced at the
cabin of Thomas and his wife, Sarah. They were happy in their
rough-hewn home, with a young son, John, to care for and increase their mutual love. Polly, at the age of seventeen, was quite
interested in a young man named Hardesty, from Wheeling. Sally
and Susannah and Drusilla and Prusilla laughed and chattered as
they ate. Lorenzo was quiet, as were Caleb and Elijah. Susannah
held William and broke the meat and beans and pone into small
morsels for him.

In due time, the supper was concluded, the table was cleared,
and all leftovers were carefully preserved. At bedtime, when the

children were secure, John and Susannah said their nightly prayers together, embraced each other with love and tenderness—and slept.

X

ADVENTURES AND AMOUR

THE INDIANS OF THE VALLEY were in an extreme state of disagreement in regard to the ceding of Northwest Territory lands as provided for in the Treaty of 1785 at Fort McIntosh the previous January. They also considered the Treaty of Fort Stanwix, previously agreed to by representatives of the Iroquois Nation and a few Shawnees in 1783, to be invalid. The Treaty of Fort Finney,[1] which took place near the mouth of the Great Miami River, with only chiefs and subchiefs of the Shawnee Nation in attendance, was accomplished by coercion and threats. When the Shawnees finally assembled at the fort in January of 1786, they were quite dismayed at the terms announced by the congressional commissioners—General Richard Butler outlined the conditions of the treaty, as follows:

> The Shawnee must recognize that all lands east of the Great Miami are the property of the United States by right of conquest; the Shawnee would be protected and punished in accordance with the laws of the Congress of the Confederation of States; and finally, only upon the return of all white prisoners would Indian hostages be released.

The Shawnee chief, Blue Jacket, and his warriors were appalled at the terms of the treaty. Blue Jacket was adamant.

"The Shawnee do not give hostages and, although you may have conquered the British, the land remains ours, as God has provided. You may keep the goods that you say you have for our families; give them to others—we do not need them."

Colonel Butler retorted angrily, "The destruction of your families and their happiness in the future is directly related to your choice. Peace or war you desire. Determine for yourselves the end result."

Blue Jacket, at the moment outnumbered ten to one, had no choice, but the silent anger in his breast would not subside. He replied softly, "Brothers, you are powerful—we now see that you, indeed, have a right to this land. We, therefore, agree to what you propose and ask that you spare our families with the hope that the Americans and the Shawnees may live in peace."

The war chief of the Shawnees signed the Treaty of Fort Finney with concealed rage and hatred in his heart, and western settlers were not long in learning the insincerity of the treaty.

Fortunately for the settlers in Tilton Territory and the surrounding areas, the Shawnees wreaked their vengeance across the southern concourse of the Ohio River.[2] And, except for the heroic efforts of Boone and Kenton and other stalwart frontiersmen, their ultimate purpose would have been accomplished.

The Reverend George Callahan came boldly into Tilton Territory in the autumn of 1787. At this time there were large settlements south and north of Tilton's claim. A settlement was established just north of Indian Short Creek by Zenas Kimberly, Benedict Wells, John McElroy, and John Humphrey. Charles Kimball and John McCormick were firmly founded in Tilton Territory.

The Reverend Callahan was a circuit rider of the Virginia District. He was born in Pennsylvania in 1766, the same year as Joseph Tilton, eldest son of John and Susannah. He was a farmer and a preacher, and the latter vocation dominated his life on the western frointier.

At Carpenter's Fort, in 1787, he held the first Methodist Episcopal Church services in the Territory Northwest of the River Ohio. Although still carrying the stigma of "squatters" on unpurchased lands in Indian country, the settlers, being strong, resolute, determined, and religious, occupied a community of permanence. Many residents of the immediate area attended the church meeting at the fort. The singing and sermon were inspiring and provided a great source of consolation to the pioneers.

They went home happy and content, and no military force or government decree would cause them to retreat from their settlements. The settlements in and near Tilton Territory were well established, well organized, and beyond question the first permanent settlements by white men in the Northwest Territory.

The hardy Hardestys of Virginia were numerous and adventuresome since they had come to the Valley of the Ohio about the year 1780.

Obediah Hardesty and his family had resided in the Wheeling area for about one year when, inspired by the munificence of the territory to the west, they crossed the Ohio and moved into the back country about seven miles south of Tilton Territory. Hardesty purchased 100 acres of land, a part of Section Twenty-four in the Third Range and Third Township, from Robert Johns. The Hardestys had a number of children, among whom were Robert, born in 1768; Ruth, probably born in 1771; and Mary, who was born in 1773.

By the year 1788, Robert Hardesty, now twenty years of age, had roamed the hills and hollows of much of the surrounding countryside in search of game and adventure. He had come to know well the settlers at Hogland's Town, Tilton's Town and other settlements. It was during these missions that he came, with intention, to know Polly Tilton, the eldest daughter of John and Susannah.

Engagements, in those early years, were not long. And in April of 1788, after the Tiltons and other residents of the area had weathered a blistering cold blast of winter winds and subzero temperatures, Robert Hardesty and Polly Tilton became man and wife. The exchange of vows was simple and expedient, with the bride's father performing the ceremony since there was no minister present in the immediate area. The next circuit rider would confirm the marriage. Another cabin was built in Tilton land, and the young couple were happy. The frivolity and merrymaking subsided and Tilton's Town became stronger.

The Johnson family was well settled and firmly established in Westmoreland County, Pennsylvania, in 1785. James Johnson and his wife had a large family among whom were John, born in September of 1775, and Henry, born on February 4, 1777. In 1785, James sold his farm and decided to explore the western lands, hopeful of finding more productive possessions, despite the perils that were always present in the Middle Ground.

Consequently, James Johnson packed his most essential articles of survival and moved westward. He crossed the Ohio and settled near Carpenter's Fort on Indian Short Creek. At this point in time, fragments of the Delaware and Shawnee tribes were quite mischievous and threatening. During the next three years, the Johnsons prospered as farmers and became prominent residents of the area.

On Saturday, October 18, 1788, James's thirteen-year-old son, John, and his eleven-year-old brother, Henry, had accompanied an older brother in search of wild game. Upon returning to their home, they discovered that one of them had lost a hat, and John and Henry decided to return to the hunting grounds, about three-fourths of a mile from their home, and recover the hat on the following day.

The next day, a crisp, cool Sunday afternoon, John and Henry took to the woods and soon found the hat. They sat down on a log and proceeded to crack some hickory nuts and eat the tasty kernels. It was while they were thus engaged that they were approached by two men who, at first glance, they thought were Mr. Russell and Mr. Perdue,[3] two of their neighbors. They soon realized their mistake as the dark complexions of the intruders became evident. Upon questioning by John, the men acknowledged that they were Indians. After inspecting the area, the larger Indian instructed the boys to accompany them. The Indians had long rifles, and the boys knew that, at this time, escape was impossible.

The complex minds of the red savage and the brave pioneer cannot be analyzed more accurately or extensively than at this encounter. The pioneers, through exposure and experience, were committed to survival—even as young boys. Each knew a tenacity of purpose, and under any circumstances they were conditioned to this end.

The foursome moved along the bank of the creek. One of the

Indians walked about ten paces in the lead and the other about ten paces behind the boys. The Indians were looking for horses.

After traveling about three miles from Carpenter's Fort, the sun was almost down and the Indians decided to rest for the night. Their concealment and shelter would be a shallow, leaf-covered hollow along the gurgling creek.

John and Henry were at this point quite concerned, not particularly for themselves but for their parents, who they knew would be quite upset that they had not returned before dark.

It was a beautiful, starlit night. The Indians had prepared a small campfire, cooked and eaten some forest victuals, talked for some time in their native tongue, and prepared to retire for the night. A plan had formed in the minds of the young captives. John talked to the Indians and they understood. He indicated he was happy to go with them, since his father was mean and made him work hard.

"I do not like hard work. I would much rather be a hunter and live in the woods," said the oldest boy.

This pleased the Indians, and they sheathed their knives and became more friendly. One of the Indians spoke good English, and he and John conversed freely. The Indian questioned John concerning the availability of horses in the area, and John replied that he knew of none. Several times the Indian asked which way their home was, and each time John would tell him a different direction. The Indians laughed. They thought the boys totally lost, but in actuality they knew the route to their home very well.

Henry became somewhat disconsolate in late evening, and John consoled him by telling him, very softly, that tonight they would kill the Indians. The boys reclined on the ground near the smoldering fire and pretended to be asleep. The Indians did likewise, one on each side of the boys to better become aware of their movements and prevent their escape. In due time, the two Indians were sleeping soundly. The boys, wide awake, arose silently and John, taking one of the Indians' guns, cocked it and aimed toward the head of a sleeping savage. He then picked up a tomahawk and prepared to cleave the skull of the other Indian.

On silent signal, Henry pulled the trigger of the gun, and John landed a series of quick, decisive strokes with the hatchet.

The boys hastily ran away from their quivering victims and moved along a path paralleling Indian Short Creek and leading to

Carpenter's Fort. They arrived at the fort just before daybreak and were greeted with great joy by their parents and neighbors. Upon relating the story of their adventure, some persons were skeptical. A small group of pioneers assembled, and John led them to the scene of their encounter. They found the toma-hawked Indian lying on the ground; the body of the other Indian was found some time later at a place where he had crawled after being fatally wounded. The Indians were great warriors of the Delaware Nation, and one of them was a chief.

In due time, the federal government, recognizing the deed of valor accomplished by the Johnson boys, granted them a tract of land which encompassed the area of their victory. The land was farmed by the Johnsons for a number of years.

Susannah Tilton was happy. At the age of almost thirty-nine and with another child due in about a month, her eyes flashed and danced, and her auburn tresses were never more beautiful. In the past two days, she had delivered two more babies to courageous mothers in the land of Tilton. With the application of bear's grease to the chest and back of a twelve-year-old girl, warmly wrapped in linsey-woolsey blankets, she comforted her; and the hot sassafras tea helped, too.

She bustled around their expanded log house, cooking, cleaning, and caring for the needs of the younger children. Sally and Susannah, now almost sixteen and fourteen respectively, helped their mother. Ten-year-old Drusilla also had her duties to perform. She assisted in feeding, dressing, and entertaining her younger sister, Prusilla, and two brothers, Caleb and William.

Life in Tilton Territory was a frolic. John and his eldest son, Joseph, spent much time in hunting and trapping, and there was always a good supply of fresh meat on hand. Lorenzo cut kindling and prepared logs for the hearthstone fire that was used for cooking and heating. He carried water from the river and milked the cows and cared for the horses. His older sisters sometimes assisted in these tasks.

In February of 1789, when Susannah gave birth to her four-teenth child, another daughter, everyone was happy. They named her Ann, and she grew strong and healthy under the watchful, flashing eyes of her pioneer mother. Although showing no evidence of the fact, Susannah had hoped for another son to name after her husband. There was still time.

Strange though it may be, since many Indian depredations were committed east of the broad Ohio in 1789 and for several years thereafter, Tilton Territory and the adjacent lands were relatively unmolested. An occasional encounter with small roving bands of Indians in search of plunder was experienced, but the solidarity of purpose of the white inhabitants soon dispersed the red men to other more lucrative and isolated areas for performing mischief.

In late May, John, wise in the ways of land seekers and convinced that the land and section survey of 1787 would remain firm under the federal statutes of the new United States of America, decided that the time had come to officially establish his claim in Ohio country. At the same time, he decided that a certain section of his land in Ohio County, Virginia, should be sold to further enhance his monetary position.

Accordingly, leaving the children in care of Joseph and the other settlers, he and Susannah traveled to Wheeling to accomplish these purposes. They were quite surprised at the number of early settlers that inhabited the community. There were many cabins and small businesses, including hostelries, markets, and taverns. Upon inquiry, they located the log building of Moses Chapline, the official clerk of Ohio County.

"My wife and I are holders of considerable land in this honorable country," said John. "Being official residents of this county, we have a friend to the north, Thomas Selman by name, whom I know to be interested in purchasing certain of our holdings."

Chapline was calm and efficient. "I know the Selman brothers," he replied, "Thomas and Adam. And only this morning I saw Thomas. Perhaps he is still here, and if you have the proper papers, the transfer of ownership can be effected today."

An assistant of Chapline's soon located Thomas Selman, and upon agreeing to the price and the acreage, the land transaction as quoted in the following passage was duly recorded:

This Indenture Made and Concluded this first day of June one thousand Seven hundred and Eighty Nine by and between John Tilton and Susannah his wife of Ohio County and State of Virginia of the one part and thomas Selman of the County and State aforesaid of the other part Witnesseth that the Said John Tilton and Susannah his wife for and in Consideration of two hundred and four pounds pens Currency to them in hand paid by the Said thomas Selman the Receipt wheareof they do hereby acknoledge doth grant bargan and Sell and by these preasants hath barganed and Sold unto the Said thomas Selman one piece parcel or tract of Land in Ohio County Containing two hundred and four Acres Laying on the waters of Buffelow Creek and bounded as followeth to wit) Beginning at a Shugartree Cornor to Said Tilton thence North Nineteen degrees East fifty Eight poles to a black Oak and ash Cornor to Alexander Wells and with his Line North thirty Seven degrees one hundred and Sixteen poles to a hickory thence west one hundred and thirty poles to a white oak thence South thirty Eight Degrees west one hundred and Sixty Six poles to a Shugartree Cornor to John Harris thence South fourteen degrees East Six poles to a Post thence South Eighty Eight degrees East two hundred and Eighty two poles to the begining togeather with all its appurtinances to have and to hold Said Tract of Land with its appurtinances unto the Said thomas Selman and his heirs to the Sole use and behoof of the Said thomas Selman his Heirs and assigns forever and the Said John Tilton and Susannah his wife and their Heirs the aforesaid Tract Peece or parcel of land with its appurtinances unto the Said thomas Selman His heirs Executors Adminnistrators or assigns against them the Said John Tilton and Susanna his wife their heirs and assigns and all persons Claiming or to Claim Said tract or parcel of land will warrent and Ever defend in Witness wheareof the Said John Tilton and Susannah his wife have heare unto Set their hands and Seals the day and years above Written

John Tilton (Seal)

hir

Susannah X Tilton (Seal)

mark

the above Indenture was Acknoledged in capen
Court at June term 1789 and ordred to be Recorded

Test

Moses Chapline Clk. O.C.[4]

John, upon completion of the deed transfer to Thomas Selman, advised Chapline that he and his family, although legally residents of Ohio County, were firmly established on claims in the Northwest Territory.

"Are these surveyed and ceded lands?" inquired Chapline.

"They are," replied Tilton. "As a matter of fact, my friend Absalom Martin, an official federal surveyor, has already established a settlement along the river about five miles south of my claim. I have conversed with him freely and am told that the land I hold embraces all of Sections Sixteen and Twenty-two of Township No. 4 and Range No. 2. It is this land which I wish to purchase."

"I will contact the proper authorities and make inquiry concerning the sale of these sections. The land offices established for sale of those lands were quite unsuccessful. However, I will investigate the matter, stressing your service in the recent war, and attempt to obtain a deed patent for you."

"Your services are much appreciated, Mr. Chapline," said John. "It appears as though this village is thriving. I have bought a good horse and salt and seeds for planting."

"That is true," said Chapline, "but we are not yet secure; the red savages are still a serious threat to our farmers north and south. The perpetrators of these dastardly deeds are small parties of renegades, mostly Shawnees, Delawares or Mingoes. They are no danger or threat to us here in Wheeling, but the isolated cabins along the northern line of our creek and the Monongahela and to the south, near Grave Creek, have been the targets of their vengeance."

"'Tis a sad state that such unjustified atrocities should occur. I was here with McColloch almost twelve years ago—I came with Williamson in '82—and I am happy that the town has flourished. It is getting late, and my wife and I must be home before dark. I will be here from time to time and look forward to your success in securing the deed to my western claim."

———————

The harvest of 1789 in Tilton Territory was abundant. The Kimballs, Carpenters, McCormicks, Tiltons, and other residents of the area filled their cabin attics with corn and long beans and pumpkin and Indian squash. The Indian smoke signals to the west were no longer evident, and the winter of 1789-90 was spent in peace, tranquility, and friendship.

In the spring of 1790, Sally married Jacob Reilly,[5] a young frontiersman whose family had settled in Western Virginia about two years earlier. The usual wedding festivities prevailed. Eventually, a cabin was built and the stars were their servants, the bear and panther their challenge, and the Indian their thirst. Their honeymoon in Tilton Territory was not long, and upon agreement, they bartered deer and beaver skins for a pack horse and moved, with high hopes, deeper into the interior of the Northwest Territory. They went with the blessing of Sally's parents.

The passage of the Ordinance of 1787, and the subsequent sale of lands in Ohio country by the United States government, did much to solidify the early settlements along the western bank of the Ohio River. As a result, certain written records were kept of land transactions and other official business conducted within the settlements.

John Tilton, Joseph Tilton, Thomas Tilton, John Carpenter, George Carpenter, William Bailey, James Clark, George Atkinson, John Buchannan, William Wallace, Jesse Edgington, and Robert Hill are known to have settled on these western lands prior to 1785.

In 1789, George Carpenter sold a portion of his claim north of Zenas Kimberly's grant to Jacob Miller. George frequented the house of John Tilton on many occasions. He became a close friend of Joseph, who was only one year his junior, and together they spent many hours roaming the western hills on exploratory and hunting missions. George could not help noticing the blooming beauty of fifteen-year-old Susannah; she had inherited many of her mother's outstanding characteristics. Nor was Susannah unaware of his manly attributes, for he was strong, quiet, and ruggedly handsome. They had walked the worn paths of Tilton Territory, talking and laughing. The talk was usually lighthearted—of moonlight and stars and violets and daffodils. The laughter resulted from the flapping departure of a startled quail or the playful antics of a tree squirrel. But, if the truth be known, they became quite fond of each other.

As time went on, the fondness turned to love, and in early 1791, George, with common courtesy, asked Susannah's father for her hand in marriage. John was not surprised; he did not question the potential groom, but he did inquire of his daughter as to her feelings toward George Carpenter.

"I am strong—I am almost sixteen—and I love him, Father," replied Susannah.

And so it was agreed. About a year after her sister, Sally, had married and moved west, Susannah became the bride of George Carpenter. John Carpenter, an authorized justice of the peace, performed the ceremony, and the young couple settled in George's blockhouse.

Joseph Tilton, now twenty-five years old, was still residing in his father's house, as were his sisters Drusilla, Prusilla, and Ann, and his younger brothers, Lorenzo, Caleb, Elijah, and William. He was in the prime of life, strong and robust and quite conditioned to hunting alone and living alone in the surrounding forests. He roamed the hills and dales along the broad Ohio from Fort Steuben, about fifteen miles north of his father's settlement, to Kirkwood's settlement,[6] seven miles to the south. He had explored westward across the hills and down in the valleys, and he knew the settlers in the whole region.

His father, John, at the age of fifty-two, was, after much experience, quite shrewd in the ways of the surrounding inhabitants be they white or red. He was content, however, to work his garden, remain in the company of his wife and children, and let Joseph provide the larder with fresh meat.

It was on this type of hunting expedition to the south that Joseph came to know Mary Hardesty, whose brother had married his oldest sister, Polly. Consequently, his hunting jaunts in the summer of 1792 were more frequently to the south, and a new era in the already expansive outgrowth of the Tiltons in the Territory Northwest of the River Ohio would be the end result!

XI

SORROW AND CEREMONY

IT WAS IN THE EARLY SUMMER of 1792 that John Tilton confided to his wife, "Susannah, I think it would be proper if I learned the state of my brother, Thomas. The people from the east have been coming to the areas of Redstone and Catfish in droves, and I feel almost compelled to investigate his status in that area."

"My husband," replied Susannah, "I know the affection you had and still have for your brother. As you know, the colony boundaries have been settled. Virginia and Pennsylvania have settled their differences on this matter. We know, too, that twenty years ago Thomas was a resident of Tyrone Township in Bedford County. Pennsylvania has been divided into new counties.[1] I agree that you should learn the whereabouts of your brother, but I beg you be careful. You and I have heard of the recent Indian murders in that area."

"I will be careful, and my heart is heavy to leave you, but Joseph is a strong defender."

"He is our son, and I love him—but he is not you, John. I tell you now that, although the children have given me much pleasure, my greatest source of joy and consolation has been you. In two or three months, we will have another child. That is when I need you most."

"This I know well, dear wife. Do not let the tears stain your face and flood your flashing eyes. Say 'don't go' and I will stay."

"No," said the charming daughter of grace with a twirl of her auburn tresses, "I am content with your mission. But spare no time in returning to my side."

And so it was that John Tilton, taking a good horse, crossed the broad Ohio, and investigated his land holdings in Ohio County,

Virginia. He found Thomas Selman secure on the land he had purchased, and wended his way to the town of Washington, formerly called "Catfish" and recently changed to honor the first president of the United States.

He was quite amazed at the number of cabins and log houses that were clustered along the banks of the Monongahela, and others in the outlying areas. After many inquiries at local taverns, markets, and blacksmith shops, he learned that his brother was located in Washington County on a farm to the northeast.

He rested the night at a local hostelry and resumed his quest in the morning. It was midday before he found the house of Thomas, and their reunion was quite jubilant.

"Thomas, even though I felt it necessary to inquire of the local citizens as to your whereabouts, I must admit I am surprised to find you here. Your house appears strong and in good repair. What of your wife and children?"

Thomas, although happy at seeing his brother, appeared nervous and the exposed portion of his face, the part unconcealed by a shaggy growth of hair, seemed pale and unexpressive.

"Come in, John. Sit with me and I will recount the events of yesteryear. Although I am not old, as old might be defined, I am not in the best state of health. At first we were happy in this western land. How well I remember those early days. You see the state of my house on the inside—it lacks a woman's touch. She has been gone for over a year, John."

" 'Tis a sad thing," said John. "But is there not someone else who could lend you consolation and add purpose to your life?"

"No one—and I will have no other. Perhaps I grieve too much, but so be it. My mind is sound, John, and soon I will make my will and you will see that it is administered properly. Your visit has filled my heart with joy, because I knew that soon I must confide in someone, and my first choice in this matter would be you."

"It is as I told Susannah," said John. "It was as though some unseen force compelled me to seek you out. However, I wish you would be more optimistic for the future. Are you in dire need of anything, Thomas?"

"Oh, no. I have two good cows, a horse, and a productive garden, even though I do not always care for these assets the way I should. But I am content. And there are things I feel it important that you know and make note of. Our first son, John, was born on May 17, 1768, in Maryland, and as you recall, about three months later, we came to this area. You know well that it was a hazardous existence, and often we thought of returning to the east. Six years later, Richard was born, on May 30, 1774. I will remember all their birthdays until I am gone."

Thomas wiped a tear from his eye, and John was downcast.

"William was our third son—he was born on October 30, 1776; and a fourth son, Elijah, became a member of our household on March 27, 1778. All are gone now—seeking their fortunes to the west. Let it not be said that they were not good sons: to the contrary—a father could not ask for more. They performed their chores faithfully and contributed much to our success as settlers and farmers. But with the passing of their mother, they became more adventuresome and independent. Sensing their inclinations, I gave them my blessing, as one by one they left this house which was once a home. I tell you these things, John, that you may know and understand my status in this life and the ultimate concessions I will make."

John Tilton stayed with his brother longer than he had intended—about ten days. At the end of that time, he saw no improvement in the gray pallor that was so evident in the face of Thomas.

It was a sad and final parting when John, after beseeching the neighbors to look after his brother, bade a sorrowful farewell. Before returning, he stopped in Washington, made the village officials aware of who he was, where his residence was located, and asked them to consult him by messenger if anything should happen to his brother or if he should be in need. He, of course, agreed to pay whatever expenses might be incurred, and to this request they agreed.

Upon returning to his home in Tilton Territory, John related his experiences at the village of Washington and the house of his brother. Susannah greeted him with a strong embrace, and the children with chants of "Father, Father." Susannah was depressed by the condition of John's brother and impressed by the stories he told of the bustling community of Washington. And in this mixture of sorrow and adulation, life in Tilton's Town and the settlements at the mouth of Short Creek and south in the adjacent territorial villages continued to flourish and prosper.

Although distraught by the condition of his brother, John knew that his first obligation was to Susannah and his children. He hoed the corn and cared for his garden and livestock while consoling himself with the thought that he had done his best. He had even offered to bring Thomas to his home, and the proposal had been refused; the other arrangements were made without the knowledge of his brother.

In early August the corn was head-high and the large golden fruit was free from contamination by insects or other blotch-infesting creatures. The older boys were helpful in the harvesting, and Drusilla and Prusilla helped their mother husk and strip and prepare the corn for pone or meal or mush.

Before the harvest had been completed, Susannah, with some difficulty, had provided, through love and obligation, a new sister for the children of the Tilton home. But the problems she experienced in this heroic deed, were insurmountable, even with the wives of Carpenter and Kimball at her side. The baby girl, Susan, lived only a few days and was buried in a large grassy area at the base of the large Indian burial mound near her brother, Jackson.

In due time, Susannah resumed her chores near the cabin. The older girls were grinding corn, Caleb was in the field with his father, and William and Elijah were playing nearby. One of the local villagers, noted for his ill manners, came by and admonished, "Do not be sorrowful, Mrs. Tilton—it was only a girl."

Susannah's eyes flashed as never before, her auburn tresses quivered, and with an oath of disgust and anger, she responded, "Tempt me not, young rascal, or I shall encumber you with a broken head from this log—my daughters are as strong and even more brave than you. Be on your way, braggart, before I carry out my threat!"

The rogue laughed softly and started to retreat, and Susannah hastened his departure by firing a wooden missile with her strong right arm. It just missed connecting with his head as he vanished into the forest.

That evening, John consoled her and commended her for her action.

The summer of 1792 passed quickly. The garden harvest had been fruitful, and once again the larder of Tilton's house was overflowing.

On a cool October morning, James Howlet, a young settler in Ohio County, Virginia, visted the residence of John Tilton. Howlet introduced himself as John was stretching and cleaning a deerskin on a wooden rack.

"My name is Howlet—James Howlet—from across the river. The other settlers tell me that you be John Tilton, and my neighbor, Selman, tells me you hold title to much of the territory in that area."

"I am glad to meet you Mr. Howlet," said John, "and you are right. I know the Selmans well, and about three years ago I sold Thomas some good land in that area. Are you settled nearby?"

"Yes, and it is not my intent to poach. I am interested in buying a section of land near Thomas Selman's"

"Land in that area is not cheap, as it once was," replied John. "Selling for a little less than one pound per acre."

"I am aware of that and prepared to pay a reasonable price."

"The land must be surveyed unless you are interested in all the land to which I have title, which is over five hundred acres."

"Oh, no," explained Howlet. "There is a section along the creek and south which I desire."

"I know the area well, Mr. Howlet. In due time, I shall have the section surveyed and, if you are willing to pay the price, an indenture of transfer will be prepared in Wheeling."

"Have the deed prepared, and I will meet your price," responded Howlet.

After the surveying had been completed and the price agreed upon, the following document was prepared and recorded in the Ohio County Court House at Wheeling:

This Indenture made this fifth day of November in the Year of our Lord one thouSand Seven hundred and Ninety two Between John tilton and Susanna his Wife of the one Part and James Howlet of the other Part Witnesseth that the Said John tilton and Susanna his Wife for and in Consideration of the Sum of one Hundred and twenty four Pounds Ten Shillings Pensylvania Currancy to me in hand

Paid by John Howlet Do give Grant bargain & Sell to the Said James Howlet and his heirs One Parcel of Land in the County of Ohio containing one hundred & Sixty Six acres three Quantéres, and Eleven Poles and Bounded as followeth Beginning at a ash adjoining Lands of Samuel Bruce thence North Seventy Seven Degrees West one Hundred and Six Poles to a White oak thence South Twenty Eight Degrees West one Hundred and Eighty five poles to a Black Locust thence South one Hundred and Sixty one Poles to a White walnut thence North fifty Eight Degrees East thirty four Poles and an half to a White oak thence North twenty Eight Degrees East three hundred and ten Poles to the Beginning with its Appurtinances to the Said James howlet and his heirs to the sole use and Behoof of the Said James howlet and his heirs the Said John Tilton and Susannah his Wife Do Covenant with the Said James howlet and his heirs that the Said John tilton and Susanna his Wife and their heirs the Said Parcel of Land with its appurtinances from them and their heirs to the Said James howlet and his heirs and will forever Warrant and Defend in witness here of the Said John tilton and Susanna his wife have here unto SubscriBed their Names and afixed their Seals the Day and year above writen.

Sealed signed and Delivered)
in the PreSents of us)

                    John tilton   (Seal)
                          her
                    Susanna X tilton (Seal)[2]
                         mark

Even after selling this tract of land of land to James Howlet, John still retained the ownership of almost four hundred acres of land in Ohio County, Virginia. His permanent residence having been over eleven years in Tilton Territory on the west side of the Ohio, he and his family were officially recognized as citizens of Virginia in the County Ohio.

It was late in the afternoon of November 7, 1792, when John and Susannah approached their log house in the west. The air was fresh and clean and cool, and there was a trace of snow in the soft breeze from the north. The fragrant odor of parched corn and roasting venison and chestnuts was evident.

When within about one hundred yards of the house, they were sharply stopped by a loud halloo, "Halt! Identify yourselves and your intentions!"

John was pleased. He knew the voice. It was his friend Kimball, and the vigilance of the settlers was reassuring.

"Kimball, it's me—Tilton and my wife."

Upon recognition, the Tilton children, led by Lorenzo, were permitted by Kimball to leave the house and welcome their parents. This they did in a rather boisterous manner, laughing and chattering to express their happiness at their return from Wheeling. Kimball held the tiny hand of three-year-old Ann, and they too greeted John and Susannah.

Tilton and Kimball shook hands.

"We are much obliged for the protection you have given our children," said John. "Perhaps we may return the favor in some manner."

" 'Twas no bother. Your children are well mannered and other neighbors were helpful. Joseph is back at your house, and I think he has something to tell you."

John allowed the wrinkles to furrow his brow.

"Oh—is he sick or injured?"

"Quite the opposite," replied Kimball. "You will be happy with what he has to say."

As they moved closer to the house, Joseph emerged through the open doorway, accompanied by a young woman.

"Father—Mother," he said, "I would have you meet Miss Mary Hardesty whom, with your blessing, I will take to wife."

Susannah's eyes sparkled. She looked at her oldest son, tall and robust, clad in buckskin breeches and a warm linsey-woolsey shirt, his dark hair reaching his shoulders. There was a twinkle of love and respect in his eyes and a slight tremor in his voice. She looked at Mary, whose braided light brown tresses fell almost to her waist. Her cheeks were of scarlet tint, and her voice was gentle as she bashfully acknowledged the presence of John and Susannah.

Susannah had known that, in due time, Joseph would marry.

She also knew that this girl—this Mary Hardesty—was right for him. But she would always remember the great source of hope and faith and love that Joseph had been as a young man and a son. He was now twenty-five years old and soon would be twenty-six.

She embraced Joseph's fiancée tenderly.

"How old are you, Mary?"

"I'm nineteen, Mrs. Tilton, and I will be twenty next September."

"A good age," proclaimed John, as he shook hands with his son. "Yes, you both have my blessing, and when will the wedding be?"

"In the next few days, Father," said Joseph. "I intend to seek out my friend, Joseph Doddridge, across the river. I have heard that he has become a minister of the gospel. I know you are acquainted with the Doddridges, Father."

"Ah, yes. They came almost twenty years ago to western Pennsylvania. I knew quite well Joseph's father, John Doddridge,[3] he died only last year. I believe they live just north of our old settlement on Buffalo Creek."

"I'm not sure, Father. It has been some time since I have seen him and at that time he and his brother, Philip, were considering attending a nearby academy to further their studies. But Mary and I have decided to seek him out."

"So be it." John's voice was firm. "I trust you will return upon accomplishing your mission."

"Yes," replied Joseph. "We have decided to stay in this rich land."

And so after several days of travel throughout the hills and valleys of Ohio County, Virginia, Joseph and Mary located the young Reverend Doddridge, who performed a simple rite of holy matrimony.

Over two months later, the minister visited Wheeling and officially recorded the marriage of Joseph Tilton and Mary Hardesty at the courthouse:

> I do hereby Certify to all to whom it may Concern that on the 13th day of November 1792 I have agreeably to the

Laws of Virginia and by virtue of a licence Directed to any
authorized Minister of the gospel in Ohio County issued by
the Clark of Sd County on the 13th day of November 1792
solemnised the Right of Marriage between Joseph Tilton
and Mary Hardisty [Hardesty] both of the County aforesaid
given under my hand this 1th day of March 1793

Joseph Doddridge—

Moses Chapline Clark of Ohio County—

Upon returning to his father's land, Joseph, with the help of his
father and the local inhabitants, proceeded to build a cabin on
the extreme southern section of Tilton Territory.[4] And after the
usual feasting and housewarming and jubilation associated with a
wedding on the early frontier, the young couple settled down to
raise a family and supply their daily needs from the good earth
and the western forests. The ingenuity, courage, strength, and
knowledge of Joseph led them in due time to extensive material
success and prosperity.

The winter of 1792-93 passed in comparative comfort for the
settlers on the west side of the Ohio. The population of the area in
and around the Tilton settlement was increasing, and many brave
souls had congregated near the mouth of Indian Short Creek just
north of Tilton's claim.

In early March of 1793, a messenger arrived from the town of
Washington, in western Pennsylvania, to inform John that
Thomas had died. John had been named administrator of
Thomas's estate, and it was necessary that he journey to
Washington to perform this function.

Consequently, after arranging for the security and comfort of
Susannah and the children, and receiving the usual entreatment
from his wife to "return in due haste," John crossed the river and
traveled to Washington on horseback, in the company of Thomas
Bines, the messenger.

Upon arriving at his destination, John was once again
fascinated by the growth and prosperity of this village. He
located the House of Law and reviewed the last will and

testament of his brother. Before being granted permission to administer his brother's will, John was required to sign a Condition of Obligation which read as follows:

Know all Men by these Presents, That we *John Tilton Thomas Bines and William Sprey all of Washington County in Pennsylvania* are held and firmly bound unto James Marshel, Esquire, Register for the Probate of Wills and granting Letters of Administration in and for the county of Washington, in the commonwealth of Pennsylvania, in the sum of *Five Hundred & Fifty*—pounds, to be paid to the said James Marshel, his Successors, administrators or assigns: To the which payment well and truly to be made we bind ourselves jointly and severally, for and in the whole, our heirs, executors and administrators, firmly be these present. Sealed with our Seals. Dated the *Seventh* day of *March* in the year of our Lord one thousand seven hundred and ninety *three*.

The Condition of this Obligation is such, That if the above bounden *John Tilton* administrator of all and singular goods, chattels and credits of *Thomas Tilton* deceased, do make or cause to be made, a true and perfect inventory of all and singular the goods, chattels and credits of the said deceased, which have or shall come to the hands, possession or knowledge of *him* the said *John Tilton* or unto the hands and possession of any other person or persons for *him* and the same so made do exhibit, or cause to be exhibited into the Register's Office in the county of Washington, at or before the *Seventh* day of *April* next, ensuing; and the same goods chattels and credits, and all other goods, chattels and credits of the said deceased, at the time of *his* death, which at any time after shall come to the hands or possession of the said *John Tilton* or into the hands and possession of any other person or persons for *him* do well and truly administer according to law, and further do make, or cause to be made, a true and just account of *his* said administration, at or before the *Seventh* day of *March, 1794* and all the rest and residue of the said goods, chattels and credits which shall be found remaining upon the said administrator's account (the same being first examined and allowed by the Orphan's Court of the county of Washington) shall deliver and pay unto such person or persons respectively, as the said Orphan's Court by their decree or sentence, pursuant to the true intent and meaning of the several laws now in force in this commonwealth, shall limit and appoint. And if it shall hereafter appear, that any last Will and Testament was made by the said deceased, and the executor or executors therein named, do exhibit the same into the said Register's Office, making request to have it allowed and approved accordingly; And if then the above bounden *John Tilton* being thereunto required, do render and deliver the said letters of administration (approbation of such testimony being first had and made in the said Register's Office) then this obligation to be void and of none effect, or else to remain in full force and virtue.

Sealed and Delivered in Presence of

Alex Miller	John Tilton	(L.S.)
Geo Caton	Thos. Bines	(L.S.)
	William Sprey	(L.S.)

The assets of Thomas had dwindled somewhat; nevertheless, John oversaw their distribution and made certain that outstanding debts were paid, as attested to by the following notation in his own handwriting:

I promise to pay unto Christey Millor the just and full Sum of four Dollars for Value Rec. as Witness My Hand this 19 of March—1793————John Tilton/s/

Witt
Henry Smith
    The Admr. States this note was given
    & paid for owing two Vendees the Estate
    of the Decsd

After completing his administrative duties in Washington and purchasing certain commodities that Susannah had requested, John began his homeward trek. He took the route he knew best—the Buffalo Creek Trail.

It was a cold and lonely journey. However, John could not resist a feeling to revisit his early settlement. The grotesque brown leafless branches of the trees and the frozen, uneven terrain made his exploration even more difficult. His old cabin had disappeared, and there was much evidence of camp-fires and burned trees in the area. He saw no sign of human life in the highlands or lowlands, of which he still held deed to almost four hundred acres.

Knowing the terrain well, he decided to move south and west of the creek to a point where he had secured his raft near the mouth of Short Creek on the Virginia side. In so doing, he suddenly became aware of two men, dressed as frontiersmen and not as Indians, in a small clearing just ahead. He moved forward cautiously and soon recognized them as Howlet and Selman—the same men to whom he had sold land not long ago.

Startled by Tilton's appearance and after grabbing their guns and scurrying for cover, they recognized him and quickly breathed sighs of relief and welcomed him warmly.

The three men conversed.

"I am returning from Washington, where I was called to administer my late brother's estate," explained John. "My raft is beached just south and west of here. I hear that renegade bands of the red savages are still wreaking havoc along some of the remote camps on the river east of here. I trust you are taking the necessary precautions to avert this invasion of your lands."

"I guess we have been fortunate," said Howlet. "We have not been threatened by intruders. Our crops and families are doing well."

Selman interjected, "I was to Wheeling recently. The towns-people say that General St. Clair is not doing well in the western territory and the Indians are getting stronger. There is much concern."

"We are now a free and independent nation," said Tilton. "I am sure that, in due time, the Army of the Confederation will be victorious and establish the boundaries for white and red occupation. Three years ago, I applied for the purchase of my claim west of the Ohio. I have heard nothing yet, but the time will come."

John's visit with Howlet and Selman had been pleasant and a brief reprieve on his return home. The Virginia settlers had supplied him with a fresh supply of jerky, and he resumed his journey with renewed vigor.

Before nightfall he was across the river and back home again with his happy wife and children. It was a night for love and affection. The moon was bright, the stars twinkled, the children slept, and John and Susannah accepted the invitation of the moon and the romantic silent shadows of their surroundings.

XII

HAPPENINGS AND HAPPINESS

THE SUMMER OF 1793 in the rich bottom land west of the beautiful Ohio was a happy time for John and Susannah. Often they would be hoeing in their corn patch, insulating their log dwelling with clay and moss from the river, or harvesting a crop of beans when, not far distant, they would hear the thump of an axe as it proceeded to accurately design the fall of a mighty oak or a sapling elm. And always this indicated that some brave woodsman was in the process of providing timber for a new cabin; and always it provided strength and encouragement to those who had already settled in the territory.

At this point in time, neighbors were not far distant. Every able-bodied man made some contribution to the construction of a new cabin. Upon completion of the cabin, the pre-established pioneers would engage in the boisterous frolic and sincere welcome for the new inhabitants. Susannah and the other women would assist in the candle-making and other activities which were necessary in order to subsist on the western frontier.

After the autumn harvest, which was somewhat of a communal affair, the harsh winter was spent in the relative security and warmth of a strong log house, which was only occasionally vacated by the men in search of fresh meat, or the children for a frolic in the snow.

In the fall of 1794, Charles Kimball, having recently returned from Wheeling, visited the house of John Tilton. Susannah and her daughters were engaged in spinning yarn and preparing new clothing for the family.

"Kimball, come in and sit; you have been absent from this area for some time. I believe your wife told Susannah you were in Wheeling."

"Yes—that I was; and that village is expanding, and Colonel Zane is to be commended. They have a post office, and soon you will see mail boats from Pittsburgh. But all the talk now is of our new general of the western army—Anthony Wayne.[1] Only last year, he led twenty-five hundred men from Pittsburgh to Cincinnati and letter bearers from the west say he recently won a great victory over the Indians."[2]

"Good news—very good news," said Tilton. "Maybe that will keep the red man in his place and away from our doorstep."

"I am sure it will help. They say this Wayne is quite shrewd in the ways of Indian warfare and that he has recruited some of the finest scouts in the land, including Simon Kenton and William Wells."

"I suppose that is why we have seen so little of the savages in recent years."

"Probably," replied Kimball.

"This western land is becoming quite populated, Charles, particularly the area near the mouth of Indian Short Creek. Some land is changing hands. I am still awaiting approval of my application to purchase the two sections of land in this vicinity; I am sure it will come. Meanwhile, John Brown, who recently came west, is settled on my Virginia claim near Selman and Howlet. I am considering the sale of a certain parcel of land to him, as he requested."

"Your home is here, John—as is mine—where the game is plentiful on yonder hill, the soil is rich and fertile on the bottom land, and your friends are close."

Kimball arose to depart and graciously declined Susannah's invitation to stay for supper. Picking up his rifle and bidding goodbye, he moved swiftly and silently in the direction of his cabin near the river.

John was thoughtful as he ate, and by nightfall he had decided to sell the Ohio County acreage that John Brown desired to own.

The parcel of land which John Brown proposed to buy from the Tiltons was accordingly surveyed, the deeds to the land were prepared in the presence of Moses Chapline, Clerk of Ohio County, Virginia, and the land transfer was effected as follows:

This Indenture made this fifth day of January in the Year

of our Lord one thousand Seven hundred & Ninety five Between John tilton & Susannah his wife of Ohio County & state of Virginia of the one part & John Brown of County & state aforesaid of the other part witnesseth that the Said John tilton & Susannah his wife, for & in Consideration of the Sum of four hundred & fifteen pounds twelve shillings & Six pence pensylvania Currency to them in hand paid by the said John Brown the Receipt whereof is hereby acknowledged do give grant bargain Sell & Convey & by these doth grant Bargain Sell & Convey to the Said John Brown One Certain tract or parcel of land lying & being situate in Ohio County on Buffaloe Creek & Bounded as folleth (towit) Beginning at a Maple on the land of John tilton four hundred Acre tract thence South Eighteen West one hundred poles to a hickory thence South forty six degrees West Ninety Six poles to a white oak corner to Beard & with his line South forty Six Degrees East two hundred & Ninety seven poles to a white oak Corner to tiltons original line & with the same North twenty Eight degrees East one hundred & one poles to a white oak Corner to hawlet & with his lines North fifty Eight degrees West thirty four & a half poles to a white walnut on the bank Of the Ceek thence down the Creek North one hundred & sixty one poles to a Black locust on Bank north twenty Eight degrees East one hundred and Sixty three poles to a small Beach & two white oaks thence leaving hawlets lines South seventy four & half Degrees West one hundred & fifty seven poles to a white oak thence North Sixty Degrees West Sixty four poles to the Beginning Containing three hundred and fifty Acres to have and to hold the said tract of land with its appurtainances To the said John Brown his heirs & assigns forever to the only Propper use and behoof of the said John Brown his heirs & assigns forever and the said John tilton & Susannah his wife doth Covenant & promise to & with the said John Brown that they the said John tilton & Susannah his wife the above Described tract or parcel of land with its appurtainances to the said John Brown his heirs & assigns shall & will warrant and forever Defend against themselves their heirs & assigns & all & every other persons whatsoever claiming the same in testimony whereof the aforesaid John tilton and Susannah his wife have hereunto set their hands & seals the Day & year above Writen—

John tilton (Seal)

hir

Susannah X tilton (Seal)

mark

A Copy from the original Indenture
which was acknoledged in Court by
John Tilton and Susannah his wife at January
Term 1795 and or dred to be Recorded and at
the same Time the said Susannah being
Examined apart from hir husband Relinquished
hir Right of dower to the aforesaid tract of land——

Test

Moses Chapline Clk.[3]

With the completion of this sale of land in Ohio County to John Brown, John still retained a small deeded claim of almost thirty acres. His coffer of currency was heavy, and he awaited, with some anxiety, the opportunity to purchase the sections of land he had claimed in the Northwest Territory. He was well aware that other settlers had applied for similar grants and purchases of the rich bottom land in the Territory Northwest of the River Ohio. In June he was even more perturbed when he learned that Ephraim Kimberly had been granted 300 acres near Indian Short Creek by President George Washington.

He visited Kimberly, whose grant was north of the creek and adjacent to the river, to discuss the matter. Kimberly explained:

"I had a land warrant issued to me as a soldier of the Revolution and made application to exercise it—oh, about a year ago from last April, as I recall. Personally, I feel the Congress and certain influential men in the east are responsible for the lack of consistency and the haphazard manner in which the territorial lands are being dispersed. But I do have a legitimate deed, which I obtained at Wheeling, and I am sure it is authentic. Would you care to see it, Mr. Tilton? It's here in my trunk."

"I do not question the validity, Mr. Kimberly," said John. "But it's been five years since I made my application for purchase."

"I hear from authorities in Wheeling, and according to my

deed, further action by the Congress, which regards these lands
for grant or sale, has been adopted."

Kimberly produced his written claim to the land and John read
as follows:

In the name of the United States of America.
To all to whom these presents shall come.

Whereas in pursuance of an act of Congress passed on the
eighteenth day of April in the year of our Lord one thousand
seven hundred and ninety four, entitled "An Act to
authorize Ephraim Kimberly to locate the land warrent
issued to him for services in the late American army" permission was granted to the said Ephraim Kimberly then and
still resident on the west bank of the Ohio near Indian Short
creek within the Territory north west of the Ohio to locate
the land warrant issued to him for three hundred acres of
land for his services in the late American Army. So as to include the land where he resided or as convenient thereto as
may be, provided he does not interfere with any existing
claim location or survey: And whereas the said Ephraim
Kimberly has procured the said land to be surveyed by Absalom Martin in the manner by me directed from the return
of which survey it appears that the said land is com-
prehended and contained within the following described
lines and bounded that is to say,—

Beginning on the said Ohio River at a Sycamore tree four
feet in diameter standing on the west side of the said River,
thence up the said river the several courses thereof, that is to
say, north forty three degrees east six chains to the mouth of
Indian Short Creek, thence north thirty seven and a half
degrees, east three chains to the north bank of said creek,
thence north thirty five degrees and a half east three chains
and fifty links, thence north forty four degrees east five
chains and fifty links; thence north thirty six degrees east
five chains and fifty links; thence north thirty three degrees
east three chains, thence north seventy nine degrees and
three quarters and four chains and fifty links, thence north
thirty two degrees and a half east twelve chains, thence
north twenty seven degrees east five chains, thence north
thirty two degrees east five chains, thence north twenty
eight degrees and a half east eight chains, thence north
twenty five degrees east five chains to a sugar tree twenty

nine inches in diameter and marked on the south west and north sides with three notches, thence west thirty five chains to a sugar tree twenty inches in diameter and marked on the east and southwest sides with two notches, thence south fifty degrees and eighty nine chains to a stone marked E.K. thence east sixty six chains to the Sycamore at the beginning which is marked on the west and north sides with two notches, containing three hundred acres.

And whereas by the oath of the Absalom Martin it appears that the said land is situate in the fourth township of the second range and that the location of the said warrent does not interfere with any existing claim location or survey, And whereas the Secretary of the Treasury has certified to me that the said Ephraim Kimberly has returned his said Warrant into the Treasury of the United States.

Now Know ye that I George Washington President of the said United States by virtue of the above recited act do hereby grant and convey unto the said Ephraim Kimberly the said tract of land containing three hundred acres as the same is ascertained and described by the location and survey aforesaid, excepting and reserving to the said United States one third part of all gold, silver, lead and copper mines within the same for future sake and disposition.

To Have and to Hold the same to the said Ephraim Kimberly his heirs and assigns forever.

In testimony whereof I have caused these letters to be made patent and the seal of the United States to be hereunto affixed.

L. S.

Given under my hand at the City of Philadelphia the eighth day of June in the year of our Lord one thousand seven hundred and ninety five and of the Independence of the United States of America the nineteenth.

G. Washington
President of the United States.[4]

John Tilton was impressed with the document.

"There is no question that you have proper title to this land and my friend, Martin, has surveyed it accurately. What are your intentions toward the residents of this area?"

"I have no ill will toward these settlers," said Kimberly. "I have had the deed put on record at Fort Steuben, and, by the way, they tell me it is the first officially recorded deed at that town. I like the lay of the land, and the creek provides a good source of power for grist mills. The river will provide transportation for salable products, and the land is rich for crops. I foresee a good future here, Mr. Tilton. I need but little land for myself; I will sell certain sections upon opportunity."

"Your intentions are honorable and just, Mr. Kimberly. I hope you will visit my house at some future time. My family and I would be much pleased."

Kimberly acknowledged the invitation and, after a brief meeting with his friends the Carpenters, John Tilton returned to his home.

At the age of forty-five, Susannah Tilton, although enduring the hardships and discomforts associated with life on the western frontier, was a lady of charm and grace. Her auburn tresses and flashing eyes were unchanged. She was a tall and contoured picture of femininity fifteen years her junior. Out of necessity and out of love, she was active and vigorous—but gentle and consoling. When not about her normal household duties or working the garden, she visited her friends, welcomed newcomers to the lush, enchanted valley, administered her magic to the sick, and brought strong, healthy babies into the world.

She was quite comfortable and confident astride a strong steed, with or without a saddle. On special occasions Sally and Jacob would ride in from their land claim, almost one hundred miles west of the river, and, at the conclusion of their visit, Susannah, if time permitted, would ride with them for some distance. Frequently on such occasions Susannah and her daughter would engage in a horse race. Flying over grassy plains and wending their way through foliage-laden thickets, the mother could easily have prevailed. But the vivacious, talented wife of John, instinctively knowledgeable of psychology and diplomacy, permitted the race to end evenly or with a slight advantage to her daughter.

On the return journey, Susannah traveled alone—unafraid but

with dispatch. Her horse could sense the presence of danger, be it Indians or other circumstances, and always, upon arriving safely at her house, she offered a prayer of thanks and a promise of trust.

Many of the early settlers in the Territory Northwest of the River Ohio could attest to the vivaciousness and charm of the Lady of Legend. She knew not fear nor desperation in the face of adversity; she supplied life and hope and wise counsel to many—including the Carpenters, the Kimballs, the Mc-Cormicks, the McClearys, the Buchanans, and many others.

And they would also say, "There is no equal to the wife of John Tilton in the matter of ministration or consolation in this land of danger and primeval existence."

It was in the autumn of 1795 that the sprightly Susannah learned that she was once again pregnant. Surprised and happy, she deemed this unusual experience a sign of hope and predestination. And on that chilly November evening, when she conveyed the message to her husband, she proclaimed, "It will be a son, and we shall call him John."

By the end of the year 1795, an aura of peace had settled over the broad region of the Upper Ohio Valley. General Anthony Wayne had soundly trounced the Indians at the Battle of Fallen Timbers, and the Treaty of Greene Ville was signed. All of the Seven Ranges and more expansive land acreage to the north and south and west was now firmly and uncontestably open to settlement by white men. The menace of the savage redskin in the area of Tilton Territory and other lands, which would eventually form the state of Ohio, was no longer present.

As news of the treaty became apparent, settlers from the east infiltrated the ceded lands in huge numbers, and in a short time cabins and log houses became quite numerous. The newcomers from the east moved deeper into the untainted territory of the Seven Ranges.

Just north of Indian Short Creek and Ephraim Kimberly's grant, a settlement was growing. Robert McCleary had migrated

from York County, Pennsylvania when he was thirty years old
and settled in this area in 1790. Benedict Wells, John Humphrey,
John McElroy, and Zenas Kimberly also had cabins not far
distant from McCleary's.

Meanwhile, John Tilton was concerned about his application
to purchase the section of land he had claimed. He had heard
nothing from his friend Lamb in Wheeling, and almost seven
years had elapsed. Upon inquiry at Wheeling, he learned that the
sale of lands in the officially surveyed area of the Seven Ranges
had lasted only intermittently about two years from 1787 to 1789
in New York. Quite evidently, his application to purchase had
been forwarded to the president of the United States and
pigeonholed. John insisted that William Lamb contact President
Washington in regard to his land purchase application, and
Lamb agreed to do so.

————————————

In late spring of 1796, when the black and yellow bumblebees
were still feasting on the flower of the locust, and the cool evening
breezes were still blowing gently from the northwest, Susannah
gave birth to her sixteenth and last child. It was a son, as she had
predicted, and they named him John. Now forty-six years old,
Susannah knew that, unless by some further miracle, this would
be her last contribution to perpetuating the Tilton name in Ohio
country. With the utmost care, she nurtured the child as only a
daughter of the primeval forest could, and the baby boy responded with strength and vigor.

In May of 1796, the Congress of the United States confirmed
the Ordinance of 1785 by adopting "An act providing for the sale
of lands of the United States in the Territory Northwest of the
River Ohio and above the mouth of Kentucky River."

John Tilton was impatient but frugal. He still owned about
thirty acres of land in Ohio County, Virginia. It was only after
assurance from Lamb that his claim to Ohio lands would be
honored in the near future that he agreed to sell his remaining
acreage in Ohio County. Adam Selman had, for some time, been
interested in buying the tract along the Buffalo. Once again, after

survey, Moses Chapline, the Clerk of Ohio County, prepared the following deed:

> This Indenture Made this fifth day of September in the year of our Lord one thousand Seven hundred and ninety Six between John Tilton and Susannah his wif of ohio county and state of virginia of the one part and Adam Selmon of the county and State aforesaid of the other part Witnesseth that the sd. John Tilton & Susannah his wife for and in consideration of the sum of One hundred and fiftey Dollars to them in hand paid by the sd. Adam Selmon the receipt whereof is hereby acknowledged have given granted bargained Sold & conveyed & by these do give grant bargain sell and Convey to the sd. Adam Selmon one certain tract or parcel of land lying & being Situate in ohio County on the waters of buffalo Creek and bounded as followeth (towit) beginning at a white oak corner to the Survey that Selmon Now lives on thence N74 1/2 E157 poles to a small beech & whiteoak thence N 28 E. 20 ps. to a White Oak thence N 30 W 88 poles to a black oak thence S 44 W 102 poles to the beginning Containing twenty nine Acres & three fourths by survey being part of a tract of Land Containing four hundred Acres granted by Sd. Henry Esqr. governor of virginia to John Tilton party to this deed by pattent bearing date 15th day of July 1786 to have & to hold the sd. tract of Land with its appurtainances to the sd. Adam Selmon on his heirs & assigns forever to the only proper use and behoof of the sd. Adam Selmon his heirs and assigns forever & the sd. John Tilton & Susannah his wife do covenant and promise to & with the sd. Adam Selmon that they the sd. John Tilton & Susannah his wife the above described tract of land with its appurtainances to the said Adam Selmon his heirs and assigns Shall and will warrant & forever defend against themselves their heirs & assigns & every other person or persons whatsoever In testimony where of the aforesaid John Tilton & susannah his wife have hereunto Set their hands and seals the day and year above written
> Signed Sealed Acknowledged & delivered
> In presents of   John Tilton (Seal)
> Philip Dodridge   hir
> Moses Chapline   Susannah X Tilton (Seal)
> Elbgey Swearingen   mark

A Copy from the oridgnial Indenture Which was Acknoledged in Court by John Tilton & Suseannah his wife at September Term 1796 And ordred to be Recorded & at the Same Time the Said Susanah being Examined apart from hir husband Relinquished hir Right of dower
Test
Moses Chapline Clk[5]

Thus, John and Susannah sold the balance of their once extensive land holdings in Ohio County, Virginia.

"John," said Susannah, as the Tilton family assembled at their rough-hewn table laden with venison, potatoes, succotash, and pone, "I have never questioned your judgment in these matters, but tell me now—are we secure in this territory?"

"Dear lady of my life, queen of frontier mothers and silent source of my determination, I implore you—be not concerned. In a short time the land in this territory will be ours."

"I am much relieved," replied the daughter of the wilderness. "Upon our return from Wheeling, when you were at the Kimballs today, I learned our sons, Lorenzo and Elijah, are intent on seeking their fortunes to the west."

John was surprised.

"Is this what you wish, my sons?"

"Yes, Father," Lorenzo responded. "I am a man and it is our wish—Elijah's and mine—that we move westward, farther into the Middle Ground. Do not for a moment think that we are not grateful for the love and good things you have given us—but the urge is strong."

"And you, Elijah—you are but a boy."

"Although young in years, I am strong," said the eleven-year-old. "Lorenzo and I can fend for ourselves. You have taught us well the ways of the woodsman."

John looked at Susannah—her eyes sparkled and her auburn tresses encircled a knowing smile.

No word was spoken.

"As you wish, my sons, so shall it be," said John.

The girls, Drusilla, now seventeen, and Prusilla, fifteen, were sad, as was thirteen-year-old Caleb. They knew that, in the past few years, a close relationship had developed between Lorenzo and Elijah, but the announcement of their intentions stimulated tears in their eyes.

What their brothers had said was true. They had spent much time together in hunting and fishing and exploring the western hills. Elijah was almost as tall as Lorenzo and quite mature. The magic of pioneer life on the western frontier seemed to have created this posture.

Caleb could not contain himself.

"Will you not wait 'til spring, when the fish are firm and the tree fruits ripe?"

"No, Caleb," said Lorenzo. "The weather is good, the ground is warm, and by the time of the great snows and cold winds we will be well located. Elijah and I have discussed this adventure for some time. We will visit our sister Sally some distance west of here, and then move on toward the country of the Illinois. The threat of tomahawk or scalping knife holds no fear for us. Our preparations are complete. In a few days, we will bid you farewell.

In mid-September, Lorenzo and Elijah, well clothed in new buckskin outfits and warm, woolsey undergarments fabricated by Susannah—and well stocked with provisions—left Tilton Territory after embracing each of their brothers and sisters and receiving the traditonal wish and blessing from their parents.

Never again would they return to the bottom land bordering the Great Blue River.

In early November of 1796, John Tilton received word from Moses Chapline, the Clerk of Ohio County, Virginia, that according to the recent Congressional act, a decision had been made to sell certain territorial lands to the highest bidders. The sales could be conducted in Pittsburgh under the direct supervision of Governor Arthur St. Clair. Chapline suggested that Tilton go to Pittsburgh to insure retainment of his claim.

John did not hesitate, and Susannah was in complete accord with his decision. He outfitted a strong horse, provisioned himself for the journey, crossed the river on a raft, and after a three-day trek, without incident, he arrived in Pittsburgh.

John found the town of Pittsburgh, although thriving, to be somewhat smaller than he had expected. There were about fourteen hundred inhabitants in the borough, itself a strong fort, and over one hundred homes and buildings on the triangular point where the Monongahela and Allegheny joined to form the Ohio. John located the land office, which was not far from the fort, and made his intentions known to the commissioners.

"The sale will be conducted in due time, Mr. Tilton," responded one of the officials. "But, I tell you now, declare yourself a resident of an established county on the frontier if you wish to be successful in your purchase—the governor is highly opposed to squatters, missionaries, explorers, settlers, territorial residents, and statehood."

"I see no problem, sir," said John. "I am a resident of Washington County in the Territory."

When the auction of territorial lands was conducted in Pittsburgh on November 25, 1796, John Tilton successfully bid $4.03 per acre for Sections Sixteen and Twenty-two in the Township No. 4 of Range No. 2 of the Seven Ranges surveyed in 1787. It was far more than he had expected to pay. Nevertheless, after payment of $1,811.88, half of the full purchase price, he received a certificate, signed by St. Clair, confirming his eventual ownership of the lands which he had long ago claimed.

Shortly thereafter, he returned home to his beloved wife and children.

He bore no expression of confidence and contentment.

Susannah knew.

"What troubles you, my husband?" she inquired.

"Do not be concerned, Susannah," said John. "If the deed I have is valid, we are secure—but the whole affair appeared to be somewhat of a mockery. My first hope is in the receipt which I retain, and, secondly, in my Certificate of Intent."

"I had thought the land was safe and salable."

"And I, also," replied John, "but the shenanigans of the Governor[6] and his cohorts were unique. I am sure the president would not have condoned their procedures."

"But you have the paper confirming your intention to purchase."

"I do—and with the help of God I will fully recompense within one year."

"Then console yourself with faith and trust and love—the last of which I shall always provide—and of which I think you have much need."

Susannah's charm prevailed. She smiled; her flashing eyes sparkled as she loosened her flowing auburn tresses.

John knowingly embraced her as they entered the house.

XIII

YOUR LAND AND MINE

ON MARCH 4, 1797, JOHN ADAMS became the second president of a young United States of America. George Washington, although somewhat pressured to attempt a third term, had refused. Thomas Jefferson, a prominent, international diplomat and principal author of the Declaration of Independence, was vice president.

The governor of the Territory Northwest of the River Ohio was still Arthur St. Clair, who had held that position since the establishment of the Territory in 1787; William Hogland was the territorial governor prior to that time. Although still opposed to statehood for the Territory or any section of it, he did permit the surveying and organizing of counties. Washington County was formed in 1788; Hamilton in 1790; Wayne in 1796; and Adams on July 10, 1797.

On July 29, 1797, Jefferson County, which encompassed Tilton Territory, was officially established. The boundaries of Jefferson County, as proclaimed by Governor St. Clair, were as follows:

> Beginning on the bank of the Ohio River, where the western boundary of Pennsylvania crosses it, and down said river to the southern boundary of the fourth township west to the southwest corner of the sixth township of the fifth range; thence north along the western boundary of said fifth range, to the termination thereof; thence due west to the Muskingum River, and up the same to and with the portage between it and the Cuyahoga River; thence down Cuyahoga to Lake Erie; thence easterly along the shores of the lake to the boundary of Pennsylvania, and south with the same to the place of beginning.

It was indeed an expansive county, comprising in excess of five thousand square miles. This was the beginning; in the future, time and circumstances would materially change the area of Jefferson County in the Northwest Territory.

The Tiltons and other inhabitants of the riverfront received the news of the newly formed county with much exuberance. They considered the formation of the county as a major step toward statehood, of which there had been much discussion, particularly by citizens in the southern settlements along the Ohio River who had stopped, in repass, at the villages on Tilton's land and north of Indian Short Creek.

Once again, the rich earth in Tilton Territory and the sourrounding areas had a bountiful harvest. It was in early December of 1797 that John Tilton finally received official notification that his land purchase request had been honored. In mid-November, he had once again made the trip to Pittsburgh and paid the balance due on his sectional claim in the Northwest Territory. The payment was duly recorded on his certificate of ownership. A messenger from a mail packet bound for Wheeling and points south had delivered the long-awaited deed to Tilton Territory.

John, with trembling fingers, opened the sealed missive and read as follows:

John Adams President of the United States of America.

To all to whom these Presents shall come, Greeting.

Know Ye That in pursuance of an act of the Congress of the United States passed on the 18th day of May, 1796, entitled, "An Act providing for the sale of the lands of the United States in the Territory Northwest of the River Ohio and above the mouth of Kentucky River," there is granted to John Tilton of Washington County in the Northwestern Territory, the lots or sections numbered twenty two and sixteen in the Township numbered four in the second range of Townships, surveyed in pursuance of an Ordinance of Congress passed on the twentieth day of May, 1785, which lots or sections contain by estimation Eight hundred and ninety nine acres and twenty hundred parts of an acre, for which lots or sections there was bidd in the rate of four dollars and three Cents per acre, amounting for the lots or sections aforesaid to three thousand six hundred and twenty three dollars and seventy seven 6/10 Cents of which there was paid on account the sum of one thousand eight hundred and eleven dollars and eighty eight 8/10 Cents unto the person authorized by the President of the United States for that purpose, as appears from a Certificate of the Governor of the said Northwestern Territory and dated at Pittsburgh on the twenty fifth day November one thousand seven hundred and ninety six, and the balance being one thousand eight hundred and eleven dollars and eighty eight Cents having been paid within one year thereafter to the Treasurer of the United States appears by his receipt dated on the eighteenth day of November one thousand seven hundred and ninety seven. To have and to hold the said lots or sections with the appurtenances, to the said John Tilton and his heirs and assigns forever.

L.S.

In Witness whereof the said John Adams President of the United States of America hath caused the Seal of the United States to be hereto affixed and signed the same with his hand at Philadelphia the twentieth day of November in the year of our Lord one thousand seven hundred and ninety seven, and in the Twenty second of the Independence of the said States.

/S/ John Adams

By the President

Timothy Pickering, Secretary of State[1]

John and Susannah were happy. Their long years of waiting, sometimes in doubt and at other times with an empty feeling of insecurity, had ended. John knew what he was buying. Although the originally surveyed sections of land were supposed to contain 640 acres, the system of rectangular land survey had substantially reduced certain sections along the Ohio River. His friend, Absalom Martin, had cautioned him to this extent. It was a determined and unmindful John Tilton who outbid the intentional promoters and unintentional purchasers of territorial claims. Other lands, adjacent to and in Jefferson County, were being purchased for one dollar an acre. Although thrifty and frugal by nature, John Tilton would have paid far more than $4.03 per acre to retain his claim.

Of the two sections he had bought, Section Twenty-two was adjacent to and directly west of Section Sixteen and contained the full 640 acres. Section Sixteen included the rich bottom land along the river and included only about 260 acres.

John and Susannah Tilton had learned much about the ways of business as it was conducted during the early years on the Ohio frontier. The steady flow of settlers and land seekers from the east was most impressive.

The year 1798 was a year of development and progress in and around Tilton Territory.

Early in that year, John Carpenter received notice that his petition for a land grant in Section Seven of the same range and township as John Tilton's had been approved. Carpenter had been sent an indenture signed by President John Adams at Philadelphia on December 27, 1797.

John and Nancy Carpenter were quite joyful. In the spring of 1798, not long after receiving title to the land, they transferred a good tract to George and Susannah Carpenter. John and Nancy retained over two hundred acres for farming and pasturing. The stout palisades which had once secured Carpenter's Fort had been dismantled. The Carpenters also held claim to a small land parcel immediately west of their homestead along Indian Short Creek.

Warren Township[2] in Jefferson County was formed in 1798, and John McElroy was the tax collector; the first commissioners of the township were William Bell and Benjamin Doyle.

Meanwhile, John Tilton was approached in early March by a frontiersman who, upon close inspection, looked quite familiar to him. The frontiersman, clad in respectable linsey-woolsey garments, hailed John, who, although the day was cold and windy, had been repairing a boundary fence.

"Mr. Tilton," inquired the stranger, "do I not know you from the time you resided across the river? I am Zachariah Sprigg, and I seem to recall meeting you there."

John was thoughtful and complacent.

"If I recall correctly," said Sprigg, "I was privileged to enroll you in the militia as a soldier."

John remembered, and a smile of recognition rimmed his lips.

"I do recall the oath I took, but Mr. Sprigg, that was over twenty years ago. I have changed—you have also—but I do recall your visit. What brings you to this area, and where are you residing now?"

"I am still near Wheeling," responded Sprigg, "but I have learned that you have become the rightful owner of much land in this territory."

"That is true."

"My friends and I are interested in buying land in this area. Might you be interested in selling certain sections at a good price?"

"Susannah and I have discussed this possibility recently. My son Joseph is also interested in such a venture. As a family, Susannah and I have no need for all this land, but I will sell a certain tract for no less than I paid—$4.03 per acre. If you and your friends are interested, the area I will sell contains about three hundred acres and one outbuilding. The land I refer to also includes some frontage on the river."

"Good," replied Sprigg, "we shall return shortly to inspect the tract and make a decision."

And so it was that on or about March 12, Zachariah Sprigg and his Ohio County investors, Jacob Croes and William Skinner, crossed the river intent on inspecting the section of land which John would sell. The survey and identification of the tract were complete, and Sprigg and his friends were agreeable to the terms of purchase.

George Humphrey, a miller and authorized Justice for the County of Jefferson in Territory Northwest of the River Ohio, prepared the deed of transfer, which read as follows:

> This Indenture made this fourteenth day of March in the year of our Lord one thousand seven hundred and ninety eight Between John Tilton of the County of Jefferson in the Territory of the United States northwest of the Ohio and Susannah his wife of the one part and Jacob Croes and William Skinner and Zachariah Sprigg of Ohio County in Virginia of the other part. Witnesseth that whereas John Adams President of the United States of America by a deed made patent under the seal of the United States bearing date

the twentieth day of November one thousand seven hundred and ninety seven for the consideration therein mentioned did grant unto John Tilton and to his heirs and assigns forever all the lots or sections of land numbered twenty two and sixteen in the township numbered four in the second range of township surveyed in pursuance of an ordinance of Congress passed the twentieth day of May 1785 which deed is recorded in the office of the Secretary of State in Patent Book A. page eleven of lands sold under the act of Congress passed the eighteenth day of May 1796.

Now this Indenture witnesseth that the said John Tilton and Susannah his wife for and in consideration of one thousand two hundred and nine Dollars to them in hand paid by the said Jacob Croes, William Skinner and Zacariah Sprigg at or before the ensealing and delivery hereof the receipt whereof is hereby acknowledged (and the said Jacob Croes, William Skinner and Zachariah Sprigg are thereof acquitted and forever discharged by these presents) have granted bargained sold aliened released and enfeoffed and by these presents do grant bargain sell alien release enfeoff and confirm and warrant to defend against all persons whatsoever unto the said Jacob Croes, William Skinner and Zachariah Sprigg (as tenants in common and not as joint tenants) all that lot or tract of land being part of each of the above mentioned sections numbered twenty two and sixteen and bounded as follows, viz: Beginning at a Sugar tree nine inches diameter corner to John Waggoner on the west boundary line of Lot number twenty two, thence running east one hundred and twenty seven chains to the Ohio river passing a post on the bank and down the same with the meanders thereof and bindings thereon twenty eight chains and twenty five links to a post on the river bank just below the mouth of a gutter between a white walnut and a hickory six links from the walnut which is twenty six inches diameter and twelve links from the hickory which is ten inches diameter, thence west one hundred and fourteen chains and twenty five links to a sugar tree nine inches diameter on the sectional line and with the same north twenty five chains to the place of beginning, together with all and singular the rights liberties privileges immunities and appurtenances whatsoever thereunto belonging or in anywise appeartaining and the reversion and reversions, remainder and remainders, dowers, rents, issues and profits and also all the estate, title, interest, property, claim and demand whatsoever which they the said John and Susannah Tilton in law or equity have in or issuing out of the same. To Have and to hold the said messuage tract or lot of land containing three hundred acres more or less the hereditaments and premises hereby granted or mentioned or intended so to be with the appurtenances thereunto belonging unto them the said Jacob Croes, William Skinner and Zachariah Sprigg and to their heirs and assigns (as tenants in common) to their only proper use and behoof forever.

In Testimony whereof we the said John Tilton and Susannah Tilton to these presents have interchangeably set out hands and seals the day and date first above written.
Signed sealed and delivered in presence of us

Jess Fulton, Zachr. Biggo   John Tilton   (L.S.)

                               her
                      Susannah   X   Tilton (L.S.)
                             mark

Jefferson County, SS.

On the fourteenth day of March one thousand seven hundred and ninety eight appeared before me the subscriber one of the Justices of the Court of Common Pleas for the County aforesaid, John Tilton and Susannah Tilton and acknowledged the within indenture of Bargain and sale to be their free act and deed, at the same time the said Susannah being examined seperate and apart from her husband acknowledged that she had without compulsion subscribed the within instrument and thereby relinquishes her right of dower in the premises.

Witness my hand & seal day and date above written.

George Humphrey (L. S.)

Jefferson County, SS. Duly recorded 23d March 1798.
                  Zenas Kimberly, Recorder.[3]

The tract of land which John sold to Sprigg, Croes, and Skinner was located in the southern half of his two-section land purchase. The river frontage was about eighteen hundred and fifty feet, and the east-west boundaries spanned the full width of both sections—approximately one and one-half miles on the north section line.

John retained the acreage in the extreme southern part of Sections Sixteen and Twenty-two just north of which his son Joseph and his family had been cabined near the river for the past six years.

Joseph and Mary Tilton had prospered in recent years. He had constructed a flour mill along Fish Creek.[4] It was a sturdy and productive structure, and the settlers in the area paid him well to convert their grain into flour. Their family was growing, too, and two sons, Zaccheus and Zachariah, and a daughter, Susannah, were now members of their household.

John and Susannah were sure that Joseph would soon request the purchase of the southern section of Tilton Territory.

Ephraim Kimberly, patriot of the Revolution, was not well in late 1797. His wife had died within the past year, and despondency added to his state of being. His daughter Lucy had married Jesse Fulton. Zenas, the first recorder in Jefferson County, was of small consolation, and Phoebe Maria, another daughter, was still young when Ephraim died in early November. Except for Phoebe Maria, he was alone. He left no will.

In the same month, the first court was held in Jefferson County of the Northwest Territory by a proclamation issued by Winthrop Sargent, who was now acting governor of the Territory. The first judges in the county were George Humphries, Philip Cable, and John Moody. Two days after its first session, the court issued the following disposition:

> Ordered by the court that Absalom Martin, George Humphries, Esquires, and Dunham Martin, be appointed as commissioners to make partition of a tract of land held in coparcenary by Zenas Kimberly, Lucy Fulton, and Phoebe Maria Kimberly, at the mouth of Short Creek, the affidavit required by law being first made by said Zenas Kimberly in open court.

This action of the court, which knew full well the reputation and disposition of Ephraim, provided for the partitioning of the three-hundred-acre Washington land grant among the three

heirs of Ephraim Kimberly. Accordingly, after due study, on
January 11, 1798, the commissioners prepared an indenture and
apportioned the land as follows:

> one hundred and thirty two acres to Lucy Fulton—eighty-
> nine acres to Zenas Kimberly and eighty acres to Phoebe
> Maria Kimberly, the orphaned daughter of Ephraim.

Zenas Kimberly had obtained a choice section of land along the
river front. After hurriedly plotting the section into rough lots, he
obtained a ferry license from Acting Governor Sargent, which
allowed him to operate a ferry from Lot No. 12 or 18, across the
Ohio River. The authorization was finalized on March 15, 1798.
The town he founded was called "Warren," after the township of
the same name. Just prior to this time, on February 13, 1798, he
had secured, for a measly sum, 107 acres, as sold by Jefferson
County's first sheriff, Francis Douglas. The land was bounded by
John Carpenter's land on the south and the land of John Connell
and Francis McGuire on the north.

Zenas and his wife, Isabella, prospered from their land transactions in the town of Warren and other sections of Jefferson
County.

John and Susannah Tilton, cognizant of the fact that a
prosperous village would in time be located near the mouth of
Short Creek, were among the early purchasers of lots in Warren.
They purchased two lots, both being close to the river and adjacent to the main thoroughfare.

"In due time, we shall build a strong house on this land," said
John. "I am convinced the area will prosper."

"The survey is not complete; I think it but a scheme to entrance
the settlers," replied Susannah.

" 'Tis quite possible, my dear, but I feel the investment is good,
and most certainly the title cannot be questioned. The money has
been paid and the prothonotary seals affixed; and if I do build a
house, it will be but temporary. The black bottom land which we
own south of there will become a town!"

Susannah's auburn tresses glistened in the sunlight—her eyes
sparkled, and she smiled. She knew the sound judgment of her

husband in these matters and confirmed her agreement with a fond embrace.

———————

In late April of 1798, Joseph and Mary Tilton visited the log house of John and Susannah. After a warm welcome from his parents, Joseph, humble and conservative as always, greeted his brothers and sisters who still resided at the Tilton homestead: a light kiss on the cheek for Drusilla; the same for seventeen-year-old Prusilla; and a bear hug for sister Ann, the nine-year-old; Caleb and William received a firm handshake and a pat on the head; and two-year-old John, a slight tickle under the chin.

Susannah had prepared dinner. Delicious rabbit stew with greens, tender turkey, and roasted corn adorned the plank table outside the house. A mint-scented brew enthralled the happy reunion, and everyone partook of the bounty.

In the beginning the conversation was light and gay. After all, Joseph and Mary did not have time or occasion to visit often. Wild ducks on the river, fish in the creek, wild game on the western hills, neighbors, children, and the future—these were topics of discussion.

Finally, Joseph brought up the subject which was most important to him at the time.

"Father, the land where I am settled and on which my mill stands—is it not part of the section which you purchased?"

"No, my son," said John. "You are located south of my section line. My friend Martin, to the south, should be your guide as to the ownership of that acreage. As you have told us, we know you have prospered as a miller. I have a good parcel of over two hundred acres just north of your home. Your mother and I felt certain that, in time, you would be interested in securing this land—for even less than what I paid."

"It would be a good investment for the future, I suppose. And the price, Father?"

"Three dollars an acre—six hundred will suffice."

Joseph was persistent. "But you said there were over two hun-

dred acres. You and mother have done much for me. I insist on
paying the full amount."

"All right—so maybe two acres more—that's all."

"Have the deed prepared," replied Joseph, smiling.

And so it was that the transfer of John and Susannah's southern
most tract of land was effected by the following document:

> This indenture made the second day of May, in the year
> of our Lord one thousand seven hundred and ninety eight
> between John Tilton of the County of Jefferson in the
> territory of the United States northwest of the river Ohio
> and Susannah his wife of the one part and Joseph Tilton of
> the County and Territory aforesaid of the other part.

> Whereas, John Adams, President of the United States of
> America by a deed made patent under the seal of the United
> States bearing date of the 20th day of November in the year
> of our Lord one thousand seven hundred and ninety seven
> did grant unto the aforesaid John Tilton the lots or sections
> of land numbered twenty two and sixteen in the township
> four in the second range.

> To have and to hold to him the said John Tilton and to his
> heirs and assigns forever as by the said patent registered in
> the Department of State of the United States in Book of
> Deeds A, page eleven of lands sold under the act of Congress
> passed the eighteenth day of May one thousand seven hun-
> dred and ninety six will more fully and at large appear.

> Now this indenture Witnesseth that the said John and
> Susannah Tilton for and in consideration of the sum of Six
> hundred and six dollars money of the United States to them
> in hand paid by the said Joseph Tilton at or before the en-
> sealing and delivery of this indenture the receipt whereof
> they the said John and Susannah Tilton do hereby
> acknowledge and thereof do acquit and forever discharge
> the said Joseph Tilton his heirs, executors and ad-
> ministrators by these presents have granted, bargained, and
> sold and by these presents do grant, bargain, sell and con-
> firm and warrant, and defend unto the said Joseph Tilton
> and to his heirs and assigns all that tract of land (being part
> of sections numbered twenty two and sixteen aforesaid) con-
> tained in the following boundaries, viz:

> Beginning at a beech and thence running east four hun-
> dred and nine poles to the Ohio River; thence north 18° east

65 poles; thence north 25° east 20 poles; thence west 440 poles to a sugar tree; thence south 80 poles to the place of beginning containing 204¼ acres, together with all the rights, titles, privileges, appurtenances and hereditaments to the same belonging or in any wise appertaining, and the remainders and reversions, rents, dowers, issues and profits thereof which they the said John and Susannah Tilton in law or equity have in or issuing out of the same.

To have and to hold the said tract or parcel of land hereditaments, and premises hereby granted or mentioned to be granted with all and singular hereditaments and premises to him the said Joseph Tilton and his heirs and assigns to the only proper use and behoof of him the said Joseph Tilton and his heirs and assigns forever. And the said John Tilton and Susannah Tilton for themselves their heirs, executors and administrators do covenant and agree to and with the said Joseph Tilton and his heirs, executors, administrators, and assigns that they the said John and Susannah Tilton, the above mentioned tract or parcel of land with the appurtenances to him the said Joseph Tilton, his heirs, and assigns, against the said John and Susannah Tilton and their heirs and assigns and against all and every person or persons lawfully claiming or to claim under them or either of them will warrant and by these presents forever defend.

In Testimony Whereof, we the said John and Susannah Tilton to these presents have set our hands and affixed our seal the eighteenth day of August and year first above written.

Signed sealed and delivered in present of:	John Tilton	(L.S.)
	her	
David Vance	Susannah X Tilton	(L.S.)
Francis Hardesty[5]	mark	

Some months before, John Tilton, shortly after receipt of his sectional deed patent, had made application to operate a ferry across the Ohio River from a point on his river front property. Acting Territorial Governor Winthrop Sergeant granted the license to John on June 5, 1798.

The instructions issued in conjunction with the ferry license provided only that the craft of conveyance be kept in good repair. The ferry was permitted to be operated between Jefferson County in the Northwest Territory and Ohio County or Brooke County, Virginia. Brooke County, named after Robert Brooke, the governor of Virginia between 1794 and 1796, had been formed in 1797 from Ohio County and contained all of the area north of Ohio County in the northern panhandle which separated Pennsylvania and the Ohio River—about one hundred and eighty square miles.

The ferry business thrived as immigrants moved westward, and John's strong log raft, capable of conveying people, livestock, and wagons, was frequently in demand.

———

The next two years were periods of complacency, security, and happiness for John and Susannah as their crops thrived in the rich soil and, for the most part, their friends and relatives were not far distant.

In 1799, John Carpenter sold his small land holding about two miles west of the river on Short Creek to John Humphrey, who built a house and flour mill at this place. Carpenter was not content. His oldest son, Edward, had married and moved north, and it was only after considerable persuasion on the part of John Tilton, his oldest and closest friend on the frontier, that he tentatively consented to remain in the area.

He had reason to be discontented.

Purchasers of Zenas Kimberly's land were infringing on his property—the eastern invaders had significantly reduced the prospects of good hunting, and the area was becoming more heavily populated. He and his wife were quite disconsolate when Edward left, and John did not appreciate the aspiring land grabbers from the east. He retained his rather extensive homestead near Warren.

———

The hatred of the Indians by the white settlers is demonstrated by an incident that occurred in 1798. Several of the red men who were, at this point in time, resigned to the fact that the supremacy of the white man could not be challenged, had crossed the western hills and entered the bustling drover's village of Warren. At a local tavern they exchanged wampum and bearskin for whiskey and soon became quite intoxicated. Upon leaving the tavern and traveling toward their camp on a northern stream, they were accosted by a party of sturdy frontiersmen, who, knowing their pitiful condition, dispatched them on the spot and buried their mutilated bodies in the damp earth.

The perpetrators of this deed were not discovered, and life in Warren and Tilton Territory continued to flourish.

XIV

A CHURCH AND A STATE

THAT THE EARLY SETTLERS of Tilton Territory and Jefferson County were of strong religious faith is unquestioned. They had been well disciplined when very young, to the effect that faith and hope in God, and love of God and neighbor were of absolute necessity to maintain strength and fortitude on a frontier which offered so many threats to their safety and well-being. As early as 1785, ten years after John Tilton had built his first cabin west of the great blue river, they had conducted religious services under a spreading elm or in a cloistered vale.

General Butler, who, along with Ensign Armstrong, had traveled the Indian Short Creek area in 1785 in an effort to force the persistent squatters to the east side of the Ohio, noted in his journal that "the people of this country appear to be much imposed upon by a sect called Methodist and are becoming great fanatics."

The word *fanatics* was an exaggeration; but it was true that the pioneers of Warren Township in Jefferson County were, primarily, followers of the Methodist Episcopal faith. The Reverend George Callahan, the Methodist Episcopal missionary, will long be remembered for the sermons he preached and the conversions he made at John Carpenter's Fort in 1787. After that, the residents of Warren Township held services in private homes for many years, and finally, in the year 1798, a small log church was constructed on the western edge of Warren Ridge—a hilly section of land about three miles north and west of John Carpenter's house.

They called the place Hopewell and, although unbeknownst to them at this time, this tiny house of worship was, without question, the first Methodist Episcopal Church in the Territory Northwest of the River Ohio—and quite probably the first denominational church in the Territory.

Samuel Conaway, who later purchased a parcel of land near the Hopewell Church from Aaron Hogland, son of the Ohio Territory's first governor, and Elston Howard, had held class meetings in their homes for many years. Finally, the Pumphrey brothers, Joseph and William, were instrumental in the building of the little Methodist Episcopal Church at Hopewell. It was not much more than a rough-hewn log cabin with clay-clinked walls and two windows adorned with a linsey blind to repel the light or permit it to shine through. Only a wooden cross on the front distinguished it!

The first sermons were preached by devout men in the area of Warren and Tilton's Town and many Sunday services were disrupted by unscrupulous characters who had spent the night at the nearby tavern in the village of Warren. The log church stood strong, however, and the pious settlers attended with regularity.

Several years thereafter, McKendree Chapel, a small edifice, was constructed east of the Hopewell Church near Rush Run. It was named in honor of the venerable Bishop William McKendree,[1] who, with the Reverend James B. Finley[2] and on at least one occasion, with Bishop Asbury,[3] had frequented the Hopewell and Rush Run areas.

In the early nineteenth century, Jacob Martin led a small group of Seventh-Day Baptists into Warren Township. He directed the building of a log church and schoolhouse on Warren Ridge. Early preachers were Enoch Martin and certain advocates of this faith named Birch, Stone, and Phillips. Evidently only few of the settlers were attracted to this pioneer crusade, and after only a short existence, during which time Ezekial Palmer conducted singing schools at the meeting house in 1807, the organization failed to prosper and the persistent Baptists moved on in search of greener pastures.

Zenas Kimberly, the first treasurer of Jefferson County, was a shrewd investor in land and real estate. He resided, at this time, in the town of Steubenville, which had been designated the Jefferson County seat and he bought and sold land extensively, but with good judgment. His lots at Warren, however, did not sell as readily as expected; there was much unclaimed land to the west and north that those desirous of settling could obtain more readily and with less expense.

The pioneers in the southern section of Warren Township at this time included William McCullough, John Henderson, David Barton, Samuel Patton, Peter Snedeker, Robert McCullough, James and Alexander McConnell, James Campbell, Joseph Moore, John Edwards, and, of course, the Tilton families of John Senior, Joseph, and Thomas. Robert McCleary, who had been a resident of Warren Township for about eight years, was appointed the first justice of the peace for Jefferson County.

David Rush had crossed the mountains and built his cabin on a choice clearing near a small stream in the northern section of Warren Township; he called the place Rush Run.

The first election in the Township of Warren was held at George Humphrey's flour mill on Short Creek. Humphrey and Robert McCleary were elected justices; James Reilly, Joseph McKee, and John Patterson were selected as trustees. These events all took place in early 1799; John Humphrey, Benedict Wells, and John McElroy had served as trustees in the previous years.

Early settlers in northern Warren Township in the late eighteenth century and early nineteenth century included Daniel Scamehorn and Henry Nations, both of whom were captured by Indians and killed in 1793; Philip Doddridge, brother of the Reverend Joseph Doddridge of Charlestown, Virginia;[4] Ebenezer Spriggs; John Jackson, who operated a flour mill; John Barret; Smiley Johnson; Samuel Dean; Daniel Tarr; William Roe; Joseph Hook; William Louis; E. Willet; James Everson; Robert Shearer; John and Archibald Armstrong; Nathaniel Dawson; Henry Hicks; John Putney; James Moore; Amos Parsons; Benjamin Linton; Joseph Rose; John Jacks; James Davis; Gideon Goswell; Henry Swearingen; John Burns; Ira Dalrymple; John Rickey; Jacob Zoll; Henry Oliver; Matthew Thompson; Thomas Taylor; Harden Wheeler; Israel Cox; J. McCulley; and the Grahams, Doughertys, and Milhollands.[5]

These valiant frontiersmen are recognized because at the time of their adventures west of the Ohio River, they constituted an inherent part of Warren Township history. Time would erase their existence in the present township of Warren even though many descendants would invade, at some later date, her lush green hills and fertile bottom lands.

In 1799, Jefferson County in the Northwest Territory was a well organized section of the Territory. It still consisted of a vast area comprising most of the northeastern part of what would soon become the sovereign state of Ohio. Justices of the Court of Common Pleas were Philip Cable, George Humphries, Absalom Martin (the surveyor), John Moody, and David Vance. These distinguished gentlemen were also considered as Justices of the Court of General Sessions of Peace, in addition to James Clark, George Edie, and Jesse Fulton. The Judge of Probate and Prothonotary for the county was Bezaleel Wells,[6] one of the founders of Steubenville; the sheriff was Francis Douglas; the coroner was John McKnight and the recorder and treasurer was Zenas Kimberly.

In this same year, the Jefferson County Militia was formed and officers and members were appointed from the prestate townships in the county, which were Richland, York, Kirkwood, Wayne, Knox, St. Clair, Beaver, Cross Creek, Steubenville and Warren.

Joseph Tilton, now almost thirty-three years old and a flourishing businessman in Warren Township, was appointed as a captain in the county militia; also appointed were Thomas Howard, William Huff, David Lockwood, John Quinn, and Peter Wireck.

Joseph had expanded and embellished his original cabin into a long house, and he and Mary were quite happy and content as the population and activities in and around his father's land holdings continued to multiply.

In 1800, John Tilton built the first house in the village of Warren, which Zenas Kimberly had laid out almost two years ago. Kimberly had shown John the rough plan for his town, and the lots which Tilton had bought were numbered thirty-three and thirty-four.

John was now sixty-two years old but looked and acted much younger. He engaged several men who were handy with axe and adz and saw, and in due time a large, rough-hewn log structure was constructed. After moving furniture, utensils, and other belongings into their new home, the Tiltons abandoned their smaller house to the south and lived in Warren.

John continued to farm his land in Tilton Territory and operate his ferry. He envisioned that, at some future date, he too would survey a section of his land along the river front and found a town.

At the age of fifty, Susannah retained the spark of youth. Her auburn tresses showed no sign of gray, and her azure eyes continued to flash and sparkle. As time permitted, she visited nearby neighbors, helping them in whatever manner she could. Drusilla, Prusilla, Caleb, William, Ann, and John still continued to reside with their parents.

In the spring of 1800, a wealthy, gentleman from Baltimore, Nicholas Teal, came to Jefferson County. He and his wife, Elizabeth, found the country to their liking and decided to stay. Teal settled in Steubenville and came to know Zenas Kimberly well, and also Jesse and Lucy Fulton. On June 14 he purchased from Lucy Fulton, for the sum of $1,200, the 132 acres of land in Warren Township which she had been allotted from the original land grant of her father, Ephraim. The land was adjacent to the town of Warren. At the time it was a wise investment, since the future of the town as a major shipping port to Wheeling and all points south along the Ohio and Mississippi Rivers appeared bright.

The movement for statehood in the Ohio Territory was strong. The Land Ordinance of 1787 required that 60,000 citizens be contained in a specific area before that area could advance a motion to Congress for recognition as a state in the United States of America.

Governor Arthur St. Clair remained adamant. Winthrop Sargent, who had been acting governor of the Territory, when St. Clair was confined to other duties and was in a state of ill health, was quite ineffective and uncooperative in furthering the cause.

In 1800, when William Henry Harrison[7] became secretary of

the Territory, progress was achieved. Harrison and Albert Gallatin, a Swiss immigrant who had come to the United States in 1780 and, through his eloquence and gallantry during the War for Independence, was elected to the United States Senate in 1793, were successful in achieving a new federal land law. Through this legislation, the minimum purchase of land in the Northwest Territory became 320 acres instead of 640. The law also allowed four years' credit, and new land offices were to be erected at Steubenville, Chillicothe, Marietta, and Cincinnati. With the enactment of this legislation and related contingencies, the urgency to establish a new state in the Northwest Territory, to be called Ohio, was catalyzed.

Arthur St. Clair was still the official territorial governor. Brave soldier though he was, he exhibited much inventive diligence to prevent the formation of states in the huge territory Northwest of the River Ohio. He strategically divided the Territory from time to time in order to prevent any section from attaining the necessary number of occupants to acclaim the right of statehood. As a result of his divisional policies and knowing their intent, certain respected, knowledgeable gentlemen in Chillicothe presented an alternate plan to William Henry Harrison, the congressional delegate of the Territory.

Harrison was instrumental in bringing about the Congressional Land Act of May 7, 1800, which provided for two distinct areas of government—the Indiana Territory and the Ohio Territory. By passage of this act, it was, at least, temporarily assured that the territorial seats would reamin at Vincennes for Indiana and Chillicothe for Ohio.

Political factions clashed, and St. Clair, a strong Federalist, feared that statehood for Ohio would constitute a strong Republican faction, unfavorable to the colonial unity. Much political maneuvering was taking place, and strong voices were heard on both sides of the issue. Thomas Worthington,[8] a Virginia stalwart who had come to the Middle Ground in 1798, played a major role in achieving statehood for Ohio, being a member of the territorial legislature.

The political leaders at Cincinnati and Marietta were highly in favor of retaining Arthur St. Clair as territorial governor and altering the Land Act of 1800 in accordance with St. Clair's proposal. This would assure these towns of becoming major and indissoluble governmental seats. These proposals were eventually rejected after Thomas Jefferson became president on March 4, 1801. The legislative efforts of Worthington, Michael Baldwin of Connecticut, and a Virginia congressman, William B. Giles, provided the president with proper chief executive authority to approve the Enabling Act of April 30, 1802. This act basically required that a convention of national congressmen be held to determine validity of statehood for certain sections of the Northwest Territory and to establish the boundaries thereof. The stage was set!

Edward Carpenter, the eldest son of John and Nancy Carpenter, visited his parents in the fall of 1801.

"I have taken a contract with the government," he told them, "to develop a roadway from Steubenville to the west. My wife and son, Edward, are quite happy to move. Upon completion of the contract, we intend settling farther west at some attractive location."

"That is good, Edward," said John. "I know you have become quite well known for this type of work. Your mother and I have thought about leaving this area for several years. With you and Elizabeth away, only Sally remains, and she is quite enamored with young Ira Kimberly. They are talking marriage in the spring."

"You would be quite welcome to come with us, Father."

"We will indeed consider your porposal, my son. If it were not for our friends, particularly the Tiltons, we would have gone before."

"Once beyond these eastern hills, the land is quite level and the soil rich," encouraged Edward.

"When will you leave?"

"In a short time, Father. No more than a month."

"Good," replied John and his wife nodded agreement. "That will provide us time to sell this house and land."

And so it was that John and Nancy Carpenter sold their

remaining property, consisting of 213⅓ acres in Warren Township, to Henry Brindley, for the sum of $500 on October 17, 1801. They trekked westward, finally settling near the old Indian town of Coshocton. Here they spent their final days and were buried near that town.

John Tilton was not idle, nor was he unaware of what was happening in the Territory, in Warren, and in the surrounding areas, including his land holdings south of Warren in Sections Sixteen and Twenty-two. For the most part, he farmed the land along the river, and his livestock grazed on the hilly western pastures.

When James McMillen approached him in early 1802 with a prospsition to purchase a section of his western land at five dollars an acre, he agreed and the following land transfer deed was prepared and recorded at Steubenville:

This Indenture made this Twentieth day of February in the year of our Lord one thousand eight hundred and two between John Tilton and wife of Jefferson County in the Territory Northwest of the Ohio River of the one part and James McMillen of the County and Territory aforesaid of the other Witnesseth that the said John Tilton and Susanna his wife for the consideration of one thousand dollars to them in hand paid by the said James McMillen the receipt of which is hereby acknowledged hath and hereby doth fully and absolutely grant, bargain, sell, release, convey and confirm unto the said James McMillen and his heirs and assigns forever a certain Tract of land situate in the Twenty second section in the fourth Township and 2d Range of Townships bounded as follows to wit Beginning at the Northwest corner of the section thence south one hundred and twenty perches, thence Two hundred and sixty six and two thirds perches, thence North one hundred and Twenty perches, thence west Two hundred sixty six and two thirds perches to the place of begining Containing Two hundred acres and bounded on the West by the lands of the heirs of Joseph McCune on the south by lands of Messurs. Sprigg, Skinner & Croes—and on the East by lands of John Tilton on the North

by lands of John McElroy, Luther Burt and Hugh Mc-
Conoghey & which lands was granted by the United States
to John Tilton by patent dated the Twentieth day of November one thousand seven hundred and ninety seven TO
HAVE and to HOLD the said described Tract of land and
premises with the appurtenances unto the said James Mc-
Millen to the only proper use and behoof of him the said
James McMillen and to his heirs and assigns forever, And we
the said John Tilton and Susanna do hereby covenant and
bind ourselves and our heirs Executors and administrators,
firmly by these presents to warrant and defend the said
Land and premises to James McMillen his heirs and assigns
forever in the full and peaceable possession of the said
described Tract of land and premises against the lawful
claim of all persons whatsoever. In Witness whereof we
have hereunto set our hands and seals the day and year first
above written. . . .

Sealed and delivered in the presence of us (I do hereby
                                          Relinquish my
John McElroy—Benj. Waggoner . . . . . . right and title
                                          of dower)

                        John Tilton   (L.S.)

                        her
                  Susanna X Tilton (L.S.)
                        mark

Territory of the United States Northwest of the River Ohio.
Jefferson County SS.

┌──────┐
│   │ Personally came befor me (one of the Justices of
│ LS │ the peace for the County aforesaid) John Tilton
│   │ and Susanna his wife the within named Grant-
│   │ ors and acknowledged the within Deed of Con-
└──────┘ veyance to be their act and Deed and at the same
Susanna Tilton being seperatly Examined and apart from
her said husband freely relinquished her right of Dower In
Testimony whereof I Peter Hone have hereunto set my hand
and seal the 20th day of February 1802.————

                                          Peter Hone

Jefferson County SS. Recorded this 10th day August 1802.
John Galbraith Recorder.[9]

After the sale of this land to James McMillen, John and Susannah still retained almost three hundred acres along the Ohio River. Many of the settlers now referred to this area as Tilton's Ferry, since the transfer of people, products, livestock, and wagons between the Ohio Country and Virginia continued to be a prosperous business.

John and his wife had been sorry to see their friends the Carpenters move west, but now, as time was fleeting and they advanced in age, John had one remaining goal—to establish a town in Tilton Territory. It would be achieved!

In April of 1802, Zenas Kimberly had his plan of the town of Warren recorded at Steubenville.[10] The plan outlined sixty-four lots, each having a fifty-foot frontage. All lots on the river front were 174 feet deep, as were also Lot Nos. 23, 24, 25, 26, 39, 40, 41, and 43. Front Street, along the Ohio River, was 80 feet wide and 890 feet long. The small village had two main streets dividing it—Second Street, which was 50 feet wide and the same length as Front Street and 389 feet west of the river; and Market Street, perpendicular to the river and 60 feet wide—except at the center, where it was 102 feet wide—and 848 feet to the west. One alley, paralleling Front and Second streets, was called Blackberry Alley and was 12 feet wide; the other alley, closer to the river, was not named on the original plan. Peach Alley was 15 feet wide and paralleled Market Street to the north; again, a similar alley to the south was not identified by name.

Kimberly's town plot was presented to Justice of the Peace John Moodey on April 3 and officially recorded on April 6, 1802.

Primarily through the influence of Thomas Worthington, the first Ohio constitutional convention was held and thirty-five delegates attended, most of them coming from the Ohio River counties—and most were Republicans.

Arthur St. Clair was permitted to address the convention, which was chaired by Edward Tiffin, a doctor of English descent who came to the Territory from Virginia in 1798. St. Clair was

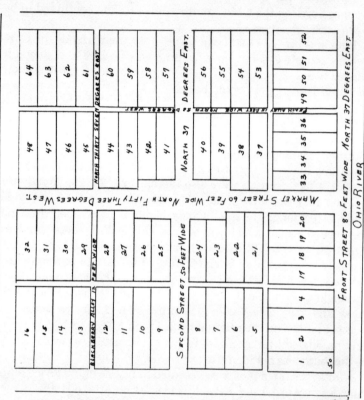

Original Town Plat: Warrenton, 1802

*Redrawn by Ethel
and Vicki Richardson*

uncouth, anti-Republican, pro-Federalist, and somewhat derogatory in his remarks. Upon learning of St. Clair's speech to the convention, Tiffin instructed the secretary of state, James Madison, to remove him from office. This Madison did by letter delivered by Charles Byrd, the territorial secretary. Upon St. Clair's removal, Byrd became acting governor.

The convention adjourned in late November, after the proposed proclamation for statehood had been signed by all delegates, and Thomas Worthington was designated to carry its message to the Congress of the United States.

After considerable debate and legislative meanderings, the seventeenth state—the sovereign state of Ohio—was admitted to the Union on the recognized date of March 1, 1803!

In the summer of the year 1802, the church at Hopewell was rebuilt to more adequately accommodate its growing congregation. The West Wheeling circuit was formed in the same year, and itinerant Methodist preachers periodically visited the meeting houses west of the Ohio. Quarterly conferences were held, and it was in September of 1803 that the famed circuit rider Bishop Francis Asbury attended such a meeting at Hopewell and dedicated the revamped church. Asbury also ordained Brother John Wrenshall as the first deacon west of the Ohio River to serve the tiny church in the wildwood.

Wrenshall wrote in his journal:

> Accordingly, on Friday (September 9), I made an early start and traveled 40 miles. Early the next morning, in company with many friends, we crossed the Ohio River and arrived at our point of destination about noon. There was a vast concourse assembled. . . . where the forest trees formed a delightful canopy over our heads. Under this canopy, surrounded by the vast multitudes, the Bishop performed on one, John Wrenshall, the rite which was responsible for being the first ordination among us in the State of Ohio. After giving me my parchment, he ordered

me to prepare for the opening of the new meeting house by preaching on that evening. Having no alternative to his request, I complied.

It was the end of a perfect day for many of the faithful in Warren Township.

XV
THE FOUNDING
OF TILTONSVILLE

IN THE SPRING OF 1804, Susannah Tilton was concerned. Her daughter, Drusilla, who was now twenty-five and who had spent much time at Martin's settlement[1] to the south and at Wheeling, visiting settlers in Virginia, still appeared quite content to remain with her parents.

It was eventide. The orange ball in the western sky moved slowly toward the peak of the western hill. John and Susannah and Drusilla were still at the table; the other children had gone to perform their evening chores or to bed.

"Drusilla," said her mother, "you have lived long with us. You have toured the countryside on both sides of the river. I must ask—with some hesitation—have you seen no young man to whom you are attracted—and has someone not been intrigued by your femininity?"

Drusilla did not blush nor blink. She did not move as she held the pewter cup of rich sassafras tea to her pale lips. Her long, dark hair was straight and glistening in the shadowy sunlight and her hand trembled, just slightly, as she set the cup down.

"Why do you ask, Mother? Have I not done my share of work at home and on the land?"

"Yes, my child. I mean no offense. Your father and I are concerned only for your future." John's head was bowed.

"You need not be. I can fend for myself if need be. It is true, I have met many young men. Some I have known well—possibly too well. But always, I have found a flaw which disturbs me greatly and deters my thoughts of wedlock. If I be a burden in your house, you need but ask and I will leave, but my love for you and Father, I cannot deny."

John looked up. His eyes were misty. He took Susannah's hand and watched two tiny tears come down her cheeks.

"As long as there is breath in my body and peace in my immortal soul, I shall protect and defend you, my daughter."

Susannah's flashing eyes were closed and tear-stained as the three of them embraced each other in consolation.

———————

The town of Warren was beginning to prosper as families moved in from the outlying areas and from Virginia. Almost overnight, new houses were built and occupied. All types of water craft, including dugout canoes, log rafts, flatboats, and, perhaps most often, the popular keelboats, plied the Ohio River southward from Pittsburgh and other stations north of Warren.

Canoes were propelled by wooden paddles; rafts usually drifted with the southward flow of the current and were often poled to their ultimate destination. Flatboats, sometimes referred to as broadhorns because of two rudders at the bow of the craft, were capable of conveying people, livestock, and commodities—on a one-way downriver journey.

In the early nineteenth century, the most effective and expeditious method of travel on the river was by keelboat—if an adventuresome family could afford it and if they could condone the boisterous antics of the muscular and mischievous operators of the craft. The keelboat was usually from forty to sixty feet long and ten to twelve feet wide. It was the first major conveyor of cattle, commodities, and colonists to southern destinations, which was accomplished with relative ease—or northern settlements, which required considerably more vigor and stamina by the keelboatmen.

The keelboat was, as occasion permitted, fitted with mast and sail to take advantage of any wind that might benefit its progress. Normally, it was constructed with separate quarters for the crew and a secluded hold for passengers and their possessions.

The men who operated the keelboats soon became a legend. The mysterious Mike Fink, publicized as the "King of the Keelboatmen," is supposed to have boasted, "I'm a Salt River roarer, half horse and half alligator, suckled by a wildcat and a playmate of the snapping turtle." Keelboat captain Meriwether Lewis was quite famous on the inland waterways. After many frustrations in having the craft constructed, he—with extreme difficulty because of the shallowness of the river—made the longest keelboat trip on record, in 1803, from Pittsburgh to St. Louis.

Keelboating upstream was a task for only the most durable of rivermen. Cargoes of sugar, whiskey, tobacco, bacon, and animal hides were stored in hickory or oak barrels and loaded on a keelboat bound for the north. As many as three hundred barrels were loaded on a single keelboat, and the journey against the current of the river could be accomplished only through strenuous effort by the hearty men of brawn and muscle. Pulling, tugging, poling, shoving, dripping, sweating, hurting, bleeding—they accomplished the task. Their wages?—about eighty cents per day.

At one time or another, every type of water craft stopped at the town of Warren. Sometimes, the travelers who came by canoe or raft stopped for information concerning the land south or west. The broadhorn immigrants were of the same nature and often abandoned their plank barge and foraged their way into the interior of Ohio.

The crews of the keelboat were distinctively different and frequently stopped at Warren on their way south. Although usually men of strength and low morals, they were not fugitives. They spent much time in a local tavern, drinking whiskey acquired from the many stills in the backwoods. When a fight erupted, it was, in most instances, among themselves. The morning after, they paid for the damage they had caused, loaded their keelboats with grain and produce from the surrounding area, and resumed their journey.

The very nature of the swarthy keelboatmen, at their time of relaxation, although not to be condoned, is somewhat counterbalanced by their achievements in these early days.

By the time the state of Ohio was officially admitted as the seventeenth state of the United States of America, Jefferson County had become considerably reduced in area from its original vast expanse. On July 10, 1800, about three years after the formation of Jefferson County out of Washington County, the territorial governor, Arthur St. Clair, proclaimed that all of the land known as the Connecticut Western Reserve was to constitute a new county named "Trumball," a name quite famous in Connecticut history. The county seat was to be at Warren, a small village platted in 1801 by Captain Ephraim Quinby, in the southern part of the new county near the Mahoning River.

On September 7, 1801, Governor St. Clair established, by proclamation, the county of Belmont out of the extreme southern section of Jefferson County. The name *Belmont* is a derivative of two French words meaning "beautiful mountain." Although quite hilly, the county contained almost six hundred square miles of good land. The first seat of justice was established at the small settlement of Pultney, which had been founded by Daniel Mc-Elherren in 1799, after considerable debate with the town of Jefferson platted by Absalom Martin in 1795 and located about five miles south of John Tilton's Section Sixteen southern boundary line which separated Belmont from Jefferson County.

Another huge parcel of land was extracted from Jefferson County when Columbiana County, located south of Trumball County, was formed. Columbiana also incorporated a section of Washington County; the recognized date of formation is March 25, 1803, less than one month after Ohio became a state. "Columbus" and "Anna" were the basis for its name. The county seat was New Lisbon, which had been founded by a Baptist minister, the Reverend Lewis Kinney.

Thus, when the county of Jefferson was divided into civil townships, in accordance with the Ohio state constitution, its land area had been reduced to less than one-fifth the size of the original county.

On May 10, 1803, Warren Township was surveyed and established as the first civil township in the county. Its boundaries were as follows:

> Beginning on the Ohio River at the lower end of the county line to the center line of the Seventh Geographical Town-

ship and Third Range; thence north with said center line until it strikes the north boundary of Eighth Township and Third Range; thence east with the township line to the Ohio River; thence down the river to the place of beginning.

The other four original civil townships in the county were Short Creek, Archer, Steubenville, and Knox.

In October, 1804, Nicholas Teal, noting the progress of Kimberly's town of Warren, surveyed part of the land which he had purchased from Lucy Fulton into lots. Kimberly's original plat had contained sixty-four lots; Teal, with Kimberly's consent, extended the town northwest by adding eighteen lots, each 50 feet wide and 200 feet long. He extended Market Street 462 feet, retained the 15-foot-wide Peach Alley to the north and the alley of the same width to the south which he called "Cherry." Included in Teal's Addition were Gooseberry Alley, 12 feet wide between Lot Nos. 65 and 66 on the southeast and Lot Nos. 67 and 68 on the northwest and an 18-foot-wide passageway, called Bridge Alley, at the extreme northwestern limits of the town. Thus, eighteen additional lots became part of Warren, and Teal officially recorded his addition in the county records at Steubenville on October 15, 1804.[2]

Warren was fast becoming a favorite point of embarkment for millers, merchants, and farmers who operated their businesses to the west, along Short Creek, and the southern and northern producers. Most of Zenas Kimberly's lots had been sold, and the lots in Teal's Addition were also being purchased, either for investment or for the building of a house or place of business.

Kimberly returned to Warren with his wife, Isabella, and their family, in 1805. He established himself as a merchant and became quite prosperous.

On May 14, 1805, Joseph Tilton purchased Lot Nos. 30 and 31 from Zenas Kimberly at a cost of $100. For Joseph, this was an investment. He and Mary continued to operate their flour mill and farm a tract of land in the extreme southern section of Warren Township and the northernmost area of Belmont County. He had previously bought 120 acres of land for $300, south of his Warren Township holdings in Section Twenty-one of Township No. 4 and

Range No. 2, from John and Eleanor Connell who lived in Brooke County, Virginia. This transaction occurred on November 22, 1804, slightly more than three years after Joseph had purchased the 100 acres on which his house was built, from Absalom Martin on August 1, 1801, also at a cost of $300. Archibald Woods and James McMillen owned the acreage adjoining Joseph's Belmont County tract.

In addition to Zaccheus, Zachariah, and Susannah, the Joseph Tilton family now included three more daughters—Cassandra, Nancy and Penelope. An unnamed child, born several years earlier, had died shortly after birth. At the time of the child's death, Joseph had staked off a small plot of land, about 150 feet wide and 225 feet long, to be used as a cemetery. It was located about a quarter of a mile north of his house and not far from the bank of the Ohio River.[3]

Susannah Tilton—pioneer lady of the west—she of the flashing eyes and auburn tresses, which at the age of fifty-five showed no sign of silver, continued her heroic efforts to console the needy, care for the sick, and bring strong, healthy babies into what was still considered the forest primeval.

She visited her married sons and daughters as time permitted. It was on one such occasion that she visited the rather humble hillside home of her second son, Thomas. He was now thirty-seven, and it was only through sheer stamina and determination that he had remained in the area of Tilton Territory.

"Thomas," said Susannah, "you do not look well. Your hands are brown but your face is pale. And where are Sarah and the children?"

"Your questions require a number of answers, Mother—some of which I hesitate to freely give. But, as my mother, I will tell you as best I can."

Rose Ann, Thomas's oldest daughter at the age of seventeen, was busy in the kitchen, while also watching her four-year-old brother, Thomas. John, Drusilla, and James were at work in the garden patch.

Thomas continued, "They have been good and mindful

children and not once have they caused me any grief or sorrow; this you know from our intercourse in past years."

"This is true, my son, but still I sense a problem."

"You have the attributes of a saint, dear mother. Can you really look into my heart and know what has happened and what will be?"

"You speak nonsense, Thomas; I am no witch or mystic. Your face tells all."

"Sarah is gone, Mother. It's been almost a week now. I have searched from hill to river and every extremity from north to south. She is not here."

Susannah was shocked, although her strong will prevented any open display of her feelings.

"Did she appear somewhat different and strange toward you in a period of time before her disappearance?"

"Yes," said Thomas. "She seemed to talk constantly of the river—its ripples, waves and blue beauty—do you suppose???"

"Do not fret, Thomas. Time will tell. Meanwhile, your father and I are close by. I urge you now—be strong, eat well, regain your strength and vigor. The children need you. I must leave now. I will see your children in the garden, and I will return soon."

It was a rather subdued and sorrowful Susannah that mounted her horse and moved slowly through the productive acres of her son's farm. She greeted each of her grandchildren as she met them, the last being Thomas's oldest son, John, who was returning from the river with a good catch of large blue catfish.

"Have you talked to my father?" questioned the fourteen-year-old.

"Yes, John," replied Susannah, "and I am sure things will work out for the best."

"Good—I must get these fish home for our evening meal." He moved away swiftly, his bare feet treading lightly on the worn path. Susannah read a different story in his worried eyes, and her flashing eyes were misty and shielded by tiny tears.

She rode slowly homeward.[4]

The year 1806 was a year of road building in and around Warren Township. Prior to that time there were certain trails that could be traveled only on foot or on horseback. Several in the Short Creek area had been widened to permit the passage of horse-drawn wagons. Before 1800, an important thoroughfare had been cut through the wilderness from Peter Henderson's land, about seven miles north of Tilton Territory, to Tilton's Ferry. In 1801, a road was established between Tilton's Ferry and Martin's Ferry,[5] about five miles to the south. Three years later, in 1804, this road was extended almost to the northern extremity of Jefferson County along the river to the mouth of Yellow Creek. Soon thereafter, it was surveyed and lengthened as noted in Book A of the Commissioner's Journal—the entry being made on June 15, 1804, by John Ward, Clerk.

> Ordered that William Wells received out of the County Treasury $9 in full for services of viewers and surveyors in laying out a road from the mouth of Yellow Creek to the western boundary of Pennsylvania.

Petitions for road right-of-ways became quite numerous and the county commissioners spent much time on these matters. On August 14, 1802, the commissioners had ordered that the road tax be uniformly half the county tax throughout the county. The federal government provided 3 percent of the receipts from land sales for road purposes.

On November 3, 1804, John Taggart complained of a road having been laid out by Robert Carothers, road commissioner, from the mouth of Short Creek to Duncan Morrison's land. Viewers were Robert Moodie, John Carr, John Adams, George Carpenter (John Tilton's son-in-law), and Thomas Harper. Over two years later, at the December session of the commissioners in 1806, John Taggart was compensated for damages sustained in constructing the part of the county road which infringed on his land.

In June, 1806, the commissioners received a request to build a road beginning at the mouth of Rush Run westward to Joseph Pumphrey's sawmill and to finally intersect the Warren Town road near "little Isaac LeMasters"; also, another road to originate near Thomas Brown's farm and to intersect a road from the mouth of Rush Run to Joseph Steer's mills, near Elias Pegg's property. George Carpenter, Joseph Boskhimer, and David Purviance were viewers and the surveyor was William Noughton.

At the same session of the commissioners (June, 1806), a petition was received to construct a road beginning at the corner of James West's field, at which point the road from Tilton's Ferry to St. Clairsville also passed. The proposed road would intersect at the road up Little Fork of Short Creek, near Henry West's mill, and continue along this road to a fording below the meeting house, eventually intersecting another road from Steer's mill to Wheeling. John McElroy was appointed surveyor and Thomas McCune, Adam Dunlap, and Joseph Tilton (son of John) were to act as viewers.

In all of Jefferson County, there were few able-bodied pioneers who were not involved with buying and selling land; building and operating flour mills, sawmills, silk mills, nail mills and woolen mills; plotting and building roads; cultivating and harvesting their crops; nurturing and increasing their livestock; repairing and operating ferry boats—and building towns!

The time had come for John Tilton to build his town.

It had been a hot summer day in late August of 1806. The orange rays of a setting sun glistened a repeat of today's weather. As the rays receded and reflections on the blue Ohio diminished, John Tilton and his family were finishing their supper.

"Susannah," said John, as his wife busied herself with clearing the table and washing the wooden plates and pewter mugs, "I think it is time that I begin fulfillment of a hope and desire which, as you know, I have had for some time."

"I know your wish, my husband, but we are not as young and strong as many of the newcomers. Do you have a plan?"

"Oh, yes." John exhibited much confidence. "In my daily visits to our ferry and farmland, I have engaged young men to remove the trees and level the land. I have talked to our son Joseph, and he is quite interested in the venture."

John produced from his linsey vest a piece of yellowed parchment. "Joseph, as you know, has had some experience in these matters and has sketched the plan in accordance with my instructions."

Susannah examined the outline of the town as drawn by her son on the rough parchment.

"In many ways, it resembles this town of Warren."

"Quite true," replied John. "Warren has been a good and prosperous town. I see no reason to change the basic plan."

Susannah's eyes flashed, and her long auburn tresses were pushed back as she faced her husband.

"Tomorrow we shall proceed to lay out your town, John—and, may I ask, what will you call it?"

"After over thirty years on this frontier—and after you and the children, who have contributed so much to my happy existence in this Middle Ground—there is only one name: it shall be called 'Tiltonsville!' "

And so it was that, shortly thereafter, Joseph came with chain and transit and two sturdy helpers to assist his father in surveying for a town. It was only after considerable labor in overcoming unforeseen barriers that the town of Tiltonsville was laid out according to John's plan. At the age of sixty-eight, John was still strong and provided considerable assistance in the surveying.

The surveyed town consisted of seventy-two lots. At the south end of the village was a street running east to west, 40 feet wide and 562½ feet long, called South Street. All lots were 150 feet deep and fifty feet wide at the front. Lot Nos. 2 through 24 were along the river bank and bounded on the west by a 60-foot-wide thoroughfare called Main Street, which extended 1,370 feet in length and paralleled the Ohio River. The 40-foot-wide Third Street was at the north end of the village, being the same length as South Street and parallel to it. In the center of the town was Market Street, 60 feet wide, running east to west. On the far western side of the town was a 40-foot-wide roadway called Middle Street, which ran the full concourse of the village, as did Main Street. Two east-to-west alleys each 15 feet wide separated the northern and southern sections of the original plat—Cherry Alley to the north and Pare (Pear) Alley to the south. Market Alley was 12½ feet wide and evenly divided Main and Middle Streets.

The complete plat of the town was not accomplished until late in the year of 1806, by which time John Tilton was not in good health. Nevertheless, the following year, a log structure was erected by relatives and friends of John and Susannah on Lot No. 12, adjacent to the path leading to Tilton's Ferry. John and Susannah Tilton, with their unmarried children, became the first occupants of the town.

John did not offer his lots for public sale by auction, as had Zenas Kimberly in Warren Town, nor did he propose to sell them at a fixed price. As a matter of fact, he planted many of them in corn and cabbage and squash and pumpkins, as he also did on his land holdings west of Tiltonsville.

"The town is laid out," he told Susannah, "but, for some reason, I cannot permit the invasion and population of this town at present."

"I well understand your feelings, John," responded Susannah. "You are not happy with the hustle and the bustle such as that which is becoming most evident at Warren Town."

"True, enough; but, eventually, I will permit it. We have enough of that now with the business of operating the ferry. I think I will discontinue that activity in due time. Also, I should record the town plat at the courthouse in Steubenville; but I am not anxious."

Susannah smiled agreement. In her heart there was a twinge of sorrow. John did not look well, and she seriously doubted if all of these plans would come to pass during the remaining years of her husband's life.

Her fears were justified!

XVI

JOHN DIES
AND PORTLAND LIVES

IN 1807, CALEB, THE SON of John and Susannah and the first white child born in Jefferson County, was married at the age of twenty-four. He and his wife, Sally, were granted by an indenture, unrecorded, but by firm agreement with his father—a sizeable tract of land in Tilton Territory. Caleb built a sturdy, square log house and cultivated the highly productive soil.

Joseph, the oldest son of the original founder of Tiltonsville, who had helped his father lay out the town, had become a most respected citizen of Warren Township and the county. As a miller, a captain in the county militia, a viewer or confirmer of road construction rights, and a consultant on land transactions, he gained a reputation for honesty and knowledge.

Meanwhile, his family was growing. Zaccheus was now fourteen; Susannah was twelve; Zachariah was ten; Cassandra was eight; Nancy was five; Penelope was three; and another daughter, Tabitha, had been born recently.

The next two years passed quickly. The season of the year did not deter the progress of the early settlers. Spring, when the white cluster of the locust tree was prevalent, was a time for high-spirited activity among the farmers who hoed their land, seeded it proliferously, and hoped for an early harvest. Summer, when the loosening of the soil around a stock of corn by stick or hoe was a monotonous task, gave vent to the feelings of the teenage boys and girls at this early time in the life of a young, but solidified, United States of America. Dried corn silk wrapped in the leaf of a walnut or elm tree provided a good smoke. The unsullied waters of the broad Ohio were ideal for swimming and many days, supposed to be spent in cultivating the crops, were primarily devoted to other, more enjoyable, experiences.

Autumn was a season when every member of the family was engaged in work: harvesting the crops of hay and oats to sustain the horses and cattle during the long winter months; bringing in the sheaves of wheat to be ground in the local grist mills; preparing the corn and beans and other vegetables for storage in the larder; and plowing the land for planting in the spring.

Winter was a time for fun, frolic, and festivities. The settlers visited their friends and neighbors and discussed their plans for the future. During the holiday season, families came together and feasted, and a plump turkey always held the place of honor on a table heavily laden with food. The taverns at Warren Town did a thriving business as the men of the area frequented these places to relax around a rough table and relate tales, sometimes exaggerated, of their accomplishments. At these sessions, whiskey flowed freely. But, for the most part, families were content to spend the long winter evenings at home around a warm fire.

The fragrant odor of toasting chestnuts enthralled the nostrils, as the head of the household told stories to the children, or the children recited the things they had learned at school. There were schools in Warren Township long before the county had been divided into civil townships, and although some children did not attend, many did.

On January 4, 1809, another son, Noah, was born to Joseph and Mary Tilton. Susannah, according to her custom, was at Joseph's house to care for the baby and the other children until Mary regained her strength. As with all her children and grandchildren, she was a master of child psychology and a rather strict disciplinarian. And they loved her—one and all. She was unpretentious and impartial in her treatment of each one, and they had high respect for her flashing eyes and the provocative movement of her hand. Joseph and Mary appreciated her assistance in their time of need, as did Thomas and Polly, the wife of Robert Hardesty; and Susannah, the wife of George Carpenter; and Caleb and her other children, still unmarried; and all the frontier mothers she had aided and consoled. Truly, a spirit of love and devotion burned within her—but she shielded the sorrow there enmeshed.

In the spring of 1810, John Tilton did not plant the furrowed ground which he, with the help of friends and relatives, had prepared the previous fall. During the early daylight hours, he was content to sit in a strong, massive rocking chair on the plank-board porch of their house in Tiltonsville and gaze upon the great blue river as its rolling surface reflected the rays of sunlight into the dense foliage of the walnut and locust trees that lined the river bank.

After an afternoon nap, he would return to the chair and look westward on his rich, unseeded land as the sun, in all its brilliant splendor, descended in the west.

Susannah, knowing John's state of body, which was quite feeble, had planted, with the help of the children still at home, a relatively small garden of corn and beans. She preferred being at her husband's side and responding to his slightest wish or whim. His mind was still sound as he proclaimed, "Dear wife, I do not expect to spend much longer on this earth. My limbs are numb, but I assure you, my mind is clear. It is my desire that the ferry become a public conveyance, and, although I will not see this town populated as I predict, I hope you do. It has been a good life—no man could ask for more—but my greatest pride and hope has been you."

Susannah cried.

John Tilton—adventurer, Indian fighter, patriot of the Revolution, scout, soldier, pioneer settler, father of settlers, and husband to the lady of flashing eyes and auburn tresses—died on July 31, 1810, only one day after he made his last will and testament. He was too feeble to write and entreated Susannah to enlist his friend, James Hindman, to write as he quoted. Hindman consented and, he, also in the presence of James Galbraith, wrote as follows:

The Last Will and Testament
of
John Tilton

In the name of God, Amen. John Tilton of Jefferson County and State of Ohio, being weak of Body but of sound and perfect mind and memory—Blessed by Almighty God for the same—do make and publish this, my last will and testament, in manner and form following (viz.)

First, I give and bequeath unto my beloved wife, Susannah, one hundred acres of land in the Bottom and privilege to get her firewood from the hill part during her life and likewise her choice of two cows, two horses, one bed and bed clothes and a sufficience of house-hold furniture for her accomodation.

Secondly, I leave unto my oldest son, Joseph Tilton, the sum of two dollars.

Thirdly, I leave unto my second son, Thomas Tilton, the one-half of my land that remains after the hundred acres that belongs to my wife and likewise the half of the stock on hand.

Fourthly, I leave unto my oldest daughter, Polly Hardesty, two dollars.

I leave unto Sally Reilly two dollars. I leave likewise unto Susannah Carpenter two dollars.

I leave unto my daughter, Drusilla Tilton, a bed and bedding and horse and saddle.

I leave unto my son, William Tilton, the one-half of my land after the hundred acres I left to my wife and half of the stock.

I leave unto my son, Caleb Tilton, all the land that he possesses at present.

I leave likewise unto my daughter, Prusilla Tilton, bed and bedding—horse and saddle.

I leave unto my son, John Tilton, the hundred acres of land I left my wife at her death.

And, likewise, I leave unto my daughter, Ann Tilton, at my wife's death, all of the stock she has and, likewise, all the house-hold furniture on hand—and my wife, Susannah Tilton, shall live during her life (if she thinks proper) in the house she now lives in and to have the third part of the peach and apple orchards during life.

In witness, whereof, I have hereunto set my hand and seal the 30th day of July, 1810.

                                                    his
                                           John X Tilton
Sealed and Delivered   mark
in presence of
(s) James Hindman
(s) James Galbraith[1]

John Tilton had been most generous to his beloved wife and apportioned the balance of his estate to those in greatest need. The will was probated at the courthouse in Steubenville on August 7, 1810.

About a quarter of a mile north of the original Tiltonsville plat, as planned by John Tilton, was a cemetery on the land then owned by John and Mary McColloch. It was a unique burial ground for many early pioneers.

In the center of the cemetery was a large mound of ancient vintage. The early settlers of Warren Township, although unaware of its true construction, recognized the distinctive difference between this monument of earth—a mound about twenty feet high, over forty feet in diameter at the base, and almost conical in overall appearance—and the flat, rectangular mounds which dotted Warren Town and the surrounding areas.

It was around this mound that many who had died from illness, old age, or violence at the hands of a red savage or a white renegade, were buried. John's sixteen-year-old son, Jackson, was buried near this mound in 1786. It was here, too, that the infant daughter of John and Susannah, who had died shortly after birth, had been buried in 1792. Elizabeth Morrison, who had come to the Ohio country at a rather advanced age, died on September 18, 1798, and was interred in the cemetery surrounding the mound.

And it was this place, also, that became the final resting place of John Tilton. There were many in attendance. A local deacon from the Hopewell Church was recruited to perform the funeral service, and he did so with solemnity and expediency by reciting the Twenty-third Psalm of the Bible, offering a short prayer for the repose of John's immortal soul, and asking the prayers of the faithful for "this righteous man of good will—this beloved husband and father."

Susannah, attired in the proper black ceremonial garb, was

there. She shielded her grief and none saw the few unrelenting tears that wet her long lashes and filled her flashing eyes. Polly and Susannah were there with their husbands; Caleb and Sally were there; as were Joseph and his wife, Mary, once again heavy with child; and the children of John and Susannah still un-married—Drusilla, Prusilla, William, Ann, and John, who was their youngest child, fourteen years old when his father died at the age of seventy-two years, were there. Many other friends and associates of John and Susannah were at the graveside.

With the passing of her husband, Susannah was content to spend more time at her home. In late fall of the year of her husband's death, Susannah briefly took respite from her mourn-ing to attend and assist in the birth of another granddaughter, Miriam, the sixth daughter of Joseph and Mary Tilton. Although two of Joseph's children had died at an early age, Miriam thrived under the deft hands of her grandmother and the rich milk from the breast of her mother.

It was almost a year before Susannah once again began her previous activities of visiting with the other inhabitants of the area and acting as doctor, nurse, and counselor to those who were ill or in need of some service she might provide. Her children were quite mature at this time, and with efficiency and dispatch, they cared for the cows and horses, planted and worked the gar-den, and did much of the routine housework. Susannah was once again the lady of solace and consolation to the residents of Warren Township. And still, at the age of sixty-one, her face was firm and her hands gentle. She retained her flashing eyes and her auburn tresses which were unblemished by streaks of gray.

The face of the river front in Warren Township was changing rapidly in the year 1811. Warehouses for storing produce, flour, whiskey, molasses, furs, and other marketable products were being built for storage.[2] Southbound keelboats stopped at Warren Town and, after thorough examination and measurement by the captains, a receipt was issued for the merchandise and the boats were loaded to capacity.

Throughout the day, and even at night, numerous horse-drawn

wagons loaded with products to be stored and shipped and sold at ports to the south, were evident on the narrow roads.

Consequently, the community of Warren Town flourished and expanded. On March 28, 1811, twenty-five new lots were laid out and included as part of the community.[3] These lots were assigned numbers 83 through 118 and were quickly purchased by settlers in the town and adjacent areas.

Also as a direct result of this increased activity, many of the sturdy, enterprising pioneers became boat builders, millers, and wagon builders. As previously noted, Joseph Tilton was a prominent miller. Also engaged in this occupation were a Mr. Nichols, William Smith, Joseph West, John Bone, Robert Patterson, Robert Sherrard, and James Hodgens.

James Hodgens and his wife, Sarah, had settled in Warren Township only about two years earlier. At the time of their arrival, James was twenty-six years old and Sarah was twenty-two. James and Sarah had acquired a small section of land north of Tilton Territory and built a substantial log house. He and his family prospered because of his untiring efforts as a miller.

It was on October 11, 1811, late in the afternoon, that the river front residents of Warren Township were treated to a display of fireworks ejected by a water craft the likes of which they had never seen before. The news of the approaching vessel of smoke and fire traveled fast, and the western bank of the Ohio was lined with people who stood or sat in awe as the smoke-belching steamboat moved slowly southward on the broad Ohio. Fiery streaks erupted from its stacks, and the driving, splashing din of the engine and paddle wheel created an aura of mysterious enthrallment among the beholders.

It was the maiden voyage of the *New Orleans*,[4] a steamboat constructed at Pittsburgh and launched only the day before, in quest of the destination for which it was named. It was also the first craft of this nature on the Ohio River, and, although many tragedies would result from this mode of travel, it would eventually predominate as a conveyor of passengers and products on the inland waterways.

The second war with Great Britain—the War of 1812—came and went, with little effect on the settlers in Warren Township. Out of the more than twelve hundred residents of Jefferson County, including one hundred and fifty-five officers who took part in this apparently inconsequential struggle, Warren Township was well represented.

Prior to the official commencement of hostilities, which occurred on June 18, 1812, many refugees from northwestern Ohio and the western territories passed through Warren Township on their journey eastward.

They related tales, almost unbelievable, of a tremendous Indian force, with the tribes consisting of the northern Delaware, Kickapoo, Wea, Potawatomi, Sauk, Fox, Piankashaw, and Shawnee, and the southern tribes of Creek, Cherokee, and Choctaw, joining forces in the northwest sector of Ohio. All of these warriors, they said, had been assembled in a spirit of brotherhood by the great Shawnee chief, Tecumseh,[5] to form a huge confederation that would side with the English. War was imminent, and they were making their way to safety.

It is said that the War of 1812 was instigated and promulgated by the western frontiersmen because of their avaricious desire to possess the rich hunting land of Canada and their dismal profits on goods transported by keelboat or flatboat and sold at New Orleans. These claims are quite inappropriate for the inhabitants of Warren Township. Their goods and produce were sold at many ports, including Wheeling, Marietta, Lousiville, and New Orleans. And always the flamboyant masters of the keelboat or the owners of the flatboats returned with just monetary rewards.

As the war progressed, word filtered back, from stragglers or travelers, which primarily concerned American victories and successful strategy: Perry's sea victory at Put-in-Bay on Lake Erie in September of 1813; Harrison's land victory at The Battle of the Thames, during which Chief Tecumseh and most of his Indian condeferation were slain; and, finally, General Andrew Jackson's triumph over the British at New Orleans. Jackson's victory had left him a national hero, but actually, his success at New Orleans in January of 1815 had occurred about two weeks after the war ended, on December 24, 1814, with the signing of the Treaty of Ghent.

The citizens of Ohio along the bank of the great blue river were slow in learning of the war's end, and, for the most part, the coming and going of an apparently senseless war was of small concern. During the whole conflict they thrived as producers, marketers, merchants, and builders of towns.

Men of means and foresight were looking to the future. They envisioned the prospering of Warren Town on the river front, and so it was that on August 12, 1811, James Galbraith filed the following authorization at the courthouse in Steubenville:

> James Galbraith to Joseph Steer: Know all men by these presents that I, James Galbraith, of Jefferson County and State of Ohio reposing just confidence in the integrity of my friend, Joseph Steer, of the County and State aforesaid do hereby constitute and appoint him the said Joseph my true and lawful attorney for me and in my name to make sale of all or any part of the lots of a new town now laying off below Short Creek of County and State aforesaid by the name of Portland and likewise to receive any money that is to be received on acct. of the sale of lots of said town and upon receiving the same, he is hereby authorized to make and execute such receipts therefore as may be proper and necessary and such receipt or receipts in my name to sign and deliver to the person making payment. In Witness whereof I have hereunto set my hand and seal the twelfth day of August one thousand eight hundred and eleven. Sealed and delivered in presence of

Hugh Christy   (s) James Galbraith

State of Ohio
            SS.
Jefferson County

Before the subscriber, one of the Justices of the Peace of said County, personally came James Galbraith and acknowledged the within power of attorney to be his act and deed. Given under my hand and seal the twelfth day of August 1811.

Robert Patterson

Jefferson County SS. Recorded March 26th 1812 by Robert Boyd, Recorder[6]

Joseph Steer was a Quaker by faith and one of the early settlers in the Quaker town of Mount Pleasant, a small village about eight miles west of Warren Town, which had been established in 1802 by Robert Carothers and Jesse Thomas. Steer was a man of fortitude and determination, having acted as viewer or surveyor on many of the early roadways in Warren Township. He operated a flour mill on Short Creek in Warren Township and was highly respected for his ability and honesty.

As attorney for the three major landholders, James Galbraith, Joseph Jeffries, and William Jessop—the proprietors of the town of Portland—he acted with a spirit of integrity and ingenuity. After viewing the area and preparing a rough sketch, he engaged John McElroy, a surveyor of note, to construct the final plan.

McElroy was an expert at his craft. He completed that task on March 3, 1812, with notes as follows:

A Plat of the Town of Portland. The town of Portland of which the underneath is a plat is laid out by James Galbraith, Joseph Jeffries and William Jessop, Proprietor under the direction of Joseph Steer of Warren Township Jefferson County Ohio, agent for the proprietor.

March 3, 1812	James Galbraith Joseph Jeffries William Jessop	Proprietor

Lots No. 53 and 54 also 92 are reserved for the use of the town for any public use.

Lots No. 1, 2, 36, 37 & 38 Reseserved by Joseph Jeffries likewise warehouse. Lot to extend forty feet Nwestward—No. 137 to extend Seastward to the river Ohio.

The alleys are all 20 feet wide.

Plat of the Town of Portland below the mouth of Short Creek Jefferson County March 1812. The condition of the sale of the lots in the town of Portland are as follows: the highest bidder is to be the purchaser and person buying and, not complying with the terms, is to pay five per cent for disappointment. The terms of sale are as follows, viz, one third in hand, one third in six months and the balance in twelve months at which time the title will be made. All the land between the west end of the Town and Robert Mc-

Cleary's line, is to be a common, also all of the land between
Wm. Jessop's part of the town and the old mill race and all
the land at the East end of the town that is not laid out in
lots, except that part lying between the warehouse lot and
the river. It is also understood that all the privileges of the
ferry are to remain the exclusive property of Joseph Jeffries
but the public are not to be subject at any time to pay whar-
fage or anything of that nature.

Given under our hands this 13th day of the fourth month
1812. N.B. The owners reserve one bid on each lot.

Joseph Steer for James Galbraith
Richard Simon
for Wm. Jessop

Jefferson County SS. Recorded March 6th, 1812
    by Robert Boyd, Recorder
              Joseph Jeffries
Recorded April 14th, 1812, by Robert Boyd[7]

Joseph Steer took no chances on assuring his friend James
Galbraith that the village of Portland had been properly platted
and that he had fulfilled his consignment. In late March, he went
to Steubenville and caused the following journal entry to be
made:

State of Ohio
        SS.
Jefferson County

L. S.

On the twenty-sixty day of March
A.D. eighteen hundred and twelve
personally appeared before me, a
Justice of the Peace for said County, Joseph Steer who acknowledged
the within to be a correct plat of
the town of Portland in the County
of Jefferson and State of Ohio as
surveyed by John McElroy and attended to by the said Joseph Steer.
Given under my hand and seal the
above written date.

J.G. Hening Justice of the Peace

Jefferson County SS. Recorded March 26th by Robert Boyd,
Recorder[8]

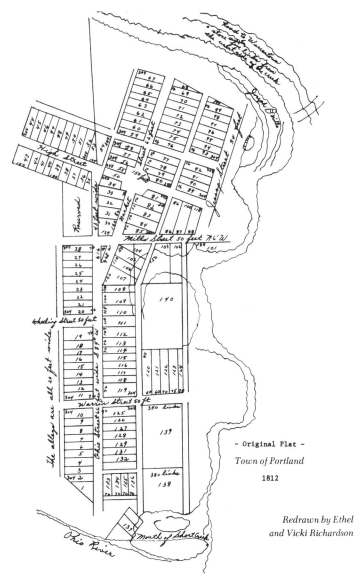

– Original Plat –

Town of Portland

1812

*Redrawn by Ethel
and Vicki Richardson*

Original Town Plat: Portland, 1812

The town of Portland in Warren Township was slow in developing. Early settlers moving westward were more interested in acquiring large tracts of land as pasture or farm land.

The proprietors had indeed undertaken a hazardous venture. Their enterprising efforts were not destined for complete failure, however, and, although the reserves on the lots were removed in due time and certain lots were combined and sold as sections, a town had been born and it would live!

XVII
JOSEPH TILTON, PROPRIETOR

IN THE YEAR 1813, WHEN THE KEELBOAT and flatboat still dominated passage on the broad Ohio, two events of particular note took place. Joel Tilton, the last child of Joseph and Mary Tilton, was born on March 10 at his parents' substantial home in Warren Township. As always, Susannah, at the age of sixty-three and still a whirlwind of charm and grace, was there. It was with a feeling of impulsive insight that she looked upon this baby boy as a future progenitor of the Tilton name and ancestry. The boy, Joel, grew strong and sturdy, and Joseph—his grist mills operating smoothly and productively—found himself more often at his mother's house in Tiltonsville. He had an insatiable desire to break the barrier of silence and inactivity that had plagued his father in the four years before his death, and to permit the pioneer families to purchase lots in the town, which was included in the land now owned by his mother.

"Mother," emphasized Joseph, during one of his frequent visits to Susannah's house, "it was Father's dream and desire!"

"Yes, and it shall be done—by you, Joseph—at the time I deem proper." Susannah's eyes flashed, and she adjusted her auburn tresses while stirring the rich stew in an iron pot.

Drusilla Tilton, after serious consideration and consultation with her mother, left her home in Tiltonsville about a year after her father's death. It is apparent that she became associated with the family of James West, who owned considerable acreage in

Section Twenty-eight of Warren Township, and eventually married a son of James West.[1]

On August 13, 1813, William Tilton, the twenty-six-year-old son of John and Susannah, was joined in holy matrimony to Miss Jane Davis, of English descent, whose family had come to eastern Ohio about six years previously. Robert Patterson, a justice of the peace and prominent landowner in Warren Township, performed the ceremony.

The usual merry-making and indulgences associated with a pioneer wedding prevailed, and within a short time thereafter, William, with the help of his friends, neighbors, and relatives, built a rough-hewn log house on the land he had inherited from his father.

With the marriage of William and his consequent removal to his own house, Susannah still enjoyed the presence of her two daughters, Prusilla and Ann, and her youngest son, John, now seventeen years of age—but not for long.

In early spring of the following year, after what had been a winter of heavy snows, but a time of peace and warmth in Susannah's house, Prusilla and her mother were relaxing in the late afternoon on the back section of the porch facing the river.

Prusilla appeared somewhat nervous as she fidgeted back and forth along the broad railing on the porch. Susannah appeared comfortable in a huge chair but she sensed the apparent solicitude of her daughter.

Finally, Prusilla spoke.

"Mother, I must tell you of my plans for the future. I hope—"

"Tell me, Prusilla, and I will listen and agree. You have been a mature and faithful daughter for many years, and my love and appreciation for all the help and consolation you have provided shall not recede—no matter what your plans."

Prusilla continued, her head bowed as she cleaned her fingernails with a pointed stick.

"I have met a gentleman in Wheeling who is quite prosperous. He is a merchant and he has offered me employment. I find no glaring flaw in his appearance or activities. Tomorrow I will go there, and I hope it is with your consent and blessing."

"Is this a fast decision? How long have you known the man? What work will you be doing?"

Susannah concealed her feelings as best she could but she was concerned.

"I have known him for some time, Mother—even before William got married. As to the work—I will do much as I have done here and also help him keep account of his business."

Susannah stood up.

"Very well. If this be your desire, you have my blessing."

Her eyes flashed, and her auburn tresses twirled as she whirled and withdrew into the house.

———

Joseph Tilton must be classified as one of the earliest entrepreneurs in a young Jefferson County and Warren Township. In addition to the purchase and sale of lands in Sections Sixteen and Twenty-two of Township No. 4 and Range No. 2, originally owned by his father, he had extended his interests to other outlying areas in Belmont County.

His original investment in 1801 of $300 to purchase 100 acres of land in Section Twenty-one of the same township and range from Absalom Martin had proved profitable; the same was true of an additional adjacent 120 acres he had bought from John Connell. On March 20, 1811, he bought one acre in Section Fifteen and 80 acres in Section Twenty from James McMillen at a cost of $1,100. All of these transactions were related to land in Township No. 4 and Range No. 2 as defined in the Survey of the Seven Ranges.

William Stringer, Jr. paid Joseph $140 for 40 acres of land in Section Twenty-one on July 20, 1812. Joseph purchased 100 acres of land in Sections Fifteen and Twenty-one from Abraham Davis on April 19, 1814, for $1,400 and on August 1, 1815, he sold 10 acres of this land to Jacob Hambler for $500.

It was in January of the year 1815 that Joseph visited his mother at her river front house on the original plat of the town planned by his father almost nine years before. The flaming locust logs in the stone fireplace generated a warm glow, and Joseph, after greeting Susannah with affection, sat next to her as

she worked on a quilt. Ann and her brother John were busy with
their chores.

"Mother," said Joseph, "I've been thinking. Is there some way
we can officially establish the town? As I have often said, it was
father's hope and desire."

"Oh, I'm sure it could be accomplished in some manner. I have
not thought much about it lately. And of course you know that
your younger brother is really entitled to this land."

"Yes, I know, Mother, and I have a plan. John is almost
nineteen now, and, although still a minor according to law, he is
mature in thought. I would propose that you appoint my brother
Thomas as John's legal guardian and provide John with a deed to
a part of the 100 acres which you now own."

Susannah pondered the suggestion.

"My needs are simple, Joseph. As to the orchards, I have no
need of them. Each year our neighbors and friends help themselves to the peaches and apples."

"I would propose that you transfer maybe only fifty acres, including, of course, this surveyed town. The balance would be sufficient for grazing and gardening. And believe me, Mother, I will
see that you want for nothing."

"And I suppose that you intend purchasing the section of land
that contains the town?"

"Yes—and I shall arrange for an official county survey as you
direct."

"I will talk to John and Thomas about this," said Susannah,
"and, if they are agreeable, so it shall be. My conscience will be
clear, as it was your father's wish that I use discretion in disposing
of the property. Meanwhile, you may arrange for the survey."

In early February, Joseph journeyed to Steubenville to engage
the services of William Lowry, the county surveyor.[2] He explained the situation, and shortly thereafter Lowry came to
Warren Township. With Joseph in attendance, he platted the
area designed by Susannah and filed a report of survey at the
courthouse, which read:

> This plat [he had prepared a sketch] represents the survey
> of lands made for Joseph Tilton containing fifty acres being
> a part of fractional section No. 16, [township] No. 4 of
> range No. 2—bounded on the East by the Ohio River, on

the south by Abner Kimble [Kimball] on the west by John Tilton [son of Thomas] [and on the north] by John Mc-Cullough [McColloch]—containing fifty acres.

Surveyed—February 18, 1815
Attest: Thos. Patton, Clk.

William Lowry
County Surveyor[3]

———

The warm springtime and the hot summertime passed quickly. Susannah had been busy with her gardening, household duties, and providing greatly appreciated medicinal and midwife services to those who requested her help.

It was a beautiful autumn day, and she was in a reflective mood. Throughout all her years on the western frontier, she had endured the drudgery of hard labor, the pangs of natural childbirth, and the heartaches associated with the loss of loved ones. But always her tremendous courage and determination had recouped the flash in her eyes and the golden tinsel in her auburn tresses. She had experienced much joy and happiness and love—and also sadness and sorrow. The decision to populate the town of Tiltonsville was hers alone, and although she had intentionally deterred the thought, after deciding positively she approached John on the subject. She explained the plan she and Joseph had discussed early in the year, and John was quite content to abide by his mother's wish.

"I am pleased, John. Let us visit Thomas and attempt to finalize the arrangements."

John saddled the horses and they rode to the house of Thomas, where they received a warm welcome.

"'Tis good to see you, Mother, and you, too, John—it's been almost—"

"Yes, I know, Thomas," injected Susannah, "but there is much to do—and also many things to think about. How is everything?"

"Oh, fine—I guess, Mother. As you know, Rose Ann recently married James Akens, a man of good repute, and I am happy for them. The children are well grown—Thomas is now almost fourteen."

"Thomas," Susannah was suddenly serious, "we have a plan to

assure the settlement of the town your father planned before he
died. It will require your help."

Susannah outlined the procedure as she and Joseph had
discussed it and as John had concurred.

Thomas was also willing to assume his role.

"You say the land has been surveyed?"

"Yes, and the survey, although unrecorded, is a matter of
record in the county surveyor's office."

"I shall petition the court as you request, Mother; however, as I
recall, the next formal session of the court will not occur until
December."

"You are probably correct, Thomas, but perform the task at
your earliest convenience."

"That I shall do," said Thomas.

After spending the evening with her son and his family, Susannah and John returned home before darkness enveloped the
valley.

It was late in the year when Thomas, who by this time had
been appointed the official guardian of John Tilton, a minor,
filed the following petition in the Court of Common Pleas at
Steubenville:

> To the Honorable, the Court of Common Pleas of Jef-
> ferson County, Ohio, at December term, 1815. The petition
> of Thomas Tilton, Guardian of John Tilton, a minor,
> represents and shows to the Court that his ward is seized as
> of fee in and to a certain piece of ground, a plat whereof is
> hereunto annexed, being part of Fractional Section No. 16,
> Township No. 4 in the Second Range and of which your
> petitioner thinks it would be of advantage to the interests of
> his ward now to have sold fifty acres thereof adjoining the
> river—that the proceeds may be vested in other property for
> him. Your petitioner therefore prays that he may be
> authorized to sell said tract of land and will ever pray, etc.
>
> Thomas Tilton

The Court concurred:

> Whereupon, it is ordered by the Court that the petition
> aforesaid be sustained and that the said, Thomas Tilton,
> proceed accordingly to law to sell the said land and make
> report to this Court at their next term, etc.[4]

The procedure for the sale of the fifty acres of land, at least a part of which contained certain lots in the town of Tiltonsville as designed by John Tilton and surveyed by him and Joseph, was prearranged. Joseph and Thomas had discussed the matter and the consternation of their mother.

"I have no choice but to comply with the request of our brother," said Thomas, as he and Joseph inspected the preliminary deed to the land. "I have been authorized by the court at Steubenville to dispose of the property."

Joseph smiled inwardly but expressed disdain. Others were present.

"But John is nineteen. He may not be recognized as an adult but he is certainly mature. Mother says he performs his chores at home with great vigor and often roams the western hills in search of game."

"The land will be sold at public auction, as of now," said Thomas strongly.

"Very well, but I think you will agree that the circumstances surrounding this event are quite mysterious," responded Joseph.

"I agree. I agree—but I am at a loss—"

"Twenty-five dollars per acre—that is what I will pay, and if you have any consideration for our mother, you will accept."

Thomas, with a weird look in his eyes, walked a short distance to a tree stump and shouted:

"Twenty-five dollars per acre I am bid for this rich bottom land on the river—do I hear further bidding?" He hesitated and glanced at the other potential buyers. They drifted away slowly, and Thomas announced:

"If not, the land is hereby sold, by deed true and proper, to Joseph Tilton."

A preliminary land transfer note was prepared, and, after receiving a receipt for partial payment of the $1,250, Joseph prepared to record certain declarations at the county seat.

At the time that William Lowry, the county surveyor, had laid out the fifty-acre tract of land for Joseph, he had also confirmed the dimensions and transit readings of the town plat. He made note of this data, as did Joseph.

In mid-February of 1816, when Joseph traveled to Steubenville to record the plat of Tiltonsville, Lowry was of much help, and, after confirming the layout, the following deed entry and plat were placed on record:

> A PLAT OF THE TOWN OF TILTONSVILLE) The Streets and alleys running with the Ohio river bears S24° W Main street is 60 feet wide Market alley 12½ and Middle street 40 the cross streets and alleys bears S66° E Market Street is 60 feet wide—South and Third streets 40 each and Pare [Pear] & Cherry alleys 15 feet—each the lots are 50 feet in front by 150 back—lots No. 60 & 61 are reserved for the use of a market house—Given under my hand and seal the 16th day of February AD 1816
>
> > Joseph Tilton
> > Wm. Lowry, surveyor[5]

Joseph, upon Lowry's confirmation of the town plat, had the layout recorded at the courthouse.

> The State of Ohio } SS Before me Joseph McGaughey a
> Jefferson County   Justice of the peace within and for
>   said County personally came
>
> [L.S.]   Joseph Tilton who being duly
>   sworn according to law declares
>   himself proprietor of the Town of
>   Tilltonsville in said County &
>   acknowledges that this is a true and
>   correct plat of the said Town and
>   that it is delivered by him as
>
> such—Given under my hand and seal the 16th day of February 1816 Joseph mcGaughey, Jus. of the peace Jefferson County SS Recorded February 17th, 1816 by Robert Boyd, Recorder J.C.[6]

After recording the town plat at Steubenville, Joseph wasted no time. He and his mother discussed the matter of selling the lots, and, as she concurred with his plans, he caused this proclamation to be recorded at the Court House:

> Joseph Tilton—Advertisement: The terms of the present sale is such—the highest bidder shall be the purchaser, the payments to be in six, twelve and eighteen months, on the purchaser giving his Notes and approved security, the lots

Original Town Plat: Tiltonsville, 1806

Redrawn by Ethel and Vicki Richardson

will be sold by their numbers, and certificate will be made out and given to the purchaser specifying each lot by its number, the Proprietor reserves the fencing and the grain which may be in the Town Plat, also the exclusive right to the public ferry on the river. Any person purchasing any lot or lots and not complying with the above terms will forfeit twenty-five per cent.

Tiltonsville, February 22, 1816
Joseph Tilton (L.S.)

Jefferson County SS Recorded November 6th, 1816 by Robert Boyd, R.J.[7]

Susannah was happy when Joseph informed her that the land transaction had been accomplished. Between them, she and Joseph now owned about two miles of bottom land along the river.

"In a short time, Mother," said Joseph, "after Thomas has filed his report of sale with the court and my advertisement has been properly acknowledged and posted, I shall proceed with the sale of lots. I have had inquiries; people are interested, and I am sure the town will prosper."

"I agree," Susannah responded with a twinkle and a twirl. "I look forward to welcoming my new neighbors."

After a brief silence and some idle chatter between Susannah and Joseph's wife, Mary, Susannah suddenly assumed a more serious mood and looked at her son.

"Joseph, have you noticed the number of boats on the river lately? Every day the number becomes greater, and, for the most part, I see young men and women and children aboard these crafts. Where are they going?"

"To the south, Mother. To the areas of rich, free land of which, I understand, there is much available. Anyhow, there is no room for them here on that type of premise—this is Tilton Territory!"

In April, Thomas Tilton returned to the courthouse at Steubenville and caused the following supplementary entry on the court dockets to appear in conjunction with his earlier entreaty to sell a certain parcel of land on behalf of John Tilton, a minor, of whom he was guardian:

Now, to wit, on the thirtieth day of April, 1816, came the said Thomas Tilton, Guardian as aforesaid, and made report in the money and figures following, to wit—In pursuance of the order of the Court after having advertised according to law, I did on the 15th day of January, 1816, on the premises—proceed to sell at public auction, fifty acres as described in the annexed plat of Survey for the sum of twenty-five dollars per acre, with the exception of the public ferry, that being the highest sum bid therefore—to be paid in six, twelve and eighteen months on instant, amounting to the sum of twelve hundred and fifty dollars.

Thomas Tilton (L.S.)

Wherefore, it is ordered by the Court that the report aforesaid be accepted and the sale confirmed.[8]

Joseph Tilton received the official deed to his fifty-acre purchase in June of 1816. Even before the recording of the deed at the courthouse on September 2, 1816, and before the recording of his pronouncement proclaiming himself as the proprietor of Tiltonsville, a number of lots in the town were sold. The word had spread quickly throughout the township that lots would be sold at public auction in the new town of Tiltonsville.

On July 27, 1816, Joseph and Mary sold two lots—Lot No. 20 to James Akens, husband of Rose Ann (daughter of Joseph's brother Thomas) for $100, and Lot No. 24 to Zaccheus Tilton, his oldest son who was now almost twenty-three years old and operating his own mill, for the same sum.

On August 12, 1816, Joseph conducted another auction, at which Joseph Jeffries of Jefferson County and one of the founders of Portland, paid $100 for Lot No. 35; on the same date, Nathan Durant of Jefferson County purchased Lot No. 40[9] for the same amount and Thomas G. Plummer of Allegheny County, Pennsylvania, was the successful bidder on Lot No. 36.

Within a few weeks after his original sale, Joseph had $500 returned on his original investment.

After another auction on September 13, 1816, when David F. Bigger bought Lot No. 44 for $100, the sale of lots in Tiltonsville became somewhat dormant. Intermediate attempts to sell the lots were unsuccessful, and the final sale in the year 1816 occurred on

December 19, at which time Benjamin Lundy,[10] a prominent citizen of Belmont County, purchased two lots—Nos. 34 and 58 for $100! On the same date, Joseph sold John Loyd of Belmont County Lots Nos. 32 and 41 for an identical fee.

Joseph and Mary spent the holiday season relaxing and enjoying the high-spirited companionship of their children. Zaccheus, their first-born, insisted on decorating their house with pine branches and holly and mistletoe, and placed tiny candles around the great stone fireplace. Zachariah assisted his older brother, as did their younger sisters, Susannah, Cassandra, Nancy, and twelve-year-old Penelope, who joined his decorating antics with much excitement and hilarity.

The queen of the frontier, Susannah, enjoyed the many visits from her children, grandchildren, and many friends. She was buoyant when they came and maintained the same attitude when they left. She treated them royally to pumpkin pie and taffy and all of the other tasty pleasures that the ingredients of a rich and productive soil would permit her to convert into uncommon delicacies.

Zaccheus Tilton possessed the business instinct of his father. He expanded his interests into farming and land clearing, and all of these ventures proved profitable. On January 8, 1817, he purchased from his parents for $1,450 a part of Sections Twenty-one and Twenty-two in Township No. 4 of Range No 2—more than 145 acres. This acreage encompassed a part of Belmont, as well as a part of Jefferson County.

The following day, Joseph and Mary sold Lot No. 11 to William P. M. Burgess, of Fredrick County, Maryland, for $100 and also Lot No. 39 to their friend from Beaver in Allegheny County, Pennsylvania, Thomas G. Plummer, for a like amount.

James Hindman, a long-time friend of the Tiltons, and the same man who had assisted in preparing the will of John Tilton, bought Lot No. 70 in Tiltonsville from Joseph and Mary on October 24, 1817, the price being $100.

The next five years were active and prosperous for the residents of Warren Township in Jefferson County, Ohio. The farmers and the millers and the flatboat builders were busy and successful. Warehouses continued to spring up, particularly at Warren Town, and the boat traffic on the river continued to increase. Taverns in the area thrived, much to the annoyance of the advocates of total abstinence. Religion remained, as it had for over thirty years, an important element in the lives of the settlers. Open-air tent meetings, conducted by circuit riders, drew huge crowds, and many were converted to the beliefs of Christianity. The leaders of the Methodists, the Presbyterians, the Baptists, and sincere advocates of other denominations were quite active in Warren Township during the early nineteenth century.

In June of 1820, Joseph and Mary Tilton sold two more lots in Tiltonsville. Caleb Dilworth, of Jefferson County, purchased Lot. No 63 for $100 on June 13, and Thomas G. Lowther, of Jefferson County, bought Lot No. 45 on June 30 for the same price.

Tiltonsville was growing, under the proprietorship of Joseph Tilton. Warren Township was also growing—but soon it would diminish in size and population!

XVII
DIVISION AND
DEVELOPMENT

THE POPULATION OF JEFFERSON County increased steadily. In the year 1800, of the seven counties in the Territory, it was the second most heavily populated with 8,766 inhabitants. Even after the formation of Belmont, Columbiana, and Tuscarawas counties, Jefferson's 17,260 residents made it the most populous county in the state, according to the census of 1810. In 1820, the population was 18,511.

Warren Township, too, was growing, and by 1823 its citizenry was estimated to number in excess of two thousand. At that time it was the largest township in the county, comprising approximately fifty square miles.

Evidently the county officials—the county commissioners were John Jackson and George Day; the clerk of courts was John Patterson—recognizing the size of the township and wishing to honor the illustrious cofounder of the county seat and one of Steubenville's most prominent legislators, Bezaleel Wells, split the township in 1823 into almost equal parts by an east-west section line about 2½ miles north of Warren Town.

The northern half of the previous Warren Township was designated as Wells Township, in honor of Bezaleel who was fifty-one years old at the time. The southern section, of course, retained the name of Warren.

In the year 1820, it had been twenty-two years since the first church building had been constructed in the township of Warren. The Hopewell Methodist Episcopal Church thrived, and many advocates of that faith traveled some distance to attend Sunday services, which were often conducted by a nomadic circuit rider.

When Bishop Asbury preached at that church in its early days, many of the worshippers stood outside to hear the magical inspiration of his message.

The bishop was a remarkable man, slight in stature but erect and dignified. His every movement was displayed in the stern brightness of his eyes and the strong, decisive nature of his actions. He died on March 21, 1816, but his name and fame will never be erased from the annals of Methodist history.

The Scotch-Irish Presbyterians, under the leadership of the Reverend John McMillan and the Reverend Thomas Marquis, were organized as the Indian Short Creek Congregation in November of 1798. The first ruling elders were Thomas McCune, James Clark, James Eagleson, and Richard McKibbon. Tent meetings were held several years prior to the organization of the congregation and even afterwards. The adventuresome Presbyterians had come primarily from the western Pennsylvania counties of Allegheny, Washington, Fayette, and Westmoreland.

Early tent meetings were actually conducted in an open clearing, surrounded by the terrestrial beauty of the forest. The "tent" or pulpit, constructed of rough-hewn logs, was somewhat elevated, so that all of the faithful could see the speaker as they reposed on a terraced, sloping hillside. A matted cover of hickory boughs and leaves covered the speaker's stand to protect the preacher from the sun and the elements.

The first house of worship for these devout people was erected of crude logs. It was built in 1800, beside the sparkling, rippling waters of a small tributary[1] of Indian Short Creek, near the western boundary of Warren Township.

And so it was that Joseph Tilton and his wife, Mary, as proprietors of the town of Tiltonsville, authorized and participated in the construction of a new church on Lot No. 14. Although a deed to the lot was not recorded at this time, Joseph and Mary had agreed to give and bequeath the lot for such purpose.[2]

A firm, clapboard-sided structure was erected, and it can be stated that without doubt the prime influence on this accomplishment was Joseph's mother. Susannah, now seventy years of age, retained the authoritative flash in her eyes, the unquestioned wisdom of her advice, and an unblemished strength of character which, even now, prevented her beautiful auburn tresses from becoming infested with signs of age.

For many years prior to the building of this Methodist Episcopal church, the settlers in and near Tiltonsville, who were of this faith, had held services in private homes, and many of the more pious had walked or ridden their horses to the little church in Hopewell.

The first pastor of the new church was the Reverend J. Stephens, a former circuit rider, who, although young, had known the famous Bishop Asbury and was well acquainted with that highly esteemed minister of the gospel, the Reverend James B. Finley.

Reverend Finley often visited eastern Ohio and Warren Township in the early nineteenth century. He knew many of the inhabitants of that area by name and face. Although only a little over seven years old when the Johnson brothers had their hazardous encounter with the Indians in 1788, he later came to know these boys quite intimately. And he took pride in relating their experience and the fact that John Johnson had become a steward in the Methodist Episcopal church and his younger brother, Henry, a preacher.

The Reverend Mr. Finley was not only a great orator in his own right, but also an impressive storyteller and writer. While encamped on a summer evening near the new church in Tiltonsville, he gave vent to his feelings and related several of his most impressive experiences associated with life among the Indians. The assembled crowd listened. He talked first of Monocue, his friend and a chief of the Wyandot Nation:

> This renowned chief of the Wyandot nation was about medium in stature, and remarkably symetrical in form. He was one of the most active men I ever knew, quick in his motion as thought, and fleet as the roe in the chase.
>
> As a speaker, he possessed a native eloquence which was truly wonderful. Few could stand before the overwhelming torrent of his eloquence. He was a son of Thunder. When inspired with this theme, he could move a large assembly with as much ease, and rouse them to as high a state of excitement, as any speaker I ever heard.

I will give a specimen—of the eloquence of this gifted son
of nature. Imagine yourself—in the depths of the forest,
surrounded by hundreds of chiefs and warriors, all sunk in
the degredation and darkness of Paganism. They have been
visited by the missionary and several converted Indian
chiefs. One after another, the chiefs rise and address the
assembly, but with no effect. The dark scowl of infidelity
settles on their brows and the frequent mutterings of the ex-
cited auditors indicate that their speeches are not ac-
ceptable, and their doctrines not believed.

At length, Monocue rises amidst confusion and distur-
bance, and ordering silence with a commanding voice, he
addresses them as follows:

"When you meet to worship God, and to hear his word,
shut up your mouths, and open your ears to hear what is
said. You have been here several days and nights worshiping
your Indian god, who has no existence, only in your dark
and beclouded minds. You have been burning your dogs and
venison for him to smell. What kind of a God or Spirit is he,
that can be delighted with the smell of a burnt dog? Do you
suppose that the great God that spread out the heavens, that
hung up the sun and moon, and all the stars, to make light,
and spread out this vast world of land and water, and filled
it with men and beasts, and everything that swims or flies, is
pleased with the smell of your burnt dogs? I tell you today,
that his great eye is on your hearts, and not on your fires, to
see and smell what you are burning. Has your worshiping
here these few days made you any better? Do you feel that
you have gotten the victory over one evil? No! You have not
taken the first step to do better, which is to keep this day
holy. This day was appointed by God himself a day of rest
for all men, and a day on which men are to worship him
with pure hearts, and to come before him, that he may
examine their hearts, and cast out all their evil. This day is
appointed for his ministers to 'preach to us, Jesus, and to
teach our dark and cloudy minds, and to bring them to
light!' "

"I have no doubt that many were convicted of sin," said the
Reverend Finley, as the sun continued its descent in the west,
"and a judgment to come."

The years passed and the little church in Tiltonsville was well
attended on Sunday morning. Susannah went regularly, as did

other townspeople. The town grew slowly, for many of the lot buyers did not build new houses immediately.

As previously noted, there were schools in Warren Township long before it had been divided. These early schools were not public nor were they free. The teacher agreed to conduct the class for a certain length of time, and the pioneers who sent their children agreed to pay from one to three dollars for each child attending. In reality, they were private schools. The schoolhouse was extremely uncomfortable and simple in structure. It was usually from fifteen to eighteen feet wide and twenty-four to twenty-eight feet long, and the roof structure was about ten feet from the ground. It was built of logs, and the floor was usually of puncheon or bare earth. Sometimes the inside walls were covered with clapboard or clay mortar, and the seats were split logs, without backs, held upright by four pegs driven into the ground. Desks were similarly constructed, and at one end of the building a huge fireplace provided the only source of warmth during the winter months. Reading, spelling, writing, and arithmetic constituted the normal course of study.

In 1821, the first state law was passed which authorized the levying of a tax for the support of schools. This law provided for the division of townships into school districts, and for the election of committees in each district to construct school buildings and affix a tax for buying land and erecting a schoolhouse. The schoolteachers were still to be paid a tuition charge for each student.

In 1825, the Ohio legislature approved a law which required that every county levy a tax of one-half mill on the dollar for school purposes; this was in addition to the township and district taxes. Shortly thereafter, Warren Township was divided into ten school districts. The districts were quite irregular in design, and District No. 1 in Warren Township enclosed most of Tilton Territory at that time.

The law enforcement of the 1825 ordinance was extremely lax, and the progress of schools with qualified instructors was slow.

Joseph and Mary continued selling the lots. On August 15, 1826, Nathaniel F. Cisco, of Jefferson County, purchased Lot No. 18 for $47 and the next year, the proprietor of the town sold the same Cisco Lot Nos. 43 and 19 for $300.

It was on April 13, 1827, that Joseph concluded, out of love and appreciation, a major land transaction with his younger brother John, who was now almost thirty-one years old.

They had discussed the matter.

"Joseph," said John, "in a short time, I will marry Hannah—you know her well—and I must secure some land and build our home."

"Hannah—Hannah Hindman. Of course, I know her, John. Have you talked to Mother?"

"Oh, yes—and she is happy. The Hindmans are of good stock, and Hannah's father helped prepare our father's will—remember?"

"I do, indeed," replied Joseph. "And I, too, am happy for you, John. I am sure we can arrange for the land."

"I have earned some money—and should tell you, too, that Mother has been helpful—in many ways."

"I suspected as much. Let us talk to her. Even now, she has the wisdom of Solomon, and we shall abide by her wishes."

Together, they rode to Susannah's house. After the usual warm greeting, John and Joseph seated themselves on a long bench stationed at the eastern end of the porch; their mother rocked.

"Has John told you?"

"Yes," replied Joseph, "and I am sure John has made a wise choice."

"I am glad, Joseph. Hannah is like a daughter to me."

John's face became quite flushed at the compliment. He fidgeted.

"Enough of the plaudits, Mother. Joseph and I have discussed my request to buy a parcel of land. What are your thoughts?"

Susannah smiled and her eyes flashed. She looked at Joseph.

"As you know, my son, some years ago John was quite agreeable to the terms which allowed you to make record of this town. I think it now appropriate that, in recompense, you consider selling some land to him—at the proper price."

Joseph knew the tone of his mother's voice. He pondered. After examining a map which he had procured from the pocket of his homespun coat, he questioned, "How much land do you need, John?"

"Oh, not a large plat—enough for our house and a good garden. I would like to invest $800."

Susannah listened quietly.

"Very well," said Joseph, "there is a good tract of land west of the town, lying adjacent to your cousin John's land, and quite a number of lots in the town are worth more than that. You may have it all because of my feelings for you—and for our mother."

John was exuberant; Susannah was pleased.

All of these arrangements had taken place in early April of the year 1827 and on the thirteenth day of that month in the same year, the official land transfer was recorded and noted as follows:

> From Joseph and Mary Tilton of Jefferson County to John Tilton of the same County for and in consideration of the sum of eight hundred dollars, a certain parcel of land—Bounded on North by Noah Zane, east by the Ohio River, south by lands of Charles Kimball and others and west by lands of John Tilton and containing thirty-one acres, two roods, 7 perches. In addition Lot Numbers 37, 38, 50, 51, 52, 53, 54, 55, 56, 64, 65, 66, 68 & 69 in the Town of Tiltonsville.[3]

It was, indeed, a bargain—as John would soon learn.

———————

That devoted Methodist missionary of God, David McMasters, once again came to Warren Township in April of 1827. He learned from his many friends in the area that John Tilton and Hannah Hindman were planning marriage. And, forthwith, he greeted them on one of their many rendezvous. It was near Susannah's house.

His mud-spattered high boots and the black kerchief tied over his long, dark hair contributed to a rather threatening appearance.

"John and Hannah, I have been told in truth you shall wed soon—let it be known that I can plant you in the vineyard of the Lord."

"But, sir," said John, "we have a church and—"

"Fine—fine—a church is good. And the pastor—?"

"We are waiting for his return."

McMasters, in a gentle but firm voice, responded, "I have a

church, too, west of here, but tomorrow at nine when the eastern
sun is rising and the blue river sparkles, underneath the broad
branches of the spreading elm, the ceremony will be performed."

It was a forceful statement and left John and Hannah slightly
confused. They looked at each other—then, suddenly, they
knowingly embraced and laughed loudly and joyfully.

"As you wish, Reverend." John's voice was loud. "At the large
tree near my mother's house at nine. And now we must take our
leave to inform our friends who will want to be there."

And so it was.

On April 24, 1827, the Reverend David McMasters, a fearless,
untiring, circuit-riding and stationary Methodist minister, married John Tilton and Hannah Hindman.

The sale of lots in Tiltonsville had been quite successful, and by
mid 1827 only few salable lots remained—and only few houses
had been built. Only recently, on May 13, Joseph and Mary had
sold the two lots they owned in Warren Town, Nos. 30 and 31, to
William Humphrey for $429. It had been almost twenty-two
years, to the day, since Joseph had purchased these lots from
Zenas Kimberly for $100. Upon completion of this sale, Joseph
confined his land investments and transfers to the southern portion of Warren Township in Sections Sixteen and Twenty-two
and Section Twenty-one in Belmont County.

By the spring of 1830, many events of concern and interest had
occurred which directly or indirectly affected the unceasing activities of Joseph Tilton and his wife, Mary. Susannah, now
eighty years of age, was concerned also, but not interested.

Joseph's brother, Thomas, had died in the fall of 1828 and been
given a proper Christian burial in the same cemetery as his
father. He was sixty years old. His children, Rose Ann (the wife of
James Akens), John, Drusilla, James, and Thomas were disconsolate, as his demise was unexpected. They were joint heirs to his

possessions, including the remaining fifty-five acres of land which he had owned. With the sons being unmarried and the married daughters materially well endowed, action on the property of Thomas was not taken at this point in time.

Zaccheus had sold an additional thirteen acres plus of his land in Section Twenty-one to his friend, Robert Clements, on April 13, 1827, for fifty-six dollars—this being the same Clements to whom he had sold over nine acres and his father over five acres in 1820.

In late spring of 1829, John B. Bayless, an abolitionist from Maryland, came to Warren Township and was immediately recognized as a gentleman of pomp and wealth. He came in a halo of aristocracy, bringing with him his third wife, Elizabeth,[4] their children and several black servants, who had refused to leave his household even though he had granted them freedom. Bayless purchased a section of land south of Short Creek and built a modest home. It was only the beginning, as the future would soon tell.

On April 19, 1830, Joseph Tilton, strong and adventuresome even at the age of sixty-three, bought forty acres of land from Caleb (his nephew) and Catherine Tilton. The land was part of Sections Sixteen and Twenty-two and was bounded on the north by the land of Joseph Tilton, on the east by the Ohio River, on the west by the lands of Samuel Biggs, and on the south by the lands of Joseph and Zachariah Tilton. He paid $600. Nathaniel Cisco, of previous note and now a renowned flatboat builder in Tiltonsville, bought Lot No. 24 from Zaccheus and Miriam Tilton on July 31, 1830, for $40.

Other boat builders in the town at this time were Thomas Liston, Joseph Large, Nathan Borran, Stephen King, James Attis, Charles Wilson, John Durant, and Joseph Hall.[5] The building of flatboats, despite competition from the famed keelboat and the explosively dangerous steamboat, thrived, and the craftsmen engaged in this occupation were justly rewarded. Charles Noble was a wagoner, and the millers and farmers of the township and points beyond employed his services to convey their goods to

Warren Town or Tiltonsville for storage and eventual shipment to southern markets.

Additional grist mills along Short Creek, Rush Run, and Fish Creek had been erected and were quite productive and profitable. Joseph Tilton's mill continued in operation. Other mills were now owned by Joseph West, William Smith, John Bone, John B. Bayless (the enterprising Marylander had built two stone mills on Short Creek), and another prominent resident of Warren Township, James Hodgens.

Hodgens had come to Warren Township from Washington County, Pennsylvania, and in only a few years he had established himself as a gentleman of distinction and respect. His sound investments yielded handsome profits. He was now forty-seven years old, and his wife, Sarah, was forty-three. Their immediate offspring included Robert W., Thomas, Helen O., John W., and Isaac N.; James Hodgens would, in due time, make a significant mark on the early settling of Warren Township.

Susannah, at the age of eighty years, was still quite active and in good health. She spent more time at her home now, where her children, grandchildren, and friends visited her often, always providing her with fresh-baked pumpkin and berry pies or a pot of turkey stew. She knew them all, mostly from their childhood, and she would firmly declare:

"Oh, you need not have done that. I am well stocked with food as provided by the garden."

But she was always glad to see them and often she and her visitors would sit for hours on the river front section of the porch and discuss a variety of subjects ranging from the significant topics of a young state in a new nation to the insignificant local incidents concerning the townspeople. The insignificant items of interest predominated in every instance.

She could sit rocking endlessly, with her toil-worn hands folded and gently resting on her lap. Usually she wore a large, bibbed cotton apron over her plain, ankle-length dress; her fading auburn tresses were mostly concealed by a a broad-rimmed sun-bonnet. Her facial features, although slightly wrinkled now, were still strong; the flashing eyes were a symbolic characteristic which she would always retain, and an authoritative motion of her hand was often noticeable as she conversed.

She expressed amazement and happiness upon learning that "Mary Smith" had twin daughters last week and that "John Smith," Mary's husband, had celebrated the occasion by becoming intoxicated in a Warren Town tavern and wreaking havoc in the place by destroying most of the furnishings. She voiced concern when a friend informed her that "Mary Ellen," the beautiful blonde temptress, an orphan, had been abducted by two sturdy keelboatmen who had boarded their partially loaded craft and floated down the river. To all of these tales she listened with heartache and happiness, and the conveyors of such stories always left Susannah's house with a feeling of exuberance and humility.

When Joseph came, with Mary, during the Christmas season of 1830, it was on a mission of joy—and how rightly so, during that all-too-short period of every year. His mother's house was not devoid of the symbols of the time. Lighted tallow candles a-dorned the stone mantle, beneath which a log fire burned briskly. A fabricated pine cone star, polished and glistening, had been placed in the center of the mantlepiece between the candles. Although it was early in the evening, Susannah was relaxed and comfortable as she contemplated the pastor's message in church that morning and concentrated on the star.

Joseph and Mary's arrival interrupted her meditation, and she greeted them with exultation.

"Mother, we will not stay long. I have here some fresh chestnuts," he said, opening a deerskin pouch. "I will cook them for you as you have done many times for me—I know you, also, enjoy the taste of this delicate tree fruit."

"I do indeed," Susannah smiled, "and there is a fresh pot of sassafras tea in the kitchen."

Mary filled the ancient pewter mugs, and Joseph roasted the chestnuts in a long-handled iron skillet over the open flame in the fireplace.

As Joseph sat on a stool near the hearthstone and Mary was seated comfortably near his mother, he announced:

"Miriam will be married next month, Mother. It was only recently that a young man, Jeff Stringer, requested her hand in the holy bonds."

"And he is quite a handsome chap," injected Mary.

Susannah was surprised, but the joy of the forthcoming event was reflected in the faces of Joseph and Mary.

"She is only a child!" Susannah's eyes flashed.

"Mother, she is now twenty years old, and her betrothed is of sturdy English stock. Mary and I are quite happy with this union. And, besides, you—"

"Yes, yes, I know, my son—I should not be selfish. Somehow I think you and Mary have been aware of my great affection for your youngest daughter."

"We know, Mother," said Joseph, and Mary agreed.

"Very well, then—a toast of tea to their future success—as lovers and architects of things to come!"

Somewhat startled by this statement of eloquence, Joseph and Mary touched pewter mugs with Susannah and drank their tea.

XIX

THE STONE HOUSE

JEFFERSON D. STRINGER, the husband-to-be of Joseph and Mary Tilton's youngest daughter, Miriam, had been born in West Fallowfield Township of Chester County, Pennsylvania, on December 1, 1800. His father, William Stringer, Jr., had also been born in that county in April of 1750[1] and had distinguished himself as a soldier of the Revolution, serving heroically under Major General Nathanael Greene.[2]

Jefferson was one of fiteen children born to William and Jane Stringer. All of the children were born at the old Stringer homestead in Chester County, Pennsylvania.

In 1805, before Jefferson was yet five years old, his father decided to move to the west and seek solace, peace, and prosperity in the new state of Ohio. William was now fifty-five years old; he had married Jane McKeown almost thirty-five years ago when she was quite young. The overland trek took some time, but eventually they reached the broad Ohio, crossed over, and decided to settle several miles west of the river on a flat hilltop plateau in the northern section of Pease Township in Belmont County.

Here they found friends of similar national origin—Scotch, Scotch-Irish and English—well entrenched, including the Clarks, Moores, Pickenses and Alexanders. Jefferson's mother died shortly after the family had settled in Scotch Ridge. The westward journey, coupled with a full life of childbearing and exhaustive toil, was too much. She was buried in a cemetery near that early settlement.

It was at this early settlement that Jefferson grew to manhood. He had watched with hope and happiness the marriage of his older brother, George Wilson Stringer, to Tabitha Tilton, the twenty-year-old daughter of Joseph and Mary Tilton, on December 6, 1827. The official act was performed by the justice of the peace, Guion Grier, of Scottish ancestry. The jubilation associated with this wedlock, it seemed, had hardly subsided when another brother, William Stringer III, married Jane Johnston, on March 19, 1829. Jefferson, now in his twenty-ninth year, knew his time would come; meanwhile, he continued to live in his father's house on Scotch Ridge.

It was from this settlement, that he often roamed, and in time he came to know Miriam Tilton, who lived with her parents several miles north and east of the Stringer home. Their courtship was not long, and on January 20, 1831, they were joined in holy matrimony by the Reverend Benjamin Mitchell, minister of the Short Creek Presbyterian Congregation.[3] At the time of their marriage, Miriam was not yet twenty-one and Jefferson had recently passed his thirtieth birthday.

They built a log house on the hillside just west of Joseph and Mary's house. Here they resided in comfort and happiness. Jefferson D. Stringer was a gentleman of strong character—sober and foresighted. He planned a prosperous future for his family.

When Miriam gave birth to their first son, William Hope Stringer, on March 25, 1832, he was overjoyed. Mary was at her daughter's house regularly and took charge of the household duties while providing every need that Miriam and her new grandson required.

Susannah, the reigning queen of Tiltonsville and Warren Township, was radiant when Joseph informed her that her most recent great-grandson had been born.

"May he have a long and fruitful life, such as mine," she said.

"I wish our new grandson the same, mother, and somehow your hopes and desires are always realized."

Susannah was nonchalant. She knew that her time on earth would ultimately cease to be, even though she was currently sound of mind and body. What she did not know was that her remaining years would contain more sorrow than joy.

———

After the marriage of Jefferson D. Stringer and Miriam Tilton, Joseph had once again resumed the sale of certain lots in Tiltonsville and outlying sections of lands which he owned.

On March 7, 1831, he sold one rood and twenty perches (a rood being a land measure equaling forty square miles, and a perch one square rod) of his hillside holdings to John Lane, of Jefferson County, for $100. James Maxwell secured the deed to Lot No. 17 in Tiltonsville by payment of $100 to Joseph and Mary Tilton on the same date.

Blair Jeffries, also of Jefferson County, purchased from Joseph and Mary a sizeable tract of land consisting of eighty-four acres, four roods, and twenty-seven perches lying west of the river, at a cost of $969 on July 27, 1831. And concurrently, Joseph and Mary's son-in-law, Jacob Wilt, who had married their daughter Cassandra, bought fifty-eight acres and twenty-two perches for $600. Part of this acreage invaded the confines of Belmont County.

Once again, it must be emphasized that Joseph was a man with a remarkable talent for business. The lands which he had sold to Jeffries and Wilt had been primarily used as pasture for his cattle. Since he had profitably disposed of this livestock, he had no further need for the property. He retained a strong team of horses to assist in cultivating his land holdings in the southern section of Warren Township.

Meanwhile, the roadbuilders of the county and township continued their activities in the name of progress and disregarded certain boundary lines. In consequence, the following petition was filed at the County Commissioner's Office in Steubenville:

The Honorable Commissioners of Jefferson County, Ohio—The remonstrance of the undersigned free holders of said County, humbly represents—That they have understood that a petition, or petitions, will be presented to your honorable board at the next session thereof, praying for the location and opening of a road to be called a "County or Township Road" and to be laid out as follows, as by advertisement (a copy of which is herewith presented)—Up and down Short Creek in Warren Township, in said county, and on the South Side of said Creek, commencing near the "—Free Church" in the Township aforesaid "thence through the lot upon which said Church stands, belonging to John B. Bayless, thence through the lands of John & Robert Bane and Co. to Banes Warehouse upon the Ohio river.

Now your petitioners would beg leave to remonstrate against said petition or petitions, particularly on account of Jesse Jeffries thro' whose land said road must pass, much to the injury of said Jeffries, he being a poor man & owning but a small farm and having a large family. The undersigned therefore; hope that you will not allow this prayer of the petitioners above referred to—And your petitioners to this remonstrance, as in duty bound will ever pray. etc.

May 2nd 1831   Warren Township, Jefferson County—Ohio

Petitioners Names

(S)   Moses C. Kimball   Joseph Tilton
      John Duff   James McCormick
      Wm. Fleming   C. A. Wayman
      John Duff 2nd   Beverly McGee
      Joel F. Martin   Joseph Smith
      John Bucan   P. McGarr
      Thos. Shannon   Henry Lally
      Alex McElroy   Adam Dunlap
      George W. McCleary   Jesse Martin
      James R. Ball   David Peck
      Francis Perdue   Geo. Beale
      Robt. Patterson   Richard Starr
      Saml. Bigger   Charles Kimball
      Samuel S. Bigger   Caleb Tilton

The petitiones against building the road thus temporarily delayed its construction, and when the road was built some four years later, it did not infringe on Jesse Jeffries' land.

———

The winter of 1831-32 had been extremely cold, and the river was frozen solid for an extended period of time. There was a preponderance of heavy snow, the like of which the local inhabitants had rarely seen. Consequently, in the spring of 1832, as the snow melted in the eastern mountains, the tributaries of the Ohio River became engorged and swiftly conveyed their overflow into the main stream.

The swollen Ohio overflowed its banks at Warren Town and did much damage to the residential section, stores and warehouses. Salvaging what meager belongings they could after the flood, many of the townspeople moved westward to higher ground in Portland. Tiltonsville, having an extremely high elevation, was unaffected by the freshet in 1832, but much of the western land south of Tilton Territory was inundated.

In 1832 and 1833, the lots in Tiltonsville continued to change ownership. Aaron Chapman of Belmont County purchased Lot No. 40 from Joseph and Mary for twenty dollars on September 25, 1832. On March 7, 1833, the proprietors of the town sold three lots for twenty dollars each—all to Nathaniel G. Cisco and being numbered 23, 47 and 48. Although most of the original seventy-two town lots had been sold, only seventeen houses had been built, and the population of Tiltonsville was 214.

In late summer, when Jefferson D. and Miriam Tilton Stringer still occupied their log house on the hill, Miriam gave birth to a second son, whom they named Joseph. William, their first child, was less than two years old. There was the usual rejoicing among the members of the immediate family.

In late November, the traditional Thanksgiving Day festivities which most of the pioneer families observed after President Washington had proclaimed the first commemoration on November 6, 1789, had been concluded. Miriam, the young mother of two sons who possessed many of the outstanding attributes of her grandmother, Susannah Tilton, was not in good health. She had developed a dry, painful cough which she concealed as best she could from her husband. After Christmas and through the long winter months, she performed her duties as a wife and mother with some difficulty.

It was in the early spring of 1834 that Miriam confided in her husband, after having fallen into a deathlike coma while performing the arduous spring planting chores. She was carried to the house and put to bed.

The rose-tinted beauty of her youthful face had faded; she was pale and still. Upon being aroused, she spoke softly as her husband sat beside the bed and held her hand.

"My husband, I am sorry that I can no longer perform my wifely duties—and I ask your forgiveness. I have endeavored to please you in all ways, and my love for you shall never wane. But I am tired—I am tired—and I cannot overcome the pain I have endured."

"Rest, my love; already I have requested the services of the doctors in Wheeling and Pittsburgh."

"It will serve no purpose—my soul has been petitioned by God, and I accept His will. Hold me close—"

Jefferson embraced her, and even he, a man rarely subject to visible displays of emotion, could not contain the freely flowing tears.

"There shall be no other," he murmured in her ear.

Miriam Tilton Stringer died two days later of tuberculosis. She was twenty-four years old. The burial service was conducted by the Presbyterian minister, Reverend Benjamin Mitchell, who only a little over three years ago had officiated at her marriage to Jefferson D. Stringer. Her earthly remains were interred in the Joseph Tilton cemetery near the road from Tiltonsville to Martin's Ferry and close to the crystal waters of the broad Ohio.

Joseph and Mary mourned.

Susannah cried.

"Dust to dust—rejoice in the faith and live—today you shall be with me in paradise—He restoreth my soul—He leadeth me beside the still waters—." The Reverend Mitchell was a great source of consolation, and the heavy hearts of the mourners were somewhat lightened as they returned to their houses.

———————

James Hodgens, of previous note, was now situated on a 400-acre tract of land immediately north of Tiltonsville and Tilton

Territory. On April 1, 1832, Hodgens had purchased the rich, productive land along the river from Richard and Mary Starr for $9,000—truly an extravagant fee since the Starrs had never occupied the land, having only secured title to it about three months previous to that date on January 7. James Chin Johnston and his wife, Sophia Zane Johnston, had sold this property to the Starrs for $700.

Noah Zane, the father of Sophia, had deeded this same parcel of land to her, out of love and affection, for and in consideration of the sum of one dollar on November 4, 1829.

The Zanes, Noah and Mary, his wife, had invested a handsome sum of $7,000 in this same land on September 19, 1819, purchasing it from John and Mary McColloch, who, eleven years previous to that, on June 7, 1808, had bought it from Joseph and Amelia Dorsey, of Washington County, Pennsylvania, for $3,200.

Joseph Dorsey was the original owner of the Hodgens tract, having been granted that section plus an additional 63¾ acres by deed patent signed by President John Adams in February of 1798. Dorsey, meanwhile, had sold the entire grant to John and Margaretta McElroy on March 13, 1803, for $1,500.

McElroy, long a resident of Warren Township and a prominent surveyor and justice of the peace, evidently became quite disillusioned with his land acquisition and exactly one month later, on April 13, he persuaded Dorsey to purchase the entire tract for one-third the price he had paid; thus, for $500, Dorsey regained possession of this valuable property.

James and Sarah Hodgens produced rich crops of corn and beans and pumpkins and squash from the black earth they now owned, and in due time they became aware of the Cemetery of the Mound, which was located in the south central section of their 400 acres. When farming they circumvented this hallowed ground which contained many tombstones of early pioneers—including that of John Tilton! It remained for their son, Isaac N., to eventually perpetuate and beautify that perfectly octagonal one acre of land.

April 10, 1834, was a significant day in the life of Joseph and Mary Tilton. At that time, they were unaware of their daughter Miriam's illness, and Joseph conducted another sale of lots in Tiltonsville.

All lots were sold for twenty dollars each, and a number of transactions took place.

John Durant bought Lot Nos. 71 and 72; G. W. Scott of Jefferson County purchased Lot No. 21; John P. Warnock of the same county was deeded Lot Nos. 22 and 46; James West, also a resident of Warren Township in Jefferson County, secured title to three lots—Nos. 5, 15 and 16; and Philip Isner, a local investor, bought Lot No. 34.

The summer of 1834 was long and hot. Joseph spent much time at the home of his mother. Mary, too, was often there.

"Our town is continuing to prosper, Mother," said Joseph, as he sat near Susannah on a warm August evening. "Most of the lots have been sold, and the population of this area is increasing rapidly."

"It is a good thing, my son, and you have done well." Susannah's eyes flashed. "I am content now, Joseph, to enjoy the companionship and happiness of my neighbors. The church and the pastor provide a stability to my remaining years; and, of course, you, my first-born, and Mary, have been very close to me."

"I have much time to think now—and to wonder. I am certain that only through the blessing of Divine Providence have I been permitted to perpetuate the name of Tilton—and I am grateful."

"But where have all my children gone? Polly—Sally—Susannah—Drusilla—Prusilla—I think I wonder about her most of all, Joseph—and, of course, Ann—"

Susannah's voice faded.

"They are well, as far as we know, Mother, but do you not think of your sons?"

"Oh, yes, Joseph—quite often—but they are all men now and quite capable of providing for themselves. I think of your sisters as little girls, and, although I love each of you, one as much as the other, my apron dried more tears and my embrace provided greater solace to your sisters."

There was a moisture-laden sparkle in Susannah's flashing

eyes, and her slim, toil-worn hands held tight to the hand of her eldest son.

"I understand, Mother—I understand."

On September 1, 1834, Joseph and Mary sold Lot No. 40[5] in Tiltonsville for twenty dollars to Thomas Liston of Warren Township and shortly thereafter, on September 30th, they sold two lots, numbered fifty-seven and fifty-eight, to Seraphim Joseph Thery at the same price per lot.

Thery was of French descent, having been born in Tiene, France, on December 25, 1799. The ambitious, flamboyant young man had come to a young United States of America in 1827, eventually migrating to Warren Township in late 1833, when the Town of Tiltonsville was but a fledgling. He took, as his first wife, Sarah Dexter. He built a good house on one of the lots he had purchased in Tiltonsville, but Sarah, being unable to cope with his passionate nature, died shortly thereafter. Later, he married Sarah Chapman, and from this union was born a son who, while still young, left the household of his parents and went to the state of Illinois to seek his fortune.

John Luther Dexter acquired river front Lot No. 10 from Joseph and Mary on March 27, 1833, and it was at this point in time that John B. Bayless, the enterprising Marylander, began to make his presence felt in Warren Township.

The Town of Portland, as designed and surveyed by Galbraith, Jeffries, and Jessop, had failed to entice potential purchasers of lots on the hilly terrain. The founders were asking high prices for the more desirable bottom lots, and interested parties soon became disinterested.

Bayless negotiated. He was eventually able to secure deed and title to almost ninety acres, much of which was in Sections Twelve, Seventeen and Eighteen and constituted most of Portland and land north and south of Short Creek. This was the land he wanted. This is where he would build a memorial for the future.

Jefferson D. Stringer, the widower of Miriam Tilton, had come to know Bayless well and he, too, had bought forty-one acres of land adjacent to the Bayless property, north of the Hodgens holdings and west of the land owned by John Bane. Portions of his land were included in Sections Eleven, Twelve, Seventeen and Eighteen.

Stringer's young sons, William Hope and Joseph, were being cared for by his sister Jane and in 1835 he built a new house in Portland where they could reside in relative comfort. To the day of his death, Jefferson D. Stringer never forgot his beloved wife, Miriam. He was quite appreciative of Jane's contribution to the care and education of his two sons. And in those early years he talked to Miriam in his nightly prayers and at Sunday services in the nearby church of the Presbyterians. He was a man of great nobility and strong character, and throughout his remaining years he remained faithful to his final vow: "There shall be no other."[4]

The intention of John B. Bayless to create a lasting monument to his presence in Warren Township was soon to be realized. He commissioned a group of local workmen, familiar with the craft of cutting and facing stone and assembling masonry structures, to open a quarry on Williamson Run, a northern tributary of Short Creek. From this quarry came the hard bedrock from which Bayless first erected a modest house about one-half mile from the Ohio River on the south bank of Short Creek.

This was only the beginning. He and his wife, Elizabeth, talked of a mansion! After sketching the design of the large structure, Bayless authorized the craftsmen to start construction. The details and intricacies of the mansion, he dictated to the builders as the structure was being erected.

The great house was completed in 1836, and it was, indeed, a masterpiece of classical colonial architecture. The stones used in construction were extremely heavy in lime content, which, consequently prevented serious deterioration from the elements. All were approximately twelve inches high and eighteen inches in depth. The length of the stones varied from two to six feet. The rock-structured base for the Bayless mansion was solidly sealed on shale and the mortar joints, enhanced with a preponderance of sand and clay, were self-sealing and unyielding. Neither rain, nor slashing sleet or heavy snow could dent their strength nor disfigure their appearance.

In overall dimension, the stone house was about fifty-two feet in width and forty-two feet in depth, leading from front to back. The full forty-two-foot-long center hallway, enhanced by a typical colonial stairway at the south end, immediately charmed the many early visitors who, after ascending a series of ornate wooden steps to the small veranda, entered the house from the front, which faced the creek.

Bayless had engaged an Italian artist to paint the main hall. The artist, a true master at his craft, painted a flowing waterfall from the peak of the stairs to the baseboard on the eastern wall. Combining silver and gold with great depth and perception, the artist portrayed, in penetrating detail, a sparkling mirage, and it was not uncommon for a visitor to shield himself from the splashing spray.

On the other side of the great hall, Bayless enshrined a replica of William Penn's treaty with the Indians and, adjacent to that, a distinctive and charming English castle and grounds. And, finally, a third panel, depicting an early grist mill and the workmen associated with its operation, was created.

The massive stone house was complete. The kitchen was located on the ground floor, as were all the provisions and utensils. Here the faithful servants of Bayless spent much time in preparing the food for the family and the many guests, some of great distinction, who visited the Bayless mansion not long after its completion. A dumbwaiter conveyed the food to the main dining room on the first floor.

This section of the house, east of the dazzling hall, was partitioned by a pair of solid, mahogany-colored sliding doors, and when the visitors were many or a party was in progress, the huge doors were opened and a vast ballroom atmosphere prevailed.

The servants who had chosen of their free will to journey westward with Bayless, were quartered in the smaller house just a short distance northwest of the mansion. Here they relaxed and rested in peace and comfort, but most of their time was spent in the bottom floor sanctuary of the great stone house. For the servants, there were two points of entry to this domain—one large and one small. The larger entrance provided access for milling equipment to be repaired, a wagon load of produce to be stored, or a sick cow to be cured.

All thirty-seven windows were similar in style: double-hung wood sash outlining prismatic, hand crafted glass. On the floor above the main floor, four large bedrooms, separated by a hall, were located. A plain, angled stairway of strong oak led to the top floor, or attic. Supporting beams, storage closets, and uniquely jointed rafters were quite prominent in the attic, much of which provided head room in excess of seven feet.

The constantly maintained, extensive flower gardens and lawn, the neatly trimmed shrubbery, and the solidly uniform gravel paths constantly reminded Bayless of his plantation in Maryland.

He, his family, and his friends, lived a full and romantic life in this Utopia of early nineteenth century Warren Township.

The Old Stone House, 1836

Photo Courtesy Mary O'Brien

XX

OF TRAGEDY AND TRIUMPH

THE FINAL YEARS IN AN ERA of competition, excitement, and land speculation in the Township of Warren in Jefferson County, Ohio, were expediently closing. On July 1, 1836, Zaccheus and Miriam Tilton, Joseph and Mary's oldest son and his wife, sold their land holdings in southern Warren Township, which consisted of 122 acres, to Henry West for $3,800. Zaccheus bade a fond farewell to his parents, and shortly thereafter he and Miriam loaded a wagon with their necessary belongings and headed west.[1]

It was not long after this land sale and the departure of Zaccheus that Mary became somewhat despondent, and on a cool evening outside their long house she expressed her concern.

"Joseph, I feel as your mother does. I know her concern, and I ask you, too—where have all *our* children gone? You are here, and I am happy for that, but the house is large, and we are its only occupants."

"Come now, Mary, do not fret. You knew that in time they would leave, and some of our sons, at least, are nearby."

"But the girls—"

"Yes, we don't see them often, I agree. Our oldest daughter, Susannah—let's see, she would now be thirty-nine. You recall her marriage to Joseph McMillan and their removal to Indiana country not many years ago with their young children, Henry and Theodosia. Cassandra and her husband, Jacob Wilt—remember, we sold them a good section of land about five years ago?"

"Yes, but they, too, have gone."

"But they are adults, Mary—young and venturesome," Joseph reflected. "Pretty Nancy—her marriage to John Green was quite an occasion; before leaving, John told me they were moving to Ashland County. Penelope and the Jeffries boy—Robert; they are still in the county. I am sure you will not forget their two daughters, Isabella and Mary."

"How could I—they were so young." Mary's eyes were full.

"Tabitha and her husband, George Stringer, are only a few miles to the south in Belmont County, and they are happy."

"It seems a great distance—we do not see them."

Joseph consoled her. "It is God's will, and I know you would be the last to defy that."

"Quite true, my husband—and I suppose that is why Miriam was not permitted to live a longer life."

"There is no question—have you not often heard the Reverend Hozen deliver such a message at Sunday services?"

"Oh, yes," Mary responded strongly, but her thinking appeared disturbed. "But even our sons are distant."

"Mary, you are distraught," said Joseph. "Zachariah went to the Ohio county of Gallia some years ago—but Noah and young Joel are still in this area and doing quite well. I well recall the happiness you displayed when Joel married Cynthia Hartzell only two years ago."

The silent, peaceful hours of eventide had passed quickly, and the silver revealing rays of moonlight now shone brightly on the dense forestry that circumscribed the outdoor clearing on the north side of Joseph's house.

"Forgive me, Joseph—I was downcast, and you have buoyed my spirits. I was sad, and you converted me to a happy state of acceptance. The time is late and we must retire. And tomorrow I shall perform my chores with great vigor and happiness, because you are, and always will be, the ultimate source of joy and comfort in my earthly life."

Mary and Joseph joined hands and walked—before embracing each other in a sincere gesture of devotion and entering the long house to retire.

———————

The year 1837 was a year of births, marriages, and deaths for many residents of Warren Township, and particularly for the Tiltons. And as usual it was a year of land transactions, involving the speculator, the profiteer, and the serious settler interested in farming and family.

On January 11, John Tilton, the son of Thomas and Sarah Tilton, was married to Sarah Rud by James McCune,[2] a local justice of the peace. Joseph and Mary's son, Noah, now twenty-eight years old, was united in wedlock with Nancy Stewart, on March 12, justice of the peace James Irvin performing the services.

Ministers of the gospel were not always available when the couples were ready to marry, and, although devout in their religious convictions, the young man and his betrothed would seek out a nearby justice of the peace to perform the ceremony. The ministers might be away on church business or riding the circuit for several months.

Once again James McCune was called upon to officiate at the marriage of Thomas (he being the second son of John and Susannah and the same who had died at the age of sixty, nine years ago) and Sarah Tilton's youngest daughter, Drusilla, to Rezin Wheeler, on June 29.

In the spring of 1837, the family of Joseph Tilton and his many relatives and friends throughout the township and the adjoining counties of Jefferson and Belmont, were stricken with grief. Mary Hardesty Tilton, wife of Joseph, died at the age of sixty-three years, eight months, and sixteen days! The date was May 11.

Joseph was quite shocked by the tragedy; but, being a strong-willed man of faith, he weathered the ordeal with a calm and subdued attitude. He was now in his sixty-ninth year, but his activities, his interest, and his dynamic vigor were always indicative of a youthful spirit.

Mary was buried in the same cemetery as her daughter, Miriam, along the quiet, pure, azure-tinted waters of the Ohio River. It was a beautiful spring day with a gentle breeze to dry a tear or wave a newborn leaf.

Foremost among the mourners was Joseph's mother, Susannah, charming and gracious in her woven black robe and matching bonnet. Her flashing eyes were, once again, blurred and the pearl-laden auburn tresses were unconcealed by her headdress and hung in splendor to her waist, as the local minister pronounced, in awesome terms: "In the sweat of your brow you shall eat bread, till you return to the ground, since out of it you were taken; for dust you are and unto dust you shall return."

Jopseph Tilton's house was quite silent and tomblike during the remainder of the tragic year of 1837. Only occasionally would his sons Noah and Joel visit while on their hunting or exploratory jaunts. Always he welcomed them with warmth and affection. On such occasions, he provided them with elderberry wine, of good vintage, and choice morsels of venison and pone. But in all too short a time they were gone.

Quite often, he visited his mother in Tiltonsville, and they would sit in handhewn rockers beside the huge, heat-providing open fireplace and reminisce. Even at this point in time, Susannah remembered her early childhood, her marriage to John at a very young age, and the happy days in Maryland before their venture to the west in 1766. And in all of their frequent conversations Joseph sensed no repetition in the undistorted tales she told of her early adventures on the western frontier.

It was in late December, over seven months after Mary's death that Susannah exclaimed to Joseph, who still enveloped himself in a cloak of sorrow, "Joseph, my son, it is time now that you once again take an interest in the land and in the people around you. Mary has fulfilled the will of God, and He now expects you to take your rightful place in continuing to settle this township—this county—and even the state and the nation. You must break loose from the bonds of sorrow. I know you have given much, you are strong and healthy—you can give more."

His mother's strong entreatment had the desired effect. He began to take more interest in his land holdings, his mills, and his crops.

On January 5, 1838, he sold Lot. No. 29 in Tiltonsville to Philip and Catharine Ellis of Jefferson County for twenty-five dollars. S. J. Thery, the Frenchman, purchased Lot. No. 59 from Joseph for the sum of forty-five dollars on March 2 of the same year. And, shortly thereafter, on March 19, Isaac Hennis, of Jefferson County, bought Lot No. 49 from the Proprietor of Tiltonsville, for thirty-five dollars.

In the spring, Joseph re-plowed a section of land and planted a

large garden of corn and beans and cabbage. He worked it well
during the summer and it produced in abundance.

During the long summer and early fall, Joseph had completely
withdrawn from his state of lethargy. He renewed acquaintances
with his friends, he visited his children and their families, and it
was a rare Sunday afternoon when he failed to see his mother.

As the weeks and months passed, he became aware of the
deteriorating state of Susannah's health. Her once robust com-
plexion seemed to fade each week. She slept longer, and although
he made sure she had plenty of food, she ate less. The signs of age:
wrinkling in the beauty of her face, silver-tinted strands
predominating in her long once-auburn tresses, and an obviously
diminishing flash in her eyes were a source of concern for Joseph
in the early fall of 1838.

In October of 1838, all the lands in the township of Warren in
Jefferson County, Ohio, were possessed by deed—true and
proper. The township was comprised of approximately twenty
full 640-acre sections and six partial sections, equivalent to about
twenty-three square miles in surface area.

In the original Survey of the Seven Ranges, the sectioning
thereof was accomplished with the crude surveying instruments
of the time—a rough transit and chain. Consequently, many of
the sections contained more or less than the standard 640 acres.
Other partitioning of the land areas in the early nineteenth century was also somewhat inaccurate.

In giving full consideration to all factors, however, including
the constant threat from Indian war parties; the awesome
weather conditions—cold, blustery winds, sleet, and rains; and
the thick undergrowth of mammoth trees in the dense, virgin
forest, the surveyors accomplished their appointed task in com-
mendable fashion. Slight inaccuracies were overlooked and supposedly corrected, as the townships of the counties became more
densely populated.

It is known that in October of 1838, the following landowners
and their families, comprising about nineteen hundred citizens,

occupied the sections of Warren Township and held deed to the acreage, as indicated:

In Fractional Section Sixteen, the heirs of John Tilton owned 114¼ acres; Thomas Mitchell held two tracts totaling 96 acres; George Wilson Stringer, who had married Joseph and Mary's daughter, Tabitha, on December 6, 1827, had purchased 40 acres; Joseph Tilton, the old pioneer, retained title to 39 acres, and the town of Tiltonsville comprised 17¾ acres. Total area: 307 acres.

In Section Twenty-two, T. McCune owned 184 acres; A. & J. McCune possessed 100 acres; Thomas Mitchell extended his land holdings by 146 acres; Joseph Tilton had not sold his title to 98 acres; Henry West now owned 80 acres; the heirs of John Tilton held deed to 23 acres; and George W. Stringer[3] owned 16 acres. Total area: 647 acres.

(These were the original sections deeded by land grant patent to John and Susannah Tilton in November of 1798 by President John Adams, and although the total acreage exceeds the original grant by about 54 acres, survey inaccuracies provide the answer. John and his son Joseph had supplemented their land holdings extensively during the interim period; except for Joseph's ownership of lots in Tiltonsville, this was the extent of Tilton Territory in Warren Township in early October of 1838—a little more than 274 acres.)

In Section Twenty-eight, Thomas McCune held the deed to 219 acres; T. McCune, Jr., owned 121½ acres; L. & C. West had attained title to 113 acres; Joseph McCune held 100 acres; and James Spencer owned 94 acres. Total area: 647½ acres.

In Section Thirty-four, at the extreme southwest corner of the township, D. Updegraff was the tittleholder to 189 acres; Clark Terrell owned 186½ acres; William Finney and J. Harrison each possessed 100 acres; L. J. (Louis Johnson) held title to 26 acres; S. McCloneghy owned 20 acres in the southwest corner of the section; J. Spencer had 12 acres; and J. M (probably Joseph McCune) 8¼ acres. Total area: 641¾ acres.

In Section Thirty-five, adjacent to and north of Section Thirty-four, Joseph McKee was the largest landholder with 234 acres; the heirs of William Finney (Sr.) had been deeded 110½ acres; O. Rieks owned 106 acres; J. Watkins held a western parcel of

98½ acres; and, north of Watkins, J. Harrison claimed title to 94¾ acres. Total area: 643¼ acres.

In Section Twenty-nine, Alexander Maxwell possessed 220 acres; James Hogg owned 138½ acres; J. McKee held title to an additional 92 acres, adjoining his land in Section Thirty-five; William Lyons had 91 acres; and R. Patterson, one of the largest land owners in the township at this time, owned 89 acres. Total area: 630½ acres.

In Section Twenty-three, Robert Patterson and I. Kelly were the only landholders, Patterson holding title to 571 acres and Kelly 79 acres. Total area: 650 acres.

In Fractional Section Seventeen, James Hodgens held deed to 247 acres; Hodgens' son Isaac N. had been sold 108 acres (the Hodgens land was immediately north of Tilton Territory); I. Kelly held 110 acres to the west; John B. Bayless, the entrepreneur from Baltimore, held deed to 46 acres connecting with his land holdings to the north; R. Patterson owned 27 acres in the northwest corner; also, along the north side of the section, J. D. Stringer held title to 29 acres; and John Blair, 14 acres, part of his tract in Section Eighteen. Total area: 571 acres.

In Fractional Section Eleven, along the river, John Bane owned 40 acres; James Hodgens retained title to 33 acres, part of his original 400-acre parcel; Isaac N. Hodgens had purchased 12 acres, adjoining his land to the west; and J. D. Stringer, whose total land ownership at this time consisted of 41 acres, a parcel being in each of four sections, owned 3 acres. Total area: 88 acres.

In Fractional Section Twelve, also along the river, Moses C. Kimball, whose uncle, also named Moses, had fought valiantly as a lieutenant in the War for Independence, held the land title to 164 acres; James McCormick, who had come to Warren Township in 1810 with his parents and was on October 3, 1838, thirty-seven years old, had secured the right of ownership to 93 acres; Joseph Smith owned 59 acres; John B. Bayless, whose land holdings embraced parts of three adjoining sections, owned 36 acres; the town of Warrenton (the spelling of the town's name was changed from Warren Town to Warrenton[4] only recently) occupied 35 acres; John Bane held two separate deeds to 35½ acres, most of which adjoined his land to the south; T. Shannon, an early settler, held the deed to 28 acres south of and adjacent to the town; D. C. Martin owned 13½ acres; J. Hutton, 7 acres; A. M. (probably Adam McCormick) 7 acres; J. D. Stringer, 3 acres; W. H. (unknown), 2½ acres; and Z. C. Yard, 1 acre. Total area: 484½ acres.

In Section Eighteen, John Blair held the deed to a large tract of 257 acres; Joseph Smith owned 198 acres; John Alexander held 79½ acres; John B. Bayless, who at this time was the dominating figure in the town of Portland, held the title deed to 53½ acres; Robert Patterson was the owner of 40 acres; and J. D. Stringer, the steadfast husband of Miriam Tilton and also a resident of Portland, had 6 acres. Total area: 634 acres.

In Section Twenty-four, William Smith possessed the largest parcel of land, consisting of 386 acres; Justice of the Peace Robert Patterson held title to an additional 131½ acres; J. Alexander owned a 100-acre tract; and Mark Burnet had a one-mile-long land claim containing 51½ acres on the extreme west side of the section. Total area: 669 acres.

In Section Thirty, David Humphrey owned 200 acres; Jonah Cadwallader, 174 acres; George Beall, 116½ acres; J. B. Bayless, 66 acres; J. McKee, 59 acres; and William McKee 52½ acres. Total area: 668 acres.

In Section Thirty-six, John B. Bayless was the major land-holder, with 228 acres; Francis Lupton owned 142 acres; Joseph Steer, a prominent miller under whose direction the original town of Portland was laid out, held the deed to 112½ acres; George Lupton had a land parcel encompassing 111 acres; the heirs of Joseph Lupton retained title to 40 acres; and J. McKee had 26½ acres adjacent to his acreage in Section Thirty. Total area: 660 acres.

In Section Thirty-one, John Neel (Neely) had the title to 263 acres; Joseph C. McCleary, who had been born here on February 14, 1812, was the owner of 140 acres; Thompson Duval owned 130 acres; and William Neely, 30 acres; T. Rouse, 20 acres; Vincent Mitchell, 19 acres; A. Tunner and V. Mitchell, 12½ acres; J. B. Bayless, 10 acres; and J. Linsey, 4 acres. Total area: 628½ acres.

In Section Twenty-five, J. Medill, who was born in Monoghan County, Ireland, and came to Warren Township about ten years earlier with his wife, Nancy Fleming Medill, and a young son, John, had now secured title to 157 acres; George Beall owned 130½ acres in this section; N. Dawson had the deed to 119 acres; T. Marshall farmed his 108½ acres; James Humphrey had 76 acres; and John Adams, 62¼ acres. Total area: 653¼ acres.

In Section Nineteen, S. Scamehorn, who had been born in Washington County, Pennsylvania, and came here in 1787, held the deed to 181½ acres; Campbell Martin had rightful claim to 180 acres; Richard Haythornwait (born in Yorkshire, England, in 1776, married Mary Parkinson in 1815, had fourteen children), who came to this area in 1820, owned 117 acres; Alanson (Absalom) Martin held title to 110 acres; William Lewis, who was born in Fayette County, Pennsylvania, in 1796, and came to the township in 1802, had 54½ acres; and John Alexander, 23 acres adjoining his land in Section Thirteen. Total area: 666 acres.

In Section Thirteen, Jacob Creamer retained title to 204¼ acres; William Lewis owned 200 acres; Jacob Calder held the deed to 149 acres; John Alexander possessed, by proper instrument, 83½ acres; and Solomen Scamehorn had the same right to 38½ acres. Total area: 675¼ acres.

In Section Seven, James Calder, who died in 1839, at the age of seventy-four years, is noted as the owner of 160 acres in early October of 1838; Henry Brindley held title to 139 acres; Thomas Shannon held the deed describing 135 acres; Jacob Creamer had purchased 125½ acres adjoining his land tract in Section Thirteen; Isaac Brindley had been deeded 74½ acres by his father; and J. M. McCormick, who had been born near Shippensburg in Cumberland County, Pennsylvania, on October 3, 1801, came with his father, Adam, to Warren Town in 1810, and married Mary McCaughey in 1824, held a small parcel of 12½ acres adjacent to his acreage in Section Twelve. Total area: 646½ acres.

In Fractional Section One, H. B. (Henry Brindley) was the sole owner of 4½ acres. Total area: 4½ acres.

In Fractional Section Two, A. M. Litton held the deed to 49 acres, David Peck had 5 acres and W. M. (probably William Morrison), about 1½ acres. Total area: 55½ acres.

In Section Eight, David Peck held separate deeds to two parcels of land, one containing 162 acres and the other 54 acres; his total acreage in this section was 219 acres, including the 3 acres covered by a third deed to his 8 acres of land in Sections Two and

Eight; Joseph Bone was the owner of 162½ acres in the northwest part of the section; Benjamin Hall held title to the northwest parcel, consisting of 133½ acres; J. Litton had 56½ acres and A. W. Litton, 41 acres; L. Browning owned 29 acres and W.M. (probably William Morrison), 1 acre. Total area: 642½ acres.

In Section Fourteen, Stephen Jones owned the largest land tract—165½ acres; Erasmus Beckett held the title to 137 acres; George Beall possessed the deed to 104 acres; Jesse Carson had lawfully purchased 84 acres; Joseph Dorsey held title to 80 acres; T. Fox had 50 acres, and W. B. (probably William Bake), 10 acres. Total area: 640½ acres.

In Section Twenty, George Beall was the titleholder to a vast tract of 306 acres; Joseph Pumphrey, an early settler and miller of note, possessed the deed to 218½ acres; and William Lewis owned the balance of the land in this section: 128 acres. Total area: 652½ acres.

In Section Twenty-six, Joseph Medill, the forthright and foresighted Irishman, owned a total of 457½ acres which was explained in two deeds; John Andrews was the rightful owner of the remaining acreage in this section—182¾ acres. Total area: 640¼ acres.

In Section Thirty-two, located in northwest corner of Warren Township, Thompson Duval held title to 302 acres; William Neely, who had come to this township early, after stopping for a short time at Middletown, Pennsylvania, owned 176 acres; Thomas Church was the owner of 100 acres; and Thomas Sixsmith, of the same family that owned a large portion of Warrenton, held the remaining 86 acres in this section. Total area: 664 acres.

Such was the state of Warren Township in early fall of 1838. John B. Bayless, who owned all of the land in the town of Portland except for a small parcel to which Jefferson D. Stringer held title was about to redesign the town. The only towns of note at this time were Warrenton and Tiltonsville. A small assemblage of houses had been constructed near the Hopewell Church, erected forty years before, and a similar arrangement had been accomplished along Rush Run; but these developments were not recorded, nor were they recognized as "towns."

Time—the essence of being—would decide their destiny.

Map of Warren Township, 1838

EPILOGUE

On October 15, 1838, Susannah Jones Tilton—the recognized and highly-respected Queen of the Ohio Frontier—died!

She of the flashing eyes and twirling auburn tresses, who had contributed immeasurably to the success and consolation of the early settlers of Warren Township and Jefferson County, was silent now. No longer would her sturdy horse or tireless tread lead her to young mothers writhing in the pains of natural childbirth, or to a sick child, or to a fever-stricken farmer. No longer would she carry an apron load of harvest fruit to someone in need—nor would she warm the hearts of children and grandchildren and friends.

She was dead! Age: eighty-eight years, nine months and twenty days.

After attending church on Sunday morning, October 14, she had returned home and spent most of the day relaxing and napping on the back porch of her house facing the river. Joseph was there for a short time.

"I will be back tomorrow, Mother."

He was concerned; he knew his mother—and the flash in her eyes, although still there, was not the same. It was a sorrowful Joseph who wended his way toward his lonely home.

Susannah had gone to bed early. It was after midnight when she awoke, and, upon arising, she exchanged her bed gown for her best dress—a charming, flowing, purple and white garment with a high neckline, ruffled bodice, and full flowing skirt. She arranged the bed and covered it with a new multihued quilt which she had kept for special occasions. She brushed her long hair with a hickory-based brush that her husband had made. Her house was in order, and now she reclined—a tinselled princess of this early life—on the new quilt, and without sound or light she forever closed her flashing eyes!

Joseph found Susannah in this position the next day. He had a strong oak coffin built and lined with soft flax covered by a white woven cloth. The people came from miles around to see her—and to cry. The auburn tint somehow returned to her hair, and there was scarcely a wrinkle on her face, but the flashing eyes were closed and her hands were folded on her breast.

When the coffin lid was closed and her mortal remains were conveyed to the Cemetery of the Mound to rest beside those of her husband, many followed in solemn procession. It was a beautiful morning. The sky was a cloudless azure, and the orange sun shed its sparkling rays of warmth. The trees on the hills and in the valley were a melancholy mixture of life and death—red and green and brown and yellow. Only the occasional tinkle of a cowbell broke the silence. The breeze was gentle, and not even a ripple creased the mirrored surface of the great blue river.

The Reverend A. L. Hozen of the Tiltonsville Methodist Episcopal Church delivered the eulogy, speaking from the thirteenth chapter of 1 Corinthians:

First, a wife, and a mother—with great Love.
For everyone, in need, she had great compassion—and Love.
Her God—and the God of all people—she loved.
She lived as a Daughter of the Wilderness—in times of
 hardship, relentless toil, danger, sorrow and
 sacred silence—but still—she loved.
She gave of herself completely in the true spirit of a soul
 endowed with boundless energy and strength.
  The reason she dispensed her mercy and tenderness so freely
  —no one was ever denied—
Can be completely summarized in the word *Love*.
She could move mountains—out of Love.
She suffered, but she was not envious; she did not brag
 nor was she conceited; she was not self-seeking
 nor ill-mannered nor irritable.
She had great trust, and she knew the value of patience.
 For her, Love will never end.
She was a woman and, out of Love, she acted as a woman.
 She knew God.

She possessed the three great virtues—Faith, Hope and
    Love—
But, in greater measure, she had—Love.

IT WAS THE END OF AN ERA.

NOTES

Prologue

1. The translation of the Old English passages referred to in the prologue must be credited to the author's friend, Mr. L. R. Jackson of Columbus, Ohio. Mr. Jackson is recognized as an expert in this field of endeavor and to him the author expresses much appreciation.

Chapter I

1. Christopher Gist, Daniel Boone and Simon Kenton were traders and explorers in Western Pennsylvania, Ohio, and Kentucky in the last half of the eighteenth century. Gist was employed by the Ohio Company, formed by several prominent Virginians in 1747 as a trading and speculating enterprise, to explore and establish land claims west of the Allegheny Mountains. He was a skilled woodsman and explored much of the western Pennsylvania and Virginia area. Richard Henderson of North Carolina, another speculator, employed Boone to secure the choice regions in Kentucky. Simon Kenton, at the age of twenty-six, invaded the Middle Ground (a term for Indian country) and, for many years, the very mention of his name wreaked fear among the savages.

2. John Carpenter, the Scotch-Irish pioneer who had accompanied Major George Washington on his tour of the French forts in 1753, was an early settler on Buffalo Creek when he was about forty-three years old.

3. Old Saint Anne's Church, located three-fourths of a mile south of Middletown, Delaware, and about three miles from the Maryland state line, was organized in 1704, and although the

church records confirming the marriage of John Tilton and Susannah Jones have been destroyed, the author accepts the place and date of the wedding as being fact—primarily because (1) Tilton knew and had attended this High Episcopal church which was near his grandfather's property in Delaware, and (2) it was the Church of England, and both he and Susannah were of that ancestry.

4. Nemacolin's Trail, laid out in 1750, is named for an Indian guide employed by Colonel Thomas Cresap, one of the agents of the Ohio Company, to clear a path for pack horses from Cumberland, Maryland, over the mountains to the Monongahela River. Nemacolin lived near the mouth of Dunlap Creek (site of Brownsville, Pennsylvania) and led Cresap along an old Indian trail which was widened slightly as they traveled. In 1755, General Braddock followed this route toward Fort Duquesne, and thereafter it became known as Braddock's Road. (The author has a distinct preference for original names and does not condone changes unless necessity demands a change.)

5. Burd's Road was blazed by Colonel James Burd of the English soldiery stationed at Fort Pitt (Pittsburgh) in 1759. This road served as a crossing between Nemacolin's Trail and Redstone Old Fort or Redstone (now Brownsville, Pennsylvania).

6. Present site of Brownsville, Pennsylvania.

7. Colonel James Paull was born in Berkeley County, Virginia, on September 17, 1760. He was the son of George Paull, who moved his family into what is now Fayette County, Pennsylvania, in 1768, and settled near the Gists. He was a member of the Continental army during the Revolutionary War, and in August of 1778 he guarded the Continental stores at Fort Burd. The browns were very early in the area of Brownsville. Wendell Brown and his sons, two of which were Maunus and Adam, came from Virginia and settled in the Mon Valley as early as 1750 or 1751.

8. Jeremiah Mason and Charles Dixon were astronomers of note in London in 1763. In August of that year, they were engaged by the Penns and Lord Baltimore to establish the division line and complete their survey. Through many depredations of the Indians, they pushed the line further west beyond the Alleghenies, encamping on the Monongahela, 233 miles from the

Delaware. The surveyors continued westward, extending the boundary line a little west of Mount Morris in Greene County, Pennsylvania. Mason and Dixon returned to the east in December of 1767 at which time they were granted an honorable discharge. The Virginia-Pennsylvania boundary dispute was not settled until 1779, with an extension of Mason and Dixon's Line and a north-south line which established the West Virginia panhandle. Boundary bickerings between the two states continued until 1784, at which time they finally agreed to their present boundaries.

9. Jacob Wolfe's Fort was a regular stockade located about five miles west of Washington, Pennsylvania, on the north side of Buffalo Creek.

10. In 1775, James Maxwell was a fugitive from Virginia, having been suspected of committing a murder in the Greenbriar country. He was a relative of Colonel Ebenezer Zane of Wheeling, who refused to harbor him and threatened to return him to the authorities to stand trial. Later, Maxwell returned to Virginia and was found innocent of the crime.

11. John McCormick, John Harris, and Charles Wells were settled along Buffalo Creek in the early 1770's. They are listed among the "Soldiers who took the Oath of Allegiance to the Commonwealth of Virginia" on October 6, 1777.

12. Camp Charlotte was located on Scippo Creek about eight miles from the town of Westfall. In November of 1774, a treaty of peace with the Indians was signed at this place, and Dunmore's War was officially concluded. Cornstalk, the principal chief and influential orator of the Shawnee, was the spokesman for all tribes. Logan, the great chief of the Mingoes, did not sign this treaty.

13. Present site of Washington, Pennsylvania.

Chapter II

1. Logan's Indian name which means "Short Dress."
2. An affluent of the Ohio River, the mouth of which is located in Saline Township, the northeasternmost township in Jefferson County.

3. Marmaduke Van Swearingen was born in 1754 of white parentage. At the age of seventeen, he was captured by a band of Shawnee warriors and inducted into that tribe. The remainder of his life was spent as a savage enemy of the whites, and he became quite famous as the war chief of the Shawnees. He died in 1810 at the age of fifty-six.

4. An early settler in Redstone Country and a relative of Wendell Brown, previously noted.

5. Wilson's Fort and Rice's Fort were both on the south branch of Buffalo Creek about twelve miles from the Ohio River.

6. Present site of Newcomerstown, Ohio.

7. Logan was camped not far from Camp Charlotte when the peace treaty was signed in 1774. Lord Dunmore sent a special envoy to meet the Mingo chieftain and ascertain his agreement to the treaty. Colonel John Gibson located Logan's camp, which was also near Scippo Creek, and conversed with him. (Some writers say Simon Kenton and Simon Girty were also present at this meeting.) Logan gave vent to his feelings:

"I appeal to any white man to say if he ever entered Logan's cabin hungry, and he gave him not meat; if ever he came cold or naked, and he clothed him not. During the course of the last long and bloody war, Logan remained idle in his cabin, an advocate of peace. Such was my love for the whites, that my countrymen pointed as they passed, and said, 'Logan is the friend of the white men.' I had even thought to live with you, but for the injuries of one man. Colonel Cresap, the last spring, in cold blood and unprovoked, murdered all the relations of Logan, not even sparing my women and children. There runs not a drop of my blood in any living creature. This called on me for revenge. I have sought it; I have killed many; I have fully glutted my vengeance. For my country, I rejoice at the beams of peace; but do not harbor a thought that mine is the joy of fear. Logan never felt fear. He will not turn on his heel to save his life. Who is there to mourn for Logan? Not one."

In later years, Logan became somewhat addicted to alcoholic spirits and was killed by another Indian in 1781.

8. Major Samuel McColloch, who had at least two brothers, Abraham and John, and two sisters—one named Elizabeth, who married Colonel Ebenezer Zane, came with his family from the

south branch of the Potomac in 1770. He was ambushed by Indians and killed on July 30, 1782, at a place called "Girty's Point," not far from Van Metre's Fort; at the time of his death, he was thirty-two years old.

Chapter III

1. Short Creek about three miles south of Beech Bottom, West Virginia.

2. This cabin may have been the house or settlement of David Rogers, a native of Ireland, who settled about five miles north of Wheeling near the Ohio River in 1775.

3. Short Creek just south of and adjacent to the present town of Warrenton, Ohio.

4. At one time the Ohio River bank was a gentle slope, and there were many broad, sandy beaches along the river. The point at which John Tilton ascended the hill was directly east of Market Street in Tiltonsville, Ohio. At the time of his ascent, and for many years thereafter, a ravine leading to the river existed.

Chapter IV

1. Washington's journey down the Ohio River occurred in 1770, and his journal indicates he was much impressed with the richness of the land and the potential it might have.

2. The mouth of Grave Creek is near the city of Moundsville, West Virginia; it was probably named after the huge Adena Indian Burial Mound which dominates this area.

3. Lewis Morris was born in 1726, graduated from Yale in 1746, and was elected to Congress in 1775. As Commissioner of Indian Affairs, he conducted the Treaty of Pittsburgh in 1775. He was one of the signers of the Declaration of Independence, served in the New York state militia, attaining the rank of major general, and died in 1798.

James Wilson, also a Declaration of Independence signer, was born in 1742 and died in 1798 after holding many important congressional offices, including that of Supreme Court Justice.

Dr. Thomas Walker was chairman of the Virginia commission to treat with the Indians.

James Wood, born in 1750, served as a captain under Lord Dunmore in 1774. He served as a colonel in the Eighth Virginia Regiment, retiring as a brigadier general. He was governor of Virginia from 1796 to 1799 and died at Winchester in 1813.

Andrew Lewis and Adam Stephen, prominent Virginia statesmen, were active participants in the War for Independence and, with Thomas Walker, were appointed by Commissioner Lewis Morris to represent Virginia at the Pittsburgh conference.

White Mingo was a Seneca chief who lived near the Allegheny a short distance above Pittsburgh. He had signed Colonel Henry Bouquet's Treaty of 1764 and died prior to 1777.

White Eyes was a prominent and eloquent spokesman for the Delaware Tribe. He was killed while on an expedition with General McIntosh in late 1778.

Shaganaba was a son of the famous Ottawa chieftain, Pontiac. Tawaas is another name for Ottawas.

Flying Crow was an influential chief of the Six Nations.

The Half-King was a principal Wyandot chief, his town being located near Sandusky, Ohio. He was prominent in the defeat of Colonel Crawford in 1782 and apparently died before General Anthony Wayne's victory in 1795.

Cornstalk was the masterful orator and spokesman for the Shawnee, and his desires were basically pro-American and peaceful. He was the principal chief of the Shawnee, and after the Treaty of Fort Charlotte, he renewed his policy of peace. Late in September of 1777, he visited his white friends at Point Pleasant, West Virginia (then Fort Randolph), where he and his son, Elinipsico, were murdered.

4. A string or a belt of wampum was created by threading and binding together strings of beads or shells. They were either black or white in color. Upon the presentation of a string or a belt during or at the conclusion of a speech, during the negotiation of treaties, the gift was considered a ceremonial pledge— white reflecting peace and black indicating disagreement, or war.

5. George Morgan was born in Philadelphia in 1742. He moved early into the Middle Ground and was living in Illinois in 1768.

Prior to the Revolution, he returned east of the Alleghenies, and in April, 1776, his appointment as Indian Agent for the Middle Department caused him to return to Pittsburgh, where he remained until his resignation in 1779. After spending some time in the Continental army, attaining the rank of colonel, he lived in Princeton, New Jersey, for a number of years. Morgan returned to Washington County, Pennsylvania, in 1796, and built an estate which he called *Morganza;* here, he died in 1810.

Chapter V

1. Presently Beech Bottom, West Virginia, located near the Ohio River about twelve miles north of Wheeling. A small fort or blockhouse had been erected, primarily for the protection of Joseph Hedges and his family.

2. Samuel Mason (or Meason) apparently lived along Buffalo Creek in the early 1770s. He moved to Wheeling and was in command of a company during the first siege of Fort Henry. In 1790 he moved south along the Mississippi River, and his lifestyle changed from hero to villain. He became the leader of a band of thieves and ultimately was killed by two of his own men.

3. John McColloch was appointed a major of the Ohio County Militia in 1795.

4. Elizabeth McColloch married Colonel Ebenezer Zane, the proprietor of Wheeling, who with his brothers, Jonathan and Silas, had come to the Wheeling area in 1769.

5. General Edward Hand was born in Ireland on December 31, 1744. He was a doctor of medicine and came to America in July of 1769 as a surgeon's mate in the Eighteenth Royal Irish Infantry. He and his fellow soldiers were immediately sent to Fort Pitt, where he became quite popular. In 1774, he resigned from the service, settled in Lancaster, Pennsylvania, and married Catherine Ewing. He enlisted in the Revolutionary War shortly after its outbreak and was appointed a lieutenant colonel in the First Battalion of Pennsylvania Riflemen. In April, 1777, he was appointed brigadier general and sent to Fort Pitt at Pittsburgh. He served throughout the war, being also at the Battle of Yorktown. Following the war, he occupied various state and fed-

eral governmental positions with honor and esteem. He died at
his home, Rockford, in 1802.

6. The author, with reservations, accepts the evidence of Butterfield and Thwaites that Simon Girty was not at the first siege
of Fort Henry; Withers and DeHass record that he was the leader
of the Indian army.

7. This grove of white beech trees is located about two miles
west of Glen Robbins in Warren Township. The names *Simon
Girty* and *Jim Girty* had been carved on the trees—the former under date of March 7, 1776, and the latter dated May 7, 1777.
Other unusual Indian carvings are apparent on several trees, and
the place provides every indication of having been an Indian
campground. Therefore, it must be concluded that Simon and
James Girty could well have been meeting with their Indian associates and active against the white settlers prior to their dates of
desertion as defined by Butterfield. (The author knows that historians have said that Simon Girty could not read or write, but
that alone does not detract from the names and figures carved
on this intriguing grove of trees.)

Chapter VI

1. David Zeisberger was born in Moravia in 1721, and in 1740
he migrated to Georgia, where his parents were located. He
worked among the Creek Indians for three years before being sent
to Pennsylvania, where he studied Indian languages at
Bethlehem. He spent some years with the Iroquois and finally
became associated with the Delawares. Their movement to the
Ohio Valley was arranged by him, and he remained with his con-
verts, called Moravians, until his death at Goshen, Ohio, in 1808.

2. Fort McIntosh was an irregular four-sided structure, being
somewhat longer on the side facing the river, built of hewn logs
and having four bastions. The fort enclosed an area of about
twenty-five hundred square yards and was well constructed and
fortified with six cannons.

3. General Lacklan McIntosh succeeded General Hand at Fort
Pitt in 1778. He was born in Scotland in 1725 and was a part of
the mass migration of the Clan McIntosh to Georgia in 1736. At

the start of the War for Independence, he joined the Colonial army, rising to the rank of brigadier general. He was an ambitious soldier, and after the construction of Fort McIntosh, his primary intent was to establish a series of forts in the Northwest Territory and, ultimately, to capture Detroit. Such was not to be. He was succeeded by Colonel Daniel Brodhead in April of 1779 and returned to Georgia, where he died at Savannah on February 20, 1806.

4. Colonel Daniel Brodhead (eventually General) became commandant at Fort Pitt in April of 1779. At that time, he noted: "Gen'l McIntosh was more ambitious. He swore that nothing less than Detroit was his object & he would have it in the winter season—in vain was the nakedness of the men—the scanty supplies worn out—Starved horses—leanness of cattle and total want of forage—difficulty under such circumstances of supporting posts at so great a distance in the enemies Country, and other Considerations urged." Brodhead is known for his Coshocton campaign of 1781. With one hundred and fifty Continental troops and almost the same number of militia, including Major Samuel McColloch and Colonel David Shepherd, he advanced toward the central town of the Delawares on April 7, 1781. Coshocton was completely destroyed—fifteen Delawares were killed, twenty prisoners taken, and plunder in the form of livestock and furs were confiscated. In November, 1781, Brodhead relinquished his post at Fort Pitt to Colonel John Gibson, a brave and battle-experienced Virginian, who had been quite active on the frontier. He died at Milford, Pennsylvania in 1809, at the age of seventy-three.

Chapter VII

1. Hacker's Creek, named after John Hacker, who settled near the creek about 1769, at which time Samuel Pringle also was in that vicinity, is an affluent of the West Fork River in the Mon Valley. Its Indian name signifies "Muddy Water." West's Fort was probably built by Charles West; Alexander West, a prominent frontier scout, had a log house about a mile east of West's Fort.

2. All of these pioneer forts—West's, Coburn's and Stradler's, were located in what is known as Tygart's Valley, south of the present Morgantown, West Virginia. The creeks were named for the fort builders, and eventually flowed into the Monongahela or Cheat Rivers. David Tygart had settled in 1754 on the east branch of the Monongahela River near the present Elkins, West Virginia, about fifty-eight miles south of the Pennsylvania state line.

3. Located on Prickett's Creek, about twelve miles above Morgantown and near the Monongahela River.

4. Present Short Creek in Warren Township, Jefferson County, Ohio.

5. Very near the present site of the Bayless Stone House, built in 1836, in Rayland, Ohio.

Chapter VIII

1. Lewis Wetzel, the most prominent and fearless Indian fighter in northwestern Virginia, was born in 1764, the son of a German immigrant, John Wetzel, who made his home on Wheeling Creek, about fourteen miles from the Ohio River. Lewis had four brothers—Martin, Jacob, John, and George—all of whom became famous in the annals of border warfare on the Upper Ohio. Jacob will be remembered as an associate of Simon Kenton, whom he often accompanied on exploits into Indian country. Some controversy exists as to the date of Lewis' death, the most reliable information appearing to be that he died in Natchez, Mississippi, in 1808.

2. Controversy also surrounds the Wallace incident. Robert Wallace, his wife, Mary, and their children lived not far from Raccoon Creek near the present town of Florence, Pennsylvania. Some writers say the Indians were of the Wyandot Nation; most say the Delawares. Withers records that Wallace and his family were killed at their settlement; the author feels that DeHass and Doyle and Doddridge have more accurately recorded this tragedy.

3. The author must agree with Butterfield (*History of the Girtys*, p. 289) when he says: "In going with the enemy to assail Fort

Henry at Wheeling, in September, 1782, James Girty, for the last time, so far as is known, marched to attack his own countrymen."

4. The Queen's Rangers were, supposedly, a group of well-disciplined English soldiers, conditioned to do battle in the traditional rank and file style. As the ranking British officer, Captain Bradt, recently sent west to assist Hamilton at Detroit, was their commander. Jim Girty, the white Shawnee, superseded Bradt and was in complete control of the joint forces at this second siege of Fort Henry.

5. The persons within the fort were: Silas and Jonathan Zane; Harry Clark; James Clark; Stephan Burkam; Jacob and George Reickart; Casper French; Conrad Stroup; Edward and Thomas Mills and old Mr. Mills; Hamilton Kerr; James Salter; Alexander McDowell; James Smith and his two sons, Henry and Thomas; John Tait; Conrad Wheat and four sons; Copeland Sullivan and two of his companions.

Most writers agree that Elizabeth (Betty) Zane, Betsy Wheat, and Lydia Boggs, in addition to other valiant women and children of whom there is no accurate record, were in the fort. Miss Boggs was seventeen years old at the time of the second siege, the same age as Betty Zane. Her testimony, supposedly given under oath in November of 1849, is completely without foundation, and DeHass, in his description of this event, is in error. Withers—p. 356:

"The dwelling house of Colonel Ebenezer Zane, standing about forty yards from the fort, contained the military stores which had been furnished by the government of Virginia; and as it was admirably situated as an outpost from which to annoy the savages in their onsets, he resolved on maintaining possession of it, as well as to aid in the defense of the fort, by preservation of the ammunition."

Lydia Boggs Cruger, at the age of eighty-four, when she asserted that Molly Scott was the heroine of Fort Henry's siege in 1782, was apparently either quite senile or jealous. Molly Scott was not even in the fort at the time.

6. With Colonel Zane at this time were his brother Andrew, who had just returned from Catfish (Washington, Pennsylvania); Mrs. Zane (Elizabeth McColloch) and her sister; George Green; and Molly Scott. The vigilant Sam, a black man, and his wife,

Kate, were also there. The author feels that DeHass has completely distorted this last battle of the revolution on the basis of falsified testimony by Lydia Boggs Cruger.

7. Betsy Wheat—the fearless, strong amazon of the frontier.

8. Caleb Tilton was the first white child born in the present county of Jefferson in the state of Ohio. Evidence to the contrary is not available.

Chapter IX

1. General William Irvine was the actual successor to General Daniel Brodhead as Commandant of the Continental Troops at Fort Pitt. Irvine, although somewhat inactive in the Indian War of 1782, was kept well informed and corresponded frequently with General George Washington. (See Butterfield's *Washington-Irvine Correspondence.*)

2. General George Rogers Clark, born in 1752, was a strong-willed Virginian, who eventually settled in Kentucky. It was his prowess and skill as a well-trained Indian fighter which ultimately led to the conquest of the Indians in the Northwest Territory. He died in 1818 at the age of sixty-six. Arthur Lee, of Virginia, and Richard Butler were the other negotiators at the Treaty of Fort McIntosh. Richard Butler, later a major general, was killed in November, 1791, while on active duty with General Arthur Saint Clair on his disastrous expedition against the Indians.

3. Colonel Josiah Harmar was born in Philadelphia on November 10, 1753. In 1789 he was made general-in-chief of the United States Army and was at least partially successful in his encounters with the Indians. He died on August 20, 1813.

4. Ensign Ebenezer Denny was an aide to Colonel Harmar. Denny kept a military journal, which is now in the possession of the Historical Society of Pennsylvania. Prior to his appointment as captain, Denny had toured the eastern section of Ohio while associated with Harmar.

5. Captain Pipe was a Delaware war chief who continuously opposed peace between Indians and whites. His village was located near Sandusky, and he was influential in the burning of

Captain William Crawford. He attended the Treaty of Fort McIntosh in 1785 and Fort Harmar in 1789—always extending a black belt. Evidently, he died before the Treaty of Greene Ville in 1795.

6. Legend—related to reason that Thomas Tilton is authentically listed as having a cabin in Warren Township in 1785.

7. Rush Run.

8. Colonel James Monroe became the fifth president of the United States in 1816. He was born on April 28, 1758, in Westmoreland County, Virginia, and died in New York on July 4, 1831.

9. Jackson Tilton was killed on a hillside in the southwest section of the present incorporated vallage of Rayland, Ohio.

10. The Indian mound referred to is of the Adena culture, a prehistoric tribe which populated certain sections of North America, between the years 800 B.C. and A.D. 700. The area surrounding the mound became a burial place for early pioneers and was used as such until the middle of the twentieth century. James Hodgens eventually owned this land, and he enclosed the cemetery in a perfect octagon of stone posts and timber cross braces (ultimately replaced by iron pipe). The octagon enclosed exactly one acre of land, and each side was ninety feet in length. This enclosed area soon became known as The Old Family Graveyard and today is known as the Mound Cemetery in Tiltonsville, Ohio. In the 1890s the mound was partially opened and stone implements and specimens of peculiar pottery were found. Over the years, erosion has uncovered a human skull and various bones which were identified as being human. Many other rare geological and mineralogical specimens were found, as well as teeth and bones of prehistoric animals.

When James Hodgens died in 1856, he was buried in The Old Family Graveyard, and a section of his land surrounding and including the cemetery was willed to his son, Isaac N. Hodgens. Isaac and his wife, Mary, sold 130 acres of land around the graveyard and mound to Joseph C. and Isabel B. McCleary on April 1, 1861, for the sum of $9,600. However, Isaac and Mary willed The Old Family Graveyard to the public forever, as can be seen in the following quotation from the original deed, which is now in possession of the author:

Said county of Jefferson and State of Ohio and bounded

and described as follows "To Wit" being part of Section No. 17, Township No. 4, and Range No. 2. Beginning on the Bank of the Ohio River on the Section Line, between the Sections No. 16 & No. 17, thence west along said Section Line 178 perches to a Stone. Thence North 1 (and) East 129½ perches to a Stone. Thence South 76 (and) East 225 perches to the Ohio River. Thence down said River South 21¼ (and) West 6-4/10 perches. Thence continuing down said River South 30¼ (and) West 80 perches to the place of beginning, containing one hundred and thirty acres. Allways excepting however out of the land above described, one acre of land known as the Old Family Grave Yard, formerly owned by James Hodgens "deceased" and reserving also a right of way by foot path, there-to to the public forever. Which said acre of land is bounded by eight lines, drawn parallel to the eight lines of Fencing which now surround the Mound and enclose the Grave Yard now on said premises, and at such distance from the lines of fencing aforesaid as will enclose one acre.

11. Virginia State Library, Richmond, Virginia, Deed Book 1, pages 318, 319.

12. William McMahon, of Scotch-Irish descent, and his brother, John, had settled early in western Pennsylvania (Crooked Creek in 1772 and Buffalo Creek in 1774). William had moved farther west along the eastern bank of the Ohio River and built a substantial log house near or within the limits of the present town of Beech Bottom, West Virginia. Certain relatives of William and John McMahon are still living in Wheeling, West Virginia, and in areas north of that city.

13. Captain Van Swearingen had distinguished himself in the War of the Revolution. He was the son of John Swearingen, of Dutch ancestry, who had migrated from Maryland in 1770 and settled in Springhill Township, Pennsylvania, on the crossroad between Cheat River and Redstone. In 1785, John was still a resident of Fayette County, Pennsylvania. Captain Van Swearingen was the father-in-law of the famous border scout, Captain Samuel Brady.

Chapter X

1. Fort Finney was named after a blockhouse built by

American troops while they were waiting for the treaty conference to convene.

2. Primarily in the present state of Kentucky.

3. William Russell and James Perdue had come early to the
Ohio country and built their cabins near the mouth of Short
Creek.

4. Ohio County Courthouse, Wheeling, West Virginia, Deed
Book 2, page 14.

5. John Tilton's will, written in 1810 by his friend, James
Hindman, since John was too feeble to write, spells the name
"Beckey" but all other evidence indicates that Sally Tilton
married Jacob Reilly and moved to the west in the present town
of Newark, Ohio.

6. Present site of Bridgeport, Ohio.

Chapter XI

1. In 1772, Bedford County encompassed all of southwestern
Pennsylvania. Westmoreland was formed in 1773, Washington in
1781, Fayette in 1783, and Allegheny in 1788.

2. Ohio County Courthouse, Wheeling, West Virginia, Deed
Book 2, page 316.

3. John Doddridge, of English decent, married Mary Wells, after which they emigrated from Maryland and settled in Bedford
County, Pennsylvania, in about 1768. Here their oldest child,
Joseph, was born on October 14, 1769. In 1773, the family moved
to the western part of what is now Washington County, Pennsylvania. Joseph at a young age became an itinerant preacher of
the Methodist Episcopal denomination and was often in the company of the famous Bishop Francis Asbury. Other children of
John and Mary Doddridge were Philip, the founder of the present
Brilliant, Ohio, in Wells Township; Ann; and Ruth.

4. Actually, this log house was just south of the present Jefferson County line in the present township of Pease in Belmont
County. McKelroy in his *Centennial History of Belmont County,
Ohio,* says it was the first settlement in that county in the year
1796. The author believes the house was constructed at least three
years earlier, in 1793.

Chapter XII

1. General Anthony Wayne was born in Eastown, Pennsylvania, on January 1, 1743. He served with extreme valor during the Revolutionary War, being with Washington at Valley Forge and assisting in the capture of Cornwallis at Yorktown. Because of his somewhat violent temper he became known as "Mad Anthony," but there is no question that he was an able and daring leader. He concluded the Treaty of Peace with the Ohio Indians in 1795 at Fort Greene Ville (now Greenville, Ohio) and died in Erie, Pennsylvania, on December 15, 1796.

2. This victory refers to the Battle of Fallen Timbers which occurred on August 20, 1794, in northwestern Ohio, near the Maumee River. The Indian army, under the leadership of the Shawnee war chief Blue Jacket, was defeated, and the Treaty of Greene Ville was signed, almost a year later, by the principal representatives of the Indian Nations and the United States.

3. Ohio County Courthouse, Wheeling, West Virginia, Deed Book 3, page 31.

4. Jefferson County Courthouse, Steubenville, Ohio, Deed Book A, page 1.

5. Ohio County Courthouse, Wheeling, West Virginia, Deed Book 3, page 344.

6. St. Clair, despite his bravery and loyalty to the cause of freedom, was a strong-willed administrator of the territorial lands. His significant contributions to the growth and prosperity of the Northwest Territory are subject to intense and objective questioning.

Chapter XIII

1. Department of State, Washington, D.C., Book of Deeds A, page 11.

2. Named after Revolutionary War hero, Joseph Warren, who was killed in the Battle of Bunker Hill in 1775. Warren, born in Roxbury, Massachusetts, in 1741, graduated from Harvard in 1759 as a physician. He was instrumental in sending Paul Revere

and William Dawes to inform his countrymen that the British were coming.

3. Jefferson County Courthouse, Steubenville, Ohio, Deed Book A, page 26.

4. Presently known as Deep Run, just south of Yorkville, Ohio, in Pease Township, Belmont County, Ohio.

5. Jefferson County Courthouse, Steubenville, Ohio, Deed Book A, pages 68, 69, 70.

Chapter XIV

1. William McKendree, successor to the famed Bishop Francis Asbury, served as the head of Methodism in America for twenty-seven years until his death in 1843.

2. The Reverend James B. Finley, who spent much time in the area of Warren Township, was born on July 1, 1781. He was an itinerant Methodist preacher in the first half of the nineteenth century and, as a presiding elder, served under Asbury and McKendree throughout the Northwest Territory and the present state of Kentucky. He was welcome in the camps of most Indian tribes, and after converting many, came to know well the tribal chieftains and their customs. Thomas Liston, the son of Ebenezer, who was born in 1809, heard Finley preach in Warren Township. Reverend Finley wrote his autobiography in 1853, at the age of seventy-two and probably died not many years thereafter.

3. Bishop Francis Asbury is known as the founder of Methodism in America. He was born in Staffordshire, England, on August 20, 1745. In 1771, he came to America as a missionary and developed the circuit-riding system of itinerant preaching. He was appointed bishop in 1785 and served the vast area of the western frontier until his death in 1816.

4. Presently, Wellsburg, West Virginia.

5. These hearty and bold pioneers, for the most part, settled in what is now the Township of Wells in Jefferson County. At the time of their settlement, they were residents of Warren Township, from which Wells Township was formed in 1823.

6. Bezaleel Wells was born in Baltimore in 1772. After

graduating from William and Mary College, he became a government surveyor and received a grant of 1,100 acres in and adjacent to the present city of Steubenville, Ohio. He and James Ross, who was born in York, Pennsylvania, in 1762, and became a noted lawyer in the Pittsburgh area and who had secured a large section of land adjacent to and north of the Wells grant, laid out the town of Steubenville and held the first sale of lots on August 23, 1797. Wells became quite wealthy and influential, as can be seen by the following letter which he wrote to Samuel Huntington of Cleveland, who became Ohio's third governor:

Steubenville 11th May 1807

Dear Sir

I am sorry to inform you that a continuance of indisposition will render it impossible for me to attend the meeting of the commissioners on the day last appointed by the 18th inst Altho I am mending, it is but slowly and my physicians insist my continuing the use of mercury for some time.

Wm. Piat, a few days since on his return informed us that Majr—Cass & Mr Adams designed attending the meeting—if they do you will not be at a loss to form a quorum to do business. Mr. Beatty has been un expectedly called over the mountains from whence he will not return for some time. Mr. Shorb has moved to Canton, which is little more than a days ride from Cleveland, I therefore expect that he will attend. I have had but little experience in Lotteries and am not able to give useful advice—It appears to me as if we think of raising the whole sum allowed by law we cannot do it by one scheme—5 or 6000 Dollars is as much as we ought to attempt at first—as little money as possible ought to be drawn out of the purchasers hands, the highest prize ought not to exceed 4 or 5000 Dollars, nor the number of tickets 8 or 10,000—Money is unusually scarce at this time it would be impossible to get through with a scheme that would embrace a very large capital, indeed in this Country we cannot expect to get through with any scheme without foreign aid—I know of no place where we would be as likely to get aid as from the City of New York; I think if a proper representative was made on the subject to the mercantile interest of that City on us vending our tickets.

Altho I cannot be at the meeting of the Commissioners, I am determined to visit Cleveland as soon as I am able to ride—which I hope will be within three weeks from this date.

> I am, Dr. Sir, respectfully
> Your Obdt—Sevt
> Bez. Wells

Colo Huntington

Bezaleel Wells died in 1846.

7. William Henry Harrison, distinguished soldier and statesman, was born in Berkeley, Virginia, in 1773. In 1841, at the age of sixty-eight, he became the ninth president of the United States. He died only a month after taking office and was succeeded by his vice president, John Tyler.

8. Thomas Worthington was the sixth governor of Ohio and occupied this high office from 1814 to 1818. He was a resident of Ross County.

9. Jefferson County Courthouse, Steubenville, Ohio, Deed Book A, page 282.

10. Jefferson County Courthouse, Steubenville, Ohio, Deed Book A, page 270.

Chapter XV

1. Martin's land, now Martins Ferry, Ohio, is about five miles south of Tiltonsville and borders on the Ohio River. Absalom Martin, the New Jersey surveyor, had settled at this location in about 1794. White settlers had occupied this area many years prior to that—at least as early as 1779. It remained for Ebenezer Martin, son of Absalom, to survey the town in 1835 and lay it out into 100 lots and name it Martinsville. Not long thereafter, the name was changed to Martin's Ferry, and also in due time, the apostrophe was eliminated.

2. Jefferson County Courthouse, Steubenville, Ohio, Deed Book A, page 351.

3. The Joseph Tilton cemetery was 1,650 feet south of Public Road in Yorkville, Ohio. A year or two after Wheeling Steel Cor-

poration purchased this cemetery and the land surrounding it from the Wheeling Steel & Iron Company on May 31, 1923, care was taken to transfer the remains of most of those buried in this small plot, and the tombstones, to Upland Cemetery, located on a hill on the west side of Yorkville. (Jefferson D. Stringer and his wife, Miriam, were exceptions, as will be noted later.)

4. The incident relating to the disappearance of Sarah Tilton must be categorized as legend. Relatives of the author often referred to this event, always indicating that Sarah committed suicide by drowning herself in the river.

5. Martin's Ferry in the town of Jefferson, now Martins Ferry, Ohio, was operated by Absalom Martin.

Chapter XVI

1. Jefferson County Courthouse, Steubenville, Ohio, Will Book No. 1, page 68.

2. Primarily, along the river front at Warrenton, Ohio.

3. Jefferson County Courthouse, Steubenville, Ohio, Deed Book C, page 323.

4. The *New Orleans*, the first steamboat on the Ohio, was completed at Pittsburgh under the direction of Nicholas J. Roosevelt. Categorized as a vessel of over 300 tons, it was launched at Pittsburgh on October 10, 1811, to make its maiden voyage. This historic craft made several trips between Pittsburgh and Cincinnati before completing a full run to Natchez in January of 1812.

5. Tecumseh, the great chief of the Shawnees, was born in 1768 near the Scioto River, about two miles south of the present Circleville, Ohio. He died in the Battle of the Thames in 1813, when the American forces were under the direction of General William Henry Harrison.

6. Jefferson County Courthouse, Steubenville, Ohio, Deed Book C, page 544.

7. Jefferson County Courthouse, Steubenville, Ohio, Deed Book C, page 543.

8. Jefferson County Courthouse, Steubenville, Ohio, Deed Book C, page 544.

Chapter XVII

1. The author has not, as of now, discerned the true name of Drusilla Tilton's husband. There is no record of the marriage, although strong evidence exists that it was John, Henry, or Thomas West. Fact: "Aunt Druzy" West occupied the house on Lot Number 9 in Tiltonsville in the late nineteenth century. Legend: An Indian, bent on mischief, was killed in her backyard facing the river. Source: Miss Lorena Roth, great-aunt of the author, who, although much younger, knew Drusilla West well.

2. Indications are that William Lowry may have been acting on behalf of Isaac Jenkins, who apparently was the official county surveyor until 1816. Nevertheless, the date of the fifty acre survey is clear. Thomas Patton was clerk of courts from 1810 to 1817.

3. Jefferson County Courthouse, Steubenville, Ohio, Common Pleas Record Book C, page 192.

4. Jefferson County Courthouse, Steubenville, Ohio, Common Pleas Record Book C, page 192.

5. Jefferson County Courthouse, Steubenville, Ohio, Deed Book, E, page 460.

6. Jefferson County Courthouse, Steubenville, Ohio, Deed Book E, page 460.

7. Jefferson County Courthouse, Steubenville, Ohio, Deed Book F, page 13.

8. Jefferson County Courthouse, Steubenville, Ohio, Common Pleas Record Book C, page 192.

9. Sale of Lot No. 40 to Nathan Durant is recorded in Deed Book E, page 624. This lot was later resold to the proprietors of Tiltonsville, Joseph and Mary Tilton.

10. Benjamin Lundy was an outspoken abolitionist who established the first society dedicated to the antislavery cause, at St. Clairsville, Ohio, in 1815. He was a leader in the Union Humane Society, which was dominant in many of the communities in eastern Ohio. Lundy was quite influential and converted many of the townspeople to the purpose in which he vigorously believed. In the village of Mount Pleasant, Ohio, he began publication of a newspaper, *The Genius of Universal Emancipation*, in 1821. There is no record which reveals the feelings of the Tiltons on this important issue; the author can

deduce, however, knowing the Tiltons as he does, that they were quite sympathetic toward the antislavery movement. Ratcliffe, Donald J., *Captain James Riley and Antislavery Sentiment in Ohio, 1819-1824*, Ohio History, Vol. 81, No. 2, 1972, pps. 80, 89.

Chapter XVIII

1. Little Short Creek in southwestern Warren Township.

2. Although no authentic record exists as to the actual transfer of Lot No. 14 for the purpose of building a church, much evidence exists to substantiate the fact that this lot was specifically designated as land for a church. The author has searched the Jefferson County Courthouse records in great detail and has been unable to discern that a private dwelling ever existed on these premises prior to 1892, when a new Methodist Episcopal church was built on Lot No. 81 in Mary Norman's addition to the Town of Tiltonsville. The deed to Lot No. 14 was acquired by the Church Board of Trustees on June 24, 1851, at which time it was recorded at the courthouse in Steubenville, Ohio.

3. Jefferson County Courthouse, Steubenville, Ohio, Deed Book K, page 227.

4. Her name, prior to marriage, was Patterson.

5. It is not the author's intent to provide complete genealogical data relative to these early settlers; however, a few comments are appropriate. It is known that Thomas Liston was born in 1809, the son of Ebenezer. Large's Hill, adjacent to and just west of Rayland, Ohio, was named for Joseph Large. Stephen King, born in Massachusetts in 1791, came to Warrenton in the early nineteenth century, had ten children, and died in 1868. He was buried in the Warrenton Cemetery.

Chapter XIX

1. Differences of opinion surround the year in which William Stringer, the father of Jefferson D. Stringer, was born. Other years quoted are 1740 and 1752; however, since the DAR accepts the year as 1750, the author will concur.

2. Major General Nathanael Greene was born in Warwich,

Rhode Island, on August 7, 1742. He joined a military company in 1774 and the following year was appointed as brigadier general in command of the Continental forces in the Boston area. He served with distinction at Dorchester Heights, Trenton, Princeton, and Brandywine. In 1780, he succeeded General Gates in charge of the southern forces, and his success continued. General Greene died in Mulbery Grove, Georgia, on June 19, 1786.

3. It is quite possible that this marriage took place at a church building in Mount Pleasant. The author of the official history of the Presbyterians' activities in eastern Ohio questions whether the church was erected prior to 1834. The ceremony could conceivably have been conducted at Joseph and Mary's house just north of Deep Run (formerly Fish Creek).

4. Jefferson D. Stringer died in 1888 at the age of more than 87 years. In 1855, he acquired the Bayless Stone House, which was occupied by members of the Stringer family for 120 years until it was finally sold in 1975, after the death of Miss Edith Stringer on March 15, 1975. She was the last surviving grandchild of Jefferson D.; she was born in the year he died and was 87 years old at the time of her death. From her niece and a great granddaughter of Jefferson D., Mary O'Brien of Columbus, Ohio, the author has learned much.

5. Evidently, Lot No. 40, once owned by Nathan Durant and later returned to Joseph and Mary, who sold it to Aaron Chapman in September of 1832, had been resold, once again, to Joseph and Mary. The author found no record of Chapman's sale; however, he retains the original deed conveying Lot No. 40 to Thomas Liston on September 13, 1834. The land transfer to Chapman is recorded at Steubenville in Deed Book P, page 601; also in Deep Book P, pages 422 and 423, the deed transferring Lot No. 40 to Thomas Liston is recorded.

Chapter XX

1. Zaccheus Tilton, the oldest son of Joseph and Mary, is somewhat mysterious. It is certain that his wife's name was Miriam, but her family name could have been one of three—Pitt,

Kimball, or Hardesty. Zaccheus Tilton married Miriam Kimball on November 24, 1817; Zaccheus Tilton married Rachel Hardesty on January 23, 1816. Both marriages were performed by the Reverend David McMasters. It is certain that Zaccheus sold all of his local land holdings to Henry West on July 1, 1836, and moved westward. Zaccheus never returned to eastern Ohio and apparently died prior to his father's death in 1860; his father left no will. There was considerable controversy over the apportionment of Joseph Tilton's estate, but neither Zaccheus nor his wife or children are mentioned as ultimate beneficiaries.

2. James McCune was born on May 30, 1792, probably in Cumberland County, Pennsylvania, and came to Warren Township in 1796 with his parents, Thomas McCune and Mary Brady McCune. At the time of their immigration, James West, a prominent Warren Township landowner, accompanied them. James McCune grew to manhood at the old McCune homestead in Warren Township (Section Twenty-eight) and became a prominent citizen of the township and county.

3. In Deed Book T, page 217, at the courthouse in Steubenville, an indenture filed on February 7, 1838, shows that the fifty-six acres outlined on the 1838 map of Warren Township were actually transferred from the heirs of Thomas Tilton, Joseph's brother, to George W. Stringer and Jefferson D. Stringer.

4. The village of Warrenton, originally Warren and later Warren Town, adopted its present name to distinguish it from Warren, the flourishing county seat in Trumball County.

Epilogue

1. The date of Susannah Tilton's death is beyond question; for many years, until destroyed by vandals, a headstone confirming the date and age was quite prominent in the Mound Cemetery. The incidents relating to her death and burial must be categorized as legend; the author accepts the details as he has heard them described by his relatives and friends.

BIBLIOGRAPHY

It has been out of necessity, persuasion, patriotism, and desire, that the author has attempted, intermittently, as time and circumstances permitted, to compile into this book, important incidents and activities associated with the early history of Warren Township in Jefferson County, Ohio.

During the past six years, countless hours were spent in consulting a myriad of sources throughout the tristate area and elsewhere, in order to weave together, in logical and accurate sequence, the events, the people, and the conditions that prevailed in this area during these early years. Although not intended as a thorough genealogical study, the name *Tilton* does predominate.

Cemeteries, courthouses, and libraries were the favorite haunts of the author during his spare time—if there is such time. It may be said that very few evenings, weekends, or vacations were not, in some way, associated with the compilation of this work—the completion of which could not have been accomplished without the understanding and indulgence of the author's wife. To her, he expresses his appreciation and love.

The following bibliographical sources are listed in alphabetical order and consist of manuscripts, letters, newspaper articles, pamphlets, and books; all have been consulted in some way to confirm or validate an incident or statement which appears in this text. They are provided as a source of consultation for the student or scholar who may wish to pursue or confirm a particular incident or activity; the facts have been established.

One further comment is appropriate. The author will welcome criticism or supplementary information relating to this volume, for it has been written in a spirit of humility. He is extremely grateful that he has been permitted to retreat in time—and come to know so intimately, the truth, which will remain undistorted, and the early settlers of historic Warren Township.

List of Works Consulted

Manuscripts and Miscellaneous Sources

Carpenter, Roy R., comp. *Abstract of Title—Land Conveyed to The Pennsylvania Coal Company by John Deary and Wife by Deed dated March 31st, 1875.* (Steubenville, 1913).

"Controversy Over Village Name Extends to New Jersey." The Steubenville *Herald Star.* (Steubenville, Dec. 6, 1929).

Draper, Lyman Copeland. *Draper Manuscripts.* Archives, Wisconsin State Historical Society. (Madison).

Letroye, Marie. "Homecoming Under Way at Hopewell Church."
The *Times-Leader.* (Martins Ferry and Bellaire, Sept. 9, 1975).

Lewis, Clifford M., ed. *Wheeling Bicentennial 1769-1969.* (Wheeling, 1969).

McConnell, Mildred M and Carr Liggett. *Wheeling's First 250 Years.* (Wheeling, 1942).

Morgan, George. *Letter Books,* 1769-1779 3 vols. (Carnegie Library of Pittsburgh).

Powell, Esther. *Ohio—Records of Pioneer Families.* 3 vols. (toledo, 1960-62).

Tilton, H. G. *Letter to Floyd J. Tilton of Rochelle, Ill.* (Vermillion, South Dakota, Jan. 22, 1928).

United Methodist Church of Tiltonsville, Ohio. *A Historical Sketch.* (St. Louis, 1966).

Book Sources

Banta, R. E. *The Ohio.* (New York—Toronto, 1949).

Billington, Ray Allen. *Westward Expansion—A History of the American Frontier.* 1949. Reprint (New York, 1960).

Brant and Fuller. *History of the Upper Ohio Valley.* 2 vols. (Madison, 1890)

Butler, Richard. "Journal of General Butler," in *The Olden Time.* 1847. Reprint (Cincinnati, 1876).

Butterfield, Consul Wilshire. *History of the Girtys.* (Cincinnati, 1890).

Caldwell, J. A. *History of Belmont and Jefferson Counties, Pertaining to Border Warfare and the Early Settlements of the Adjacent Portion of the Ohio Valley.* (Wheeling, 1880).

Cochran, John S. *Bonnie Belmont—A Historical Romance of the Days of Slavery and the Civil War.* (Wheeling, 1907).

DeHass, Wills. *History of the Early Settlements and Indian Wars of Western Virginia; Embracing an Account of the Various Expeditions in the West, Previous to 1795.* 1851. Reprint (Parsons, West Virginia, 1960).

Delaware Archives. Vol. I, pp. 12, 35, 571; vol. II, pp. 986, 987; vol. III, p. 1475. (Wilmington, 1911)

Doddridge, Joseph. *Logan, the Last of the Race of Shikellemus, Chief of the Cayuga Nation.* Virginia Edition: 1823; Cincinnati, 1868; Reprint (Parsons, West Virginia, 1971).

_____. *Notes on the Settlement and Indian Wars—Of the Western Parts of Virginia and Pennsylvania from 1763 to 1783, inclusive, together with a Review of the State of Society and Manners of the First Settlers of the Western Country.* Wellsburg, 1824; Albany, 1876; Pittsburgh, 1912; Reprint (Parsons, West Virginia, 1960).

Downes, Randolph C. *Council Fires on the Upper Ohio—A Narrative of Indian Affairs in the Upper Ohio Valley until 1795.* (Pittsburgh, 1969).

_____. *Ohio's Squatter Governor: William Hogland of Hoglandstown.—Ohio Archaeological and Historical Society Publications.* vol. XLIII, pp. 273-282. (Columbus, 1934)

Doyle, Joseph B. *20th Century History of Steubenville and Jeffer-*

son County, Ohio and Representative Citizens. (Chicago, 1910).

Eckert, Allan W. *The Frontiersman.* (Boston—Toronto, 1967).

Finley, James B. *Autobiography of Rev. James B. Finley or, Pioneer Life in the West.* (Cincinnati, n.d.).

_____. *Life Among the Indians; or, Personal Reminiscences and Historical Incidents Illustrative of Indian Life and Character.* (Cincinnati, n.d.).

First Presbyterian Church, Mt. Pleasant, Ohio, formerly The Indian Short Creek Congregation. Sesqui-Centennial History. (1948).

Havighurst, Walter. *River to the West—Three Centuries of the Ohio.* (New York, 1970).

Hendelson, William H., ed.-in-cf. *The Standard International Encyclopedia.* 20 vols. (New York, 1955).

Hildreth, Samuel P. *Pioneer History: Being an Account of the First Examinations of the Ohio Valley, and the Early Settlements of the Northwest Territory.* Cincinnati, 1848; Reprint (New York, 1971).

History of Allegheny Co., Pennsylvania 1753-1876. S.W. D., ed. (Philadelphia, 1876).

Howe, Henry. *Historical Collections of Ohio.* 2 vols. (Cincinnati, 1908).

Hunter, W. H., comp. *The Pathfinders of Jefferson County— Ohio Archaeological and Historical Society Publications.* vol. VI, pp. 95-313 and vol. VIII, pp. 132-262. (Columbus, 1898 and 1900).

Hutslar, Donald A. *The Log Architecture of Ohio—Ohio History.* Vol. 80, nos. 3 & 4, pp. 172-271. (Columbus, 1971).

Inventory of the Church Archives of Delaware. The Historical Records Survey. (Wilmington, 1938).

Kellogg, Louise P., ed. *Frontier Advance on the Upper Ohio, 1778-1779.* (Madison, 1916).

_____. *Frontier Retreat on the Upper Ohio, 1779-1781.* (Madison, 1917).

Leckey, Howard L. *The Tenmile Country and Its Pioneer Families.* p. 18. (Waynesburg, 1950)

McKelvey, Hon. A. T., ed. *Centennial History of Belmont County, Ohio and Representative Citizens.* (Chicago, 1903).

Mockler, William E. *West Virginia Surnames—The Pioneers.* (Parsons, West Virginia, 1973).

Mulkearn, Lois, comp. & ed. *George Mercer Papers relating to the Ohio Company of Virginia.* (Pittsburgh, 1954).

Pattison, William D. *The Survey of the Seven Ranges—The Ohio Historical Quartely.* Vol. 68, no. 2, pp. 115-140. (Columbus, 1959).

Pennsylvania Colonial Records. 16 vols. (Harrisburg, 1851-1853).

Roseboom, Eugene H. and Weisenburger, Francis P. *A History of Ohio.* (Columbus, 1967).

Sinclair, Mary Donaldson. *Pioneer Days.* (Strasburg, Virginia, 1962).

Sparks, Jared, ed. *Correspondence of the American Revolution; Being Letters of Eminent Men to George Washington.* 4 vols. (Boston, 1853).

Stillwell, John E. *Historical and Genealogical Miscellany—Early Settlers of New Jersey and their Decendants.* Vol. 5. (New York, 1932).

Stuart, Charles A. *Memoir of Indian Wars, and other Documents.* 1833. Reprint (Parsons, West Virginia, 1971).

Thwaites, Reuben G. and Louise P. Kellogg, eds. *Documentary History of Dunmore's War, 1774.* (Madison, 1905).

————. *Frontier Defense on the Upper Ohio, 1777-1778.* (Madison, 1912).

————. *The Revolution on the Upper Ohio, 1775-1777.* 1908. Reprint (Port Washington—London, 1970).

Tilton, Francis Theodore. *History of the Tilton Family in America.* 8 vols. (Clifton, New Jersey, 1927-1930).

Veech, James. *The Monongahela of Old Or Historical Sketches of Southwestern Pennsylvania to the Year 1800.* 1858-1892. Reprint (Parsons, West Virginia, 1971).

Washington, George. *The Writings of George Washington.* Jared Sparks, ed. (Boston, 1846), 12 vols.

Whitehead, William A., ed. *Documents Relating to the Colonial History of the State of New Jersey.* vol. I—1631-1687. (Newark, 1880).

Withers, Alexander Scott. *Chronicles of Border Warfare, or a History of the Settlement by the Whites, of North-Western Virginia, and of the Indian Wars and Massacres in that Section of the State—with Reflections, Anecdotes, etc.* 1895. Reprint (Parsons, West Virginia, 1961, 1970).

Wright, J. E. and Doris S. Corbett. *Pioneer Life—In Western Pennsylvania.* (Pittsburgh, 1940).

INDEX

Boskhimer, Joseph, 187
Boyd, John, 55
Boyd, Robert, 198, 200,210
Bradt, Captain Andrew, 89
Brindley, Henry, 173, 248
Brindley, Isaac, 248
Brodhead, Colonel Daniel, 70, 77-78, 96
Brooke County, Virginia, 164, 184
Brooke, Robert, 164
Brown, Coleman, 25
Brown, Judge William, 23
Brown, John, 139-141
Brown, Thomas, 186
Brown, Wendell and sons (Adam and Maunus), 12
Browning, L., 249
Bruce, Samuel, 130
Bucan, John, 231
Buchanan, John (settled in Warren Township prior to 1785), 105, 123, 145
Buchanon's Fort, 77
Buffalo Creek, 7, 13, 17-20, 24, 30, 33, 62, 65, 73, 76, 82, 87, 104, 107-108, 121, 132, 135, 140, 146-147
Burd, Colonel James, 12
Burd's Road, 12
Burgess, William P. M., 214
Burnet, Mark, 247
Burns, John, 168
Burt, Luther, 174
Butler, Richard, 97; commissioner, 100; general, 105; at Fort Finney, 114; in Warren Township, 166
Byrd, Charles, 177

Cable, Philip, 159, 169
Cadwallader, Jonah, 247

Calder, Jacob, 248
Calder, James, 248
Caldwell, Alfred, 64
Callahan, Reverend George, 141, 166
Camp Charlotte, 20
Campbell, James, 168
Captain Pipe (Delaware chief), 23, 47, 102
Captina Creek, 23
Carothers, Robert, 186, 199
Carpenter, Edward, 19, 82, 164, 172
Carpenter, Edward (son of Edward), 172
Carpenter, Elizabeth, 82, 111, 172
Carpenter, George, 103, 123, 155, 186-187, 191
Carpenter, John, at his Buffalo Creek settlement in 1775, 8-9, 17-25, 39-43, 49, 52, 54, 57, 65, 73-74, 78-82; builds fort, 83; 84-89, 92-93, 95-96; elected justice, 100; 105, 111, 122-123, 144-145; land grant, 155; land boundary, 160; sells land, 164; 166; visit by his son, 172-173
Carpenter, Nancy (wife of John), 39-40, 42-43, 49, 73, 80, 82, 85, 88-89, 111, 122, 128, 144-145, 155, 164, 172-173
Carpenter, Sally (daughter of John and Nancy), 172
Carpenter, Susannah Tilton (wife of George), 155
Carpenter's Fort, 82-84, 88-89, 115, 118-119, 166
Carr, John, 186
Carson, Jesse, 249

125; courts and marries Mary Hardesty, 131-133; land interest, 156; flour mill on Fish Creek, 159; buys land from his father, 161-163; noted, 168; county militia captain, 169; buys lots in Warren, 183; family grows and a cemetery is platted, 184; road viewer, 187; helps survey Tiltonsville, 188-189; at his father's burial, 195; miller of note, 196; last child born, 203; land entrepreneur, 205; purchases Tiltonsville, 209-212; receives deed and sells lots, 213-215; lot for a new church, 217; land transactions, 220-224; at his mother's house (Christmas 1830), 226-227; land sales, 229-230, 232; at his daughter Miriam's burial, 233; again at his mother's house, 235-236; consoles his wife, 240-241; his wife's death and burial, 242-243; advice from his mother, 243; resumes his activities, 243-244; concern for his mother, 244; land holdings (1838), 245; at his mother's burial service, 252

Tilton, Lorenzo, 68, 73, 93, 112, 124, 131, 148-149

Tilton, Mary (wife of John of Gravesend), 3

Tilton, Mary (wife of Thomas of Del.), 4-6

Tilton, Mary Hardesty (wife of Joseph, proprietor of Tiltonsville, 159, 161, 169, 183, 191, 195 *passim;* last child born, 203; 212 *passim;* Christmas (1816), 214, 215, lot sales; new church, 217; 220, 222-223, lot sales; Christmas (1830), 226; assists Miriam, 229; lot sales, 230, 232, 235-236; despondent, 240-241; death, 242

Tilton, Miriam, 195, 227-228; marriage, 229; second son, 232; death, 233

Tilton, Nancy, 184, 190, 214, 240

Tilton, Nehemiah (son of Thomas and Mary), 4-6, 10

Tilton, Noah, 191, 241-243

Tilton, Penelope, 184, 190, 214, 240

Tilton, Polly (daughter of John and Susannah), 10, 16, 21, 34, 37, 68, 73, 79, 93, 112 *passim;* marriage, 116; 124, 191, 195, 235 *passim*

Tilton, Prusilla, 78-80, 93, 112, 119, 124, 128, 148, 161, 170, 195, 204-205, 235

Tilton, Richard, 127

Tilton, Rose Ann, 184, 207, 213, 223

Tilton, Sally (daughter of John and Susannah), 10, 18, 21, 37, 68, 73, 93, 112, 119; marriage, 123; 124, 144, 235

Tilton, Sally (wife of Caleb, son of John and Susannah), 190, 195

Tilton, Sarah (wife of Thomas, son of John and Susannah), 112, 184-185